UNTIL TUESDAY

UNTIL TUESDAY

A WOUNDED WARRIOR
and the GOLDEN RETRIEVER
WHO SAVED HIM

FORMER U.S. ARMY CAPTAIN
Luis Carlos Montalván

with BRET WITTER

HYPERION
· · · · ·
NEW YORK

Library of Congress Cataloging-in-Publication Data

Montalván, Luis Carlos.
Until Tuesday : a wounded warrior and the golden retriever
who saved him / Luis Carlos Montalván.—1st ed.
p. cm.
ISBN 978-1-4013-2429-2 (hardback)
1. Service dogs—United States.   2. Human-animal
relationships.   3. Montalván, Luis Carlos.   4. Men with
disabilities—United States—Biography.
I. Witter, Bret.   II. Title.
HV1569.6.M56 2011
362.4092—dc22
[B]
2010051147

Hyperion books are available for special promotions and
premiums. For details contact the HarperCollins Special
Markets Department in the New York office at 212-207-7528,
fax 212-207-7222, or email spsales@harpercollins.com.

Book design by Karen Minster

First Edition

10   9   8   7   6   5   4   3   2   1

For My Papá
& Tuesday . . .

CONTENTS

PART III

TUESDAY
AND LUIS

ACKNOWLEDGMENTS

My deepest thanks go to Peter McGuigan, Hannah Gordon, Stéphanie Abou, and all of the amazing people at Foundry Literary & Media. Thank you for believing in Tuesday and me.

Thank you, Bret Witter. Not only did you put up with me, but you've significantly contributed to the ongoing healing process. And, Tuesday's happy to have gained a friend forever.

To Elisabeth Dyssegaard, Ellen Archer, Kristin Kiser, Katherine Tasheff, Marie Coolman, Molly Rosenbaum, and all of the magnificent people at Hyperion—you are simply the best.

Tuesday. What would I do without my Tuesday? Thank you, you "good ole soul."

My heartfelt thanks go out to all of you below to whom I am indebted. Through the years, you've offered friendship, mentorship, support, and love.

Plinio Homero Montalván, Ruth Montalván, Sergio Miranda Ortiz, Teresa Miranda, George Plinio Montalván, Patricia Montalván, J. Plinio Montalván, Gina Montalván, Cristina Rieppi, Pablo Rieppi, Isabel Cabán, Angel Cabán, Carlos Cabán, Carmen Cabán, Esq., Maggie Dooley, Kevin Dooley, Alex Dooley, David Dooley, David Cabán, Ileana Cabán, Paul Vizcarrondo, Esq., Nina Vizcarrondo, Kevin Krufky, Esq., Tim Westhusing, Keith Westhusing, Nadia McCaffrey, Emily Pearcy, Dr. Goli Motarassed, M.D., Briah Carey, Myrtle Vacirca-Quinn, Esq., Christina Curry, Marvin Wassermann, Michael Schweinsberg, Councilwoman Sara González, Assemblyman Félix Ortiz, Lu Picard, Dale Picard, Judy Knispel,

Barbara Jenkel, Paul Jenkel, Leslie Granda-Hill, Tammy Snowden, Michelle Mullany, Jeffrey Bodley, Esq., Michele Bernstein-Goldsmith, Barry S. Goldsmith, Olga Trevizo, Angie Trevizo, Donna Kelly Thibedeau-Eddy, Tyler Boudreau, Amme Poe-Gilbert, Melody Moezzi, Esq., Matthew Lenard, Paul Rieckhoff, Ali Fawzi, Hamza Thakir, Cindy Rodríguez, Domenica Iacovone, Teresa Davis, Bronwen Pence, Amy Pence, Ted Gavin, Amy Gavin, Michael Elkin, Amy Kielman, Jarka Kristinova, Chris Lombardi, Rachel Rawlings, Joe Bello, Katie Johnson, James Bloomer III, Gary Brozek & Huck, T. J. Buonomo, Alicia Castañeda, Rolando Castañeda, Aaron Glantz, Patricia Greenwald, Mario Ruiz, Cynthia Labelle, David Lackowitz, Esq., Robert Wolf, Esq., Katie McMaster, Jeri Miller, Kristabelle Munson, Prof. Phillip Napoli, PhD, Rachel Natelson, Esq., Tony Ntellas, Marianne Perez, Joe Piazza, Ned Powell, Diane Powell, Tricia Powell, Prof. Edward Queen, PhD, Esq., David Ramsay, Gabriel Razoky, Shannon Rickey, Fred Schieck, Ben Selkow, Katharine Bailey, Dee Soder, PhD, Jose Vasquez, Mike Chung, Hwang Chung, Todd Wiseman, Jr., Milos Silber, Keely Zahn, Karin Zeitvogel, Pfc. (Ret.) Phil Bauer & Reese, Pfc. Cole Vickery & Cylis, Pfc. (Ret.) David Page, Pfc. Joseph Knott, Pfc. Robert Murray, Pfc. Wyatt Eisenhauer, Senior Airman (Ret.) Kimberly Specht & Toby, Spc. Ricky Rockholt, Spc. Hoby Bradfield, Spc. Justin Pollard, Spc. (Ret.) Tyson Carter, Spc. (Ret.) Andrew Hanson & Jackie, Sgt. (Ret.) Mary Dague & Remy, Sgt. (Ret.) Eric Pearcy, Staff Sgt. (Ret.) Rick Boone & Raeburn, Staff Sgt. (Ret.) John Davis, Sgt. 1st Class (Ret.) Kevin Epps, Sgt. 1st Class Brian Potter, 1st Sgt. (Ret.) Scott Annese, 1st Sgt. Zack Lever, Command Sgt. Maj. John Caldwell, Command Sgt. Maj. Jon Hunt, Command Sgt. Maj. (Ret.) William Burns, 1st Lieutenant Joseph D. Demoors, Capt. (Ret.) Mark Brogan, Capt. Ernie Ambrose, Capt. Adam Tiffen, Esq., Capt. Brian Schwab, Capt. (Ret.) Chris Hadsall, Capt. Joe Merrill, Capt. John Fuchko, Capt. Timothy Meier, PhD (SJ),

Maj. Fred Pasquale, Maj. Denis Lortie, Maj. Jay Baker, M.D., Maj. Doug LaBouff, Maj. Eric Gardner, Maj. Michael Martinez, Maj. Scott Pence, Maj. Bill Bainbridge, Esq., Maj. (Ret.) Donald Vandergriff, Lt. Col. Matthew Canfield, Lt. Col. Brian Steed, Lt. Col. David Causey, Lt. Col. Don Moore, Lt. Col. Michael Shinners, Lt. Col. (Ret.) Michael Sternfeld, Lt. Col. Christopher Kennedy, Lt. Col. James Gallivan, Col. Joel Armstrong, Col. Christopher Gibson, PhD, Col. Christopher M. Hickey, Col. Paul Yingling, Col. Gregory Reilly, Col. (Ret.) Mary Belmont, PhD, Col. Ted Westhusing, PhD, Brig. Gen. H. R. McMaster, Maj. General Khorsheed Saleem al-Dosekey, Mayor Najim Abid al-Jibouri, Sec. Eugene Dewey, Sen. Al Franken, Franni Franken, Prof. David Segal, PhD, Prof. Mady Segal, PhD, Prof. Winthrop Adkins, PhD, Dean Nicholas Lemann, Dean Sree Sreenivasan, Dean Melanie Huff, Dean Laura Muha, Dean Tom Harford, PhD, Prof. John Martin, Prof. Shawn McIntosh, Prof. Christopher Lehmann-Haupt, Prof. Beth Whitehouse, Prof. Elena Cabral, Prof. Rob Bennett, Prof. Mirta Ojito, Prof. John Smock, Prof. Tony Judt, PhD.

Split in Half

I happened upon a tree struck by lightning;
the aftermath of a wild and violent thing.
A tree split in half.

How do we come upon such things?

What happened here?

I have seen men and women split in half.
I've split people in half.
I am split in half.

Are two halves really a whole?

There are holes.
Deep and lonely holes,
split in half.
A tree with holes.

—Luis Carlos Montalván,
2009

UNTIL TUESDAY

THE FIRST LOOK

THE FIRST THING EVERYONE NOTICES IS THE DOG. WHENEVER I walk through my neighborhood in upper Manhattan, every eye is drawn to Tuesday. A few people hesitate, unsure of such a large dog—Tuesday is eighty pounds, huge by New York City standards—but soon even the cautious ones smile. There is something about the way Tuesday carries himself that puts everyone at ease. Before they know it, construction workers on their coffee break are yelling to him and cute young women are asking if they can pet him. Even the little kids are astonished. "Look at that dog, Mommy," I hear them say as we pass. "What a cool dog."

And it's true. Tuesday is, without exception, the coolest golden retriever I have ever known. He's big and well built, but he has a golden's innate love of life: playful, bouncy, exuberant. Even when he's walking, he looks like he's having fun. Not silly, doggy fun, though. There isn't anything loose or sloppy about Tuesday, at least when he's out on the street. Sure, he can't resist a sniff or two where the other dogs have left their mark, but when he doesn't have his nose pressed against a fire hydrant he's as regal as a Westminster show dog, walking lightly at my side with his head up and his eyes straight ahead. He keeps his tail up too; this marks his confidence and shows off his luxurious coat, which is more auburn than the usual golden and seems to shine, even in the shade.

That gorgeous coat is no accident. Tuesday has been bred for generations to impress. He has been trained for temperament and deportment since he was three days old. Not years, days. He has been groomed every day of his life for at least fifteen minutes, and twice every day since I adopted him at the age of two. Each time we return to my apartment, I clean his paws with baby wipes. I clean his ears and trim his nails at least once a week. I clip the hair from his footpads and around his ears as soon as I notice them getting long. I even brush his teeth with chicken-flavored toothpaste every night. One night, I accidentally grabbed Tuesday's toothpaste, popped a brushful in my mouth, and almost threw up. It was appalling, like eating mealy apples mixed with sand. But Tuesday loves it. He loves sitting on my lap while I groom him. He loves having Q-tips dipped down three inches inside his ears. Whenever he sees his toothbrush, his lips peel back and he shows me his teeth in anticipation of chicken-flavored sand.

But it's not just his beautiful coat, or his extraordinarily fresh breath (for a dog), or even his regal bearing that attracts the stares. It's his personality. As you can see from the photo on the cover of this book, Tuesday has an expressive face. He has sensitive, almost sad eyes—I think of them as smart-dog eyes, since they always seem to be watching you—but they are offset by a big goofy smile. Tuesday is one of those fortunate animals whose mouth forms a natural upward curve, so that even when he's just loping along he looks happy. When he really smiles, his lips push all the way up into his eyes. Then his tongue drops out. His head goes up. His muscles relax and, pretty soon, his whole body is wagging, right down to his tail.

Then there are his eyebrows, a couple of big furry knots on the top of his head. Whenever Tuesday is thinking, his eyebrows move in random order, one up, one down. Every time I say his name, his eyebrows start dancing, up-down, down-up. They also start galloping when he smells something unusual, hears something in the distance, or notices someone and wants to figure out their intentions. He never passes anyone without flashing them a sly look with those deep eyes, his eyebrows bobbing, a big natural smile on his face and his tail wagging back and forth as if to say, *I'm sorry, I see you, I'd love to play, but I'm working right now.* He makes a connection, that's the best way to say it; he has a friendly disposition. It's common for people to pull out their cell phones and take pictures of him. I am not kidding: Tuesday is that kind of dog.

And then, in passing, they notice me, the big man standing beside the star. I'm Hispanic—Cuban on my father's side, Puerto Rican on my mother's—but I'm what's known as a "white Latino," someone light enough to be mistaken for Caucasian. I'm also six-foot-two, with broad shoulders and a muscular build from decades of workouts, now regrettably in my past. I'm going a little soft, I must admit, but I'm still intimidating, for lack of a better word. That's why they called me Terminator, back in my old job with the U.S. Army. That's how I became a captain in that Army, leading a platoon of men in combat and training Iraqi soldiers, police, and border police at the regimental level. There is nothing about me, in other words—even the straight, stiff way I carry myself—that seems disabled. Instead, the first impression I give most people, I've been told, is cop.

Until they notice the cane in my left hand, that is, and the way I lean on it every few steps. Then they realize my stiff walk and straight posture aren't just pride, but a physical necessity. They don't see the other scars: the fractured vertebrae and torn-up knee that gave me this limp, or the traumatic brain injury that left me with crippling migraines and severe balance problems. Even more hidden are the psychological wounds: the flashbacks and night-mares, the social anxiety and agoraphobia, the panic attacks at the sight of something as innocuous as a discarded soda can, a com-mon IED during my two tours in Iraq. They don't see the year I spent in an alcoholic haze, trying to cope with the collapse of my family, my marriage, and my career; the months I spent trying and failing to step outside my apartment; the betrayal of all the ideals—duty, honor, respect, brotherhood—I had believed in before the war.

And because they can't see that, they never quite understand my relationship with Tuesday. No matter how much they admire him, they can never know what he means to me. Because Tuesday isn't an ordinary dog. He walks directly beside me, for instance, or exactly two steps in front, depending on his mood. He guides me down stairs. He is trained to respond to more than 150 commands and to realize when my breathing changes or my pulse quickens, so that he can nudge me with his head until I've come out of the memories and back into the present. He is my barrier against crowds, my distraction from anxiety, and my assistant in everyday tasks. Even his beauty is a form of protection, because it attracts attention and puts people at ease. That's why he was bred for good looks: not for ego, but so that people will notice him and, hopefully, the red vest with the white medical cross he wears across his back. Because beautiful, happy-go-lucky, favorite-of-the-neighborhood Tuesday isn't my pet; he's my trained-to-help-the-disabled service dog.

Before Tuesday, I caught glimpses of snipers on rooftops. Before Tuesday, I spent more than an hour in my apartment working up the courage to walk half a block to the liquor store. I took twenty medicines a day for everything from physical pain to severe agoraphobia, and even benign social encounters caused crippling migraines. Some days, I could barely bend down because of the damaged vertebrae in my back. Other days, I limped half a mile in a "gray-out," awakening on a street corner with no idea where I was or how I had gotten there. My equilibrium was so bad because of a traumatic brain injury (TBI) that I often fell, including one time down a flight of concrete subway stairs.

Before Tuesday, I couldn't work. Before Tuesday, I couldn't sleep. I drank whole bottles of rum in one sitting to escape, but still lay in bed unable to shut my eyes. And every time I did, I saw terrible things: a murderous assailant, a dead child. After one grueling therapy session I went to a coffee shop, opened my laptop, and saw the face of a suicide bomber from Sinjar, Iraq. A platoon of Iraqi soldiers partnered with our regiment had placed their rest tent too close to their vehicle checkpoint, and the bomber had blown several of them apart. When I arrived, the tent was still smoldering, sirens were blaring, and body parts were everywhere. I was stepping over a severed arm toward the blown-out frame of the suicide car when I saw the bomber. Not his body, which was obliterated. Not his head, which had been decapitated and pulverized. I saw his face, shorn clean by the blast, lying quietly on the ground in the middle of hell like a children's mask. The eye sockets were empty, but the rest was there: eyebrows, nose, lips, even his beard.

I buried that face in my mind for three years, but once it resurfaced in therapy I couldn't escape it. I saw it on my computer screen. I saw it on the television in the corner of the coffee shop. I left, but caught glimpses of it in every window I passed. I hurried to the subway station, pushing myself along with my cane. I reeled wildly into the first subway car and collapsed beside the door. I was sweating wildly, and I could smell my stink, that funky mix of adrenaline and fear. I felt badly for the impeccably dressed black woman beside me, but I couldn't speak. I couldn't lift my eyes. I tried not to move. I closed my eyes, but the suicide bomber's severed face, so evil and yet so calm, was imprinted on my eyelids. I sloshed wildly as the train caromed down the track, my head drumming and my stomach lurching, until finally, as the hydrogen bomb of a migraine exploded, I hurled myself out of my seat, threw open the emergency door, and, hunched over in the crevice between two subway cars, vomited onto the track, my life exploding out of me once again in a thousand little pieces.

I didn't pick myself up, not for real anyway, until Tuesday. I didn't start to put the pieces together, and hold them together, until this beautiful golden retriever, trained for two years to change the life of someone like me, became inseparable from my side. Tuesday gave me freedom, even from my worst fears, and by doing so he gave me back my life.

So no, Tuesday isn't my pet. He doesn't just make me laugh, or fetch my shoes, or give me someone to play with in the park. He doesn't teach me metaphorical life lessons. He doesn't greet me every time I open the door, because he is never on the other side of the door. He is with me all the time. Every second. He goes to the store with me. He goes to class with me. He rides in taxis with me and eats with me in restaurants. When I go to bed at night, Tuesday tucks me in. When I wake up, he walks to my side. When I go into a public restroom, Tuesday is there. In the stall. Right beside me.

We are bonded, dog and man, in a way able-bodied people can never understand, because they will never experience anything like it. As long as Tuesday is alive, he will be with me. Neither of us will ever be alone. We will never be without companionship. We will never have any privacy, even in our minds, because Tuesday and I are so in tune with each other after more than two years together that we can read each other's body language and know each other's thoughts.

It wasn't always like that, of course. For a year, Tuesday and I lived two hours apart, without knowing each other. For a time in 2007, we were both so damaged the people who knew us doubted we would ever make it out. That's part of our story, too: the journey we took to get here, the experiences that created the need. Because we aren't just service dog and master; Tuesday and I are also best friends. Kindred souls. Brothers. Whatever you want to call it. We weren't made for each other, but we turned out to be exactly what the other needed.

And that's why I always smile when Tuesday and I sit on the stoop of my apartment building on West 112th Street, enjoying the warmth of the sun. I smile because even more than his training, it was Tuesday's personality that broke my shell and set me free. He's a happy dog. He loves life. And when you're with someone like that every second of every day, how can you not love life too? Because of him, for the first time in a long time, I appreciate the simple moments with my dog at my side. And not just because it was so hard for Tuesday and me to achieve them, but because moments of quiet friendship are what make life—everyone's life—so grand.

"Hi, Tuesday," someone will invariably say, snapping me out of my thoughts, because even though we've lived on West 112th Street for less than two years Tuesday is already famous on the block.

When that happens, Tuesday perks up. He bobs his eyebrows a few times, the lovable rogue, but he doesn't even peek over his shoulder at me with a longing look. He's a service dog. He's too disciplined to ask for favors or be distracted by fans. But I can see from the length and speed of his tail wagging that he wants me to give him the new command, "Go say hi," the one that allows him to be petted while on duty. More often than not these days, I give it to him. Because I trust him. Because he knows his responsibilities. Because he loves his life. Because he loves to make people happy, and that makes me happy. And because I know Tuesday can rub his head under someone else's hand without forgetting that he belongs to me, just as I belong to him.

"Can I take a picture? He's an amazing dog."

You don't know the half of it, I think, as I move out of the background so the young woman can photograph Tuesday alone. *You have no idea.*

PART I
TUESDAY

CHAPTER 1

MOTHERLY LOVE

Love and work . . . work and love,
that's all there is.

—SIGMUND FREUD

TUESDAY WAS BORN ON SEPTEMBER 10, 2006, ONE OF FOUR IN a litter of beautiful purebred golden retriever pups. No, it wasn't a Tuesday. It was a Sunday, so that's one explanation for his name out the window. I have a few others I've made up over the years. I met him on a Tuesday, the day of the 2008 presidential election. I like the Rolling Stones song "Ruby Tuesday." The day was named after the Norse god of war and dedicated to the Hindu god of mischief, and both seemed appropriate.

The truth, though, is that Tuesday's name is a mystery. He may have been one of four in his litter, but he was also about the 200th golden retriever born over thirteen years at East Coast Assistance Dogs (ECAD)★, a nonprofit in upstate New York that trains dogs for the disabled. The two years and $25,000 of training it would take to turn him into a life-changing companion were paid for by an anonymous donor, so the donor named him and two of his littermates,

---

★ The name was recently changed to Educated Canines Assisting with Disabilities (ECAD).

Linus and Blue. I don't even know who the person was, much less why they chose Tuesday.

"People used to make fun of that name," an ECAD employee told me once. "Now everyone loves it."

I can only imagine Tuesday as a puppy, since I didn't meet him until he was two, but like everyone else I have seen pictures of newborn golden retrievers, their tiny hairless bodies pressed against their mother, squirming for milk. They have sleek bodies, just right for holding in your hand, and adorable faces that droop around the lips, making them sad and helpless and completely irresistible. Tuesday was more amber-colored than his siblings, and I imagine him as the goofball of the litter, rolling and nipping at his brothers and sister and then tottering off on baby legs to collapse in a bundle of happy exhaustion. Tuesday was a family dog; he loved the constant contact of his siblings. When they lay together in a heap of puppies, with heads and legs and tails sticking out in all directions, Tuesday was no doubt the one you noticed, his orange fur peeking out in several spots from the big yellow pile and his dark eyes, opening for the first time, staring at you with fascination. Even then, I suspect, his tiny brown come-hither eyes were impossible to resist.

But that wasn't the extent of Tuesday's early life. Not really. Tuesday was born to be one of the most highly developed dogs in the world—an assistance dog for the disabled—and he began his training when he was three days old, long before his eyes opened, while he was still pushing himself on his belly toward his mother's milk. Nursing is the most calming activity of an animal's life, and thus the best reward. Tiny, sightless, three-day-old Tuesday felt calm when he nursed. He felt nurtured and safe, and that was something ECAD needed him to experience with humans. So at three days old, Lu Picard, the extraordinary founder and lead trainer at ECAD, started tapping his feet as he nursed, associating human touch and smell with the pleasure of mother's milk. Tuesday was so young that his senses weren't developed. His ears were pinned to his head, his eyes shut. His feet were his most sensitive area. As a newborn, they were his guide to the world.

At fifteen days old, Tuesday's eyes opened, small and innocent. I can imagine his face: the baby fuzz on his snout, his delicate mouth, his inquisitive brown eyes fascinated by colors and shapes. At the same time, his ears opened and, for the first time, he could sense the world beyond his touch. When Lu tapped his feet now, she said "pa-pa-pa," then "smk-smk-smk," like a kissing noise. She was imitating the sound of nursing, offering him the one sound he already knew.

Now that he could sense the world, Lu gently held him back from feeding. Tuesday, like his brothers and sister, whimpered for his milk. It was all he knew; he desired its safety and comfort. But Lu touched him and said "pa-pa-pa, smk-smk-smk," until slowly, incrementally, he stopped struggling and crying. As soon as he was calm, she let him go to his mother. She was teaching him patience and manners—that self-control was rewarded while pleading and aggression were not.

At five weeks, Tuesday's formal training began with several hours of leash-walking exercises and an introduction to simple commands. He was also driven to Green Chimneys Farm, a service dog training facility where elementary-school-age children in treatment for emotional and behavior problems—the first of many people Tuesday would help—placed food in his mouth. There was no biological need. Tuesday was still a bundle of fur, barely able to see, tottering and tripping instead of walking, wholly dependent on his mother. The food was a training tool. Puppies start by eating food their mother has regurgitated; the smell of her saliva tells them the food is safe. It is a fundamental biological trust. Tuesday was learning to trust human beings as well.

He didn't want the food. At least not at first. None of the puppies ever did. They were the equivalent of seven-month-old children, and they were being fed by strangers. So Tuesday closed his mouth. He shook his head. He spat out the food when it was pushed through his lips. The children petted him, encouraged him, gave him more. He pushed it away with his tongue, coughed it out, his eyes pinched shut and his mouth hanging open as his tongue slapped in disgust.

Eventually, he started to lick the food. There was no point in resisting, and besides, he was hungry. The children said "yes, yes, yes," "good, good, good." They had been told to reinforce good behavior, but it was their excitement and joy, more than their words, that Tuesday responded to. Dogs love making people happy. They are pack animals; it's in their DNA. Even newborn puppies, barely coordinated enough to tumble, wag their tail when they experience positive reinforcement.

So Tuesday ate. "Yes, yes, good dog, good dog." Tuesday happily ate more. The children praised him again. "Good dog, Tuesday, good dog." They were both learning to focus on a task, to have patience and trust. Instead of acting out for attention, they were discovering that accomplishment was a powerful reward. Tuesday was also learning one of the primary lessons of his life, that there was a payoff for following directions: positive affection and love.

Back at ECAD, he was moved from his whelping box, where newborn puppies were cared for, to a larger indoor-outdoor area where he could totter and roll with his siblings. He was still breastfed by his mother three times a day, but since the introduction of food she no longer cleaned his messes. Mother dogs never do, once a puppy has eaten solid food, so this was another opportunity. Lu added wood shavings to the larger cage, and Tuesday, already attuned to human desires at six weeks of age, immediately understood the shavings were for poop and pee. Each day, Lu moved the

shavings farther from his mother so that Tuesday had to walk farther to relieve himself.

After a few days, a piece of wood and a piece of nubby plastic
were placed between the puppies and their mother. Instead of playing innocently in that warm pile, all legs and ears and wagging tails,
the puppies now had to negotiate an obstacle course to reach their
milk. The alpha of the litter was always the first, tottering across the
nubs and scrambling up, then collapsing over, the piece of wood.
Once he made it, the others followed. That's how I know Tuesday
was never across first. There's nothing alpha about Tuesday, which is
one reason he's a great service dog. In fact, most alphas flunk out of
service dog programs because they are too assertive. Lu's dogs were
different because, after generations of mating malleable dogs, even
her alphas were soft. From Lu, "soft" was a compliment. It meant
her dogs weren't bullheaded and dominant; they were amiable and
confident, the perfect traits for a service dog.

In Tuesday's litter, Blue was the alpha. But I always imagine
Tuesday second. Not because he was stronger, although he was always bigger than his siblings. And not because he was assertive, although he is certainly an inquisitive and opinionated dog. Tuesday's
defining trait, for me, is his desire for affection, his need to be
touched and nurtured. I was once told there are two types of dogs:
leaners and nonleaners. Leaners are always touching you, rubbing
against your hip when they walk past, flopping on your feet when
they rest, putting their paws on your lap when you sit down. Nonleaners stand a few feet away, lie near you but never on top of you.
This is not lack of affection. They are with you, but they want their
space.

Tuesday is a leaner. In fact, in the grand hierarchy of leaners,
Tuesday might be the king alpha. He craves contact. He needs it like
water or air. From the day we met, he encouraged me to touch him,
and he is constantly brushing against me or bumping me with his

head. That's why I imagine young Tuesday, his new eyes shut tight with the effort, wriggling his little butt energetically to squeeze under an obstacle or bouncing once, twice, three times, his tongue hanging out and his front paws scrambling, before flopping over on his face on the other side of a barrier. He can't stand to be alone now; it must have killed him to be separated from his mother as a tiny puppy, even for an instant. I imagine him nearly sprinting, in the lurching awkward way of very young animals, across the knobby floor and then whimpering quietly as Lu held him back until finally, finally, his mind slowed, his scrambling stopped, his breathing calmed, and he waited obediently for his turn.

It was all part of the training. Puppies like Tuesday don't just have to follow commands; they need a work ethic. They have to understand how to serve people, and they have to desire the rewards of that service. Over the next two weeks, Tuesday's training increased while his contact with his mother decreased, so by the time he was completely weaned, at about week eight as is natural for all dogs, he was in training four days a week. By then, his bond with his mother had been gradually transitioned to the person that walked by his side, giving him commands and communicating with him through the leash. He received excellent care. He was groomed twice a day; he was fed the healthiest food. He spent time with his brothers and sister when he wasn't working, so he was physically fit and intellectually challenged. But he wasn't indulged. He was part of a system, and everything within that system, even the downtime, was carefully calibrated toward creating the ideal service dog. As Lu Picard described it, in her no-nonsense suburban New York City accent: "There's a lot of affection, but there's no free love. You work, you get love. You don't get it for nothing."

Or as she told me on another occasion: "It's about the client. . . . I am trying to give my client more independence, more freedom, and more positive interaction."

Tall and thin, with a wild mop of curly brown hair, Lu doesn't glamorize what she does. She can talk about dogs like Volkswagens and Rolls-Royces when she's describing her processes, but even her clipped descriptions don't fool anyone for long. She isn't in the dog-training business for the money, and unlike some other people I've met in the field, she isn't interested in public adulation or hobnobbing with celebrities. She's in the business for the clients, and the love of the dogs, and the memory of her father.

Lu's father raised her alone after her mother died when she was a teenager. He worked hard, sacrificing for his daughter. He never remarried, but he always planned to travel, maybe move to Florida . . . someday, someday. When he retired, Lu was ecstatic. He was finally going to live his dream. Two weeks later, he had major stroke.

"I was livid," Lu told me. "I'm not self-righteous, but I will jump you if you are kicking someone when he's down. If there is a person on the ground and you are still beating him, I'm jumping in the fight, *you gotta get off now, you gotta get up*, that's just the way I am. . . . So when my father had a stroke, I was livid. I was, like, this is wrong. What happened to your golden years?"

Unable to walk or talk without difficulty, her father moved in with Lu and her husband. Within a few weeks, he fell into a deep depression.

"I should have died," he muttered over and over again. "I wish I'd just died."

Traditional care wasn't working, so Lu tried something different. She trained a dog. At the time, she was turning young dogs into well-mannered pets for wealthy suburbanites, so she had a veritable kennel in her garage. She built a mock harness with a solid handle and taught one of her best dogs to stand still—a hold, as it's called in the service dog field, although Lu didn't know that at the time.

She intended the dog to pull her father off the sofa and assist him in walking around the house. Her father was skeptical—until he tried it. The first day, with the dog's help, he was able to stand up from the couch. Within a few days, he was walking to the kitchen. More importantly, he was talking, and not in his self-pitying patter. He was talking *to the dog*. It started as simple necessity, a running conversation of commands and encouragement. But soon it was conversational. The dog gave him freedom, but he also gave him something Lu hadn't expected: companionship. He started calling the dog to his side and talking to him like a friend. They spent whole afternoons together and, before long, even slept together. As she watched the two of them walk to the kitchen one evening, smiling and happy, Lu turned to her husband and said, "This is what I should be doing with my life."

"Then do it," he replied.

A year later, after specialized training at Green Chimneys Farm, the legendary guide dog training facility in Brewster, New York (the place where Tuesday was fed as therapy for emotionally wounded children), Lu Picard founded East Coast Assistance Dogs. Her husband quit his job soon after and joined her. I can't even begin to tell you how many lives they have changed since then. A boy severely brain-damaged in a car accident. An autistic girl unable to bond with any other living thing. A teenager with cerebral palsy. A soldier with his legs blown off by an IED. I can't list the names, but I can tell you the effect on their lives. It is beyond profound: it is among the best and most important things that will ever happen to them. It is the answer to their prayer: not the "let me win this football game" prayer, but the one from the bottom of their souls. ECAD has changed the way they live every day. I know, because that's what Tuesday has done for me.

You don't create that dynamic with training alone. It's not simply a matter of instilling in a dog an understanding of people and a desire to please. There's something else vital to the relationship, too: a bond. A service dog must develop absolute devotion to its owner; it must feel a closeness with that person beyond ordinary life. In order to create that special bond, ECAD creates a need. In the first three months, a dog like Tuesday is never trained by the same person two days in a row. He is taught from three days old to find acceptance and love in humans, but he is never given a single person to bond with. He is surrounded by love, but he is isolated from the ultimate object of that affection: a constant companion.

That's a little tough for me to think about. After all, I've been there myself. I came back from two tours of duty in Iraq alienated from those around me. I cut ties with my family. I lost connection with my fellow soldiers, choosing to live in a fenced trailer thirty miles away rather than on post. I spent two years in New York City, surrounded by humanity on every side, and yet I was completely isolated. It didn't matter if I spoke with a dozen people, or attended classes at Columbia, or even, as I sometimes did, went to baseball games or concerts with my fellow veterans. Inside, I was unmoored, unable to connect, and empty.

Lu doesn't buy my worries. "Dogs aren't like people," she explained. "They live in the moment. Am I happy now? Am I getting what I want right now, in terms of food and shelter and stimulation? They don't worry about where their life is going." They need a bond, biologically, I mean, but they don't long for it like I did, because they don't miss what they have never known. "I can't give this dog every single pleasure in life," Lu explained. "He has to wait until he gets to the client to realize the grass is actually greener over there."

I know Tuesday was happy at ECAD. I mean, he goes completely nuts every time we return for a visit. We don't go often, because the three-hour round trip via public transportation from my apartment in Manhattan to the center in Dobbs Ferry, New York, is

psychologically draining, but as soon as we enter the commuter
train at Grand Central Terminal, Tuesday knows our destination.
I can see it in the way he holds his body and in the way his tail
swings so fiercely it pulls his haunches from side to side. He does a
good job sitting beneath my seat on the train because he knows I
need him to be calm in confined spaces, but as soon as we are in
the Dobbs Ferry station he begins to pull at the leash. Often, I
have to stop two or three times on the platform and tell him to
heel, which he does for a moment before springing back to the
lead. That's not like Tuesday. He knows I need him beside me; he'd
never pull me up the stairs. But sometimes, in Dobbs Ferry, he
loses himself. In the shuttle van, he has a habit of continually popping up to look out the window, his tail slapping the seat, his
tongue out, panting with excitement. This time, when we arrive
at ECAD, he leaps over the seat of the van and out the door, a serious breach of professional duty.

But I can't hold it against him, any more than I can his love of
sniffing fire hydrants and watching squirrels. My apartment is Tuesday's home, but he has a primal attraction to this place. If he were a
person, I'd say it was where he became a man. Two years for a dog,
after all, is like fourteen years for a human being. His brothers and
sisters are long gone, but Tuesday still finds sanctuary in the big concrete room with yellow training lines on the floor. He still loves to
see the dogs, even if he doesn't know them. He watches them walking with their trainers, a twinkle in his eye, as if he were an old
sergeant major watching a platoon of promising recruits. It's not just
the joy of seeing your profession well represented by fine young
men and women. It's the atmosphere. The cool breeze on a crisp
day, the late-afternoon clouds rimmed by sun, the smell of autumn
over the parade grounds, the cadence of boots. This is the world you
know.

When I sit down with Lu, Tuesday watches her intently. As we talk, his eyebrows bob double-time, like dancing caterpillars, processing everything. He has an eager sense about him, his neck craned forward slightly, his tongue hanging out so that his lips curl up into his natural smile. Eyebrows up, eyebrows down, head back and forth, looking between us.

When Lu says "my lap," Tuesday reacts. It's what he's been waiting for, and he bounces his front feet onto her knees, letting his momentum carry him forward so he can lick her once on the nose.

"I forgot that about you, Tuesday," Lu laughs. "I forgot how loving you are."

That's a funny admission, because Lu remembers everything about Tuesday. She has placed 120 trained dogs; she can talk about them like cars on an assembly line, if that's what it takes to explain a concept to you; but these aren't cars to her. Lu knows the personality and habits, both good and bad, of every dog she has ever trained. She knows what motivates them, what bothers them, and the best type of person to pair them with. She's a dog lover, after all. That's why she leash-broke them for suburban housewives; that's why she's spent seventeen years training them for the disabled. That's why, as soon as Lu gave Tuesday the opportunity, he bounced onto her lap and gave her his full-tongued love. He doesn't do that with anyone else but me. Ever.

But Lu Picard? She's special. I am Tuesday's partner. I am his best friend and companion. But Lu . . . she gave him this life. She started him down the path.

She's also the one who pushed him away. It seemed like a good idea at the time. It seemed like the right way to support a good cause. But in the end, prison wasn't the best place for a three-month-old, or at least a sensitive three-month-old golden retriever like Tuesday.

"I would have skipped it," Lu told me, laughing while Tuesday tried to maul her with his great pink tongue, "if I knew then what I know now."

I understand what she means, but given how the story turns out, I'm not sure I agree.

CHAPTER 2

PUPPY
BEHIND BARS

Ever has it been that love knows not its own depth
until the hour of separation.

—KAHLIL GIBRAN

TUESDAY WASN'T THE FIRST SERVICE DOG TO BE TRAINED BY Puppies Behind Bars. Not even close. The program had been around for ten years when Tuesday joined in 2006. It had its own wing in several New York State prisons, where prisoners trained in its intensive twelve-week program, then lived and worked with a dog for up to sixteen months at a time. It had hundreds of graduates—both canine and human—who had gone on to purposeful lives on the outside.

Tuesday was, however, in the first group of ECAD dogs to be trained by Puppies Behind Bars. The program had recently expanded to providing service dogs for wounded veterans of the Iraq and Afghanistan wars, and Lu Picard reluctantly agreed to help the cause. It wasn't that she was against giving prisoners meaningful work, life skills, and the kind of loving relationship that can open their hearts and revive their humanity after decades in the dehumanizing modern American prison system. Those were, of course, worthy goals. And she wasn't against helping wounded veterans. Who but the most hardened soul would be against that?

Lu simply used a different training method than the prison program, and she wasn't sure the two were compatible. For Lu, the elimination of premature, trainer-specific bonding was a key ingredient in creating the best client–service dog bond. With Puppies Behind Bars, a professional instructor was only at the prison for a few hours each week. The rest of the time, the dogs trained with one specific prisoner and lived in his or her cell. It was impossible, Lu figured, for longtime prisoners, offered an adoring and affectionate twelve-week-old puppy, to not fall on their knees and give that dog a hug just for being there.

She was right, of course. I saw that firsthand when I visited a Puppies Behind Bars program with Tuesday during the second week of our training together at ECAD. I hadn't expected to be moved, at least not in my heart, but when I looked around the large concrete prison room where Tuesday had received some of his training, I felt a surprising kinship with the men sitting around me. They were mostly shaven bald, and many had neck tattoos, but they weren't broken or hard. They were a lot like me and the young soldiers I had known in the U.S. Army.

It's not that hard to imagine myself in jail, because it's just one mistake. One night of drunk driving. A descent into drug addiction. Standing with the wrong person at the wrong time. A bar fight goes wrong, someone gets killed, and that's it. It's over. I mean, I've killed people in my life. I was probably the biggest killer in the room; they just never called it murder. In Iraq, a rifle went off while being cleaned and killed a twenty-one-year-old specialist in our small outpost at Al-Waleed. The shooter, a sergeant, isn't in jail. Nor should he be. Exhaustion was an official cause, so in my opinion that death is on the generals for having too many objectives and too few men in the field. And accidents happen. Terrible decisions are made. But there are no wasted lives. There remains potential. Everybody deserves a second chance.

These men were taking advantage of the opportunity. They were cast-offs who decided to give back to society, rough men softened by their companionship with dogs. They had helped train Tuesday and a hundred others like him. How many lives had they changed? How much hope and happiness had they given to the world? Did it outweigh the damage they had done?

Puppies Behind Bars, which was sponsoring the event, asked each of the wounded veterans to say something to the prisoners. There were four of us; I went last. By then, it felt intimate. Very intimate. It was just a small gathering in a concrete block prison room, but it felt like my words mattered.

"You are doing God's work," I said simply. "It is incredibly meaningful. From one brother to another, I am proud of your service. If circumstances were different, I'd take any of you to be one of my sergeants."

I noticed a few tears when I sat down. I hadn't expected that, not from prisoners. Then I felt moisture on my own cheeks. I had expected that even less. Maybe, I rationalized, it was the presence of the dogs. It is hard to be angry or cold with a puppy at your feet. During the question-and-answer session after the thank-yous, I even found myself talking freely with strangers for the first time in years. In fact, we talked so long that most of the dogs, including Tuesday, eventually fell asleep.

"So how do you maintain a young puppy's attention," I asked, "when it's tired like this?"

The men looked at each other. Then a few of them started to laugh. "Show him, Joe," someone said.

A giant of a man stood up from his chair. He looked like Curly from the Three Stooges, if Curly had been three feet taller and eighty pounds heavier and had spent twenty years lifting weights, repressing his anger, and getting tattoos on his neck.

Then he smiled. "We call this jollying," Joe said.

Next thing I knew, Tattooed Curly was on the floor, rolling and wrestling in front of his puppy while making a nonstop string of noises that, I swear, included Curly's classic "nyuk-nyuk-nyuk" and a breakdancing-inspired backspin. Every dog in the place was immediately at attention, staring at Curly Joe, because the big man could dance, or at least he could move on the floor continuously for a surprisingly long time. When Curly Joe finally stopped, every single dog was alert and ready to go.

"That's how we do it," one of the inmates said.

Jollying. I think of that crazy Curly dance every time I wrestle with Tuesday. At night, I love to lie in the bed and grab the sides of his face, rustling his fur and telling him what a good boy he is. Tuesday always gets excited and starts jumping on me, scrambling for leverage to fight back while I bite his ears like a mother dog and shake his neck, his sides, even his tail.

Jollying. That seems like exactly the right word.

But what a change it must have been for Tuesday. He was three months old when he went to prison, having lived his whole life in a place where discipline was strict. Where his life had been carefully planned since he was three days old. Where he was juggled between trainers so that he wouldn't bond with any single one of them. Where the love was abundant, but only if you worked for it.

In prison, he was in a place where the strict professional trainer was only present three hours a week. Where he spent all day with one "raiser" and even slept in his cell. Where he could be jollied not for doing something right but for being distracted and inattentive. I love Lu, but no one on staff at ECAD would ever give a dog-in-training spontaneous, unearned love. It would upset the whole course of their development. And they would never do a Curly dance on the floor to jolly their dogs. Prison was a completely different world.

Tuesday loved it. I can't imagine that he didn't. He's a very emotionally intelligent dog, or what some people might call needy, and he loved attention. No matter what Lu says, I think Tuesday felt the loss of a strong bond in his life, even if he didn't know what was missing. When he found a person who was always there with him, he immediately grew attached. By all accounts, he was a good dog, maybe even a great one. He learned his commands quickly. He always walked by his raiser's side. He was smart. He behaved. He was inseparable from his cellmate, but nobody worried much about that. They were a team; wasn't that how it was supposed to be?

Then, after three months, his cellmate was transferred to another prison.

It must have been a difficult parting. It's hard to disappoint Tuesday, especially when he looks at you with those sad intelligent eyes. There must have been tears shed as his raiser hugged him for the last time. As Tuesday stood at the door of the cell and watched him go, the poor dog's heart was breaking. You can see sadness in Tuesday; it settles all over his body. It's almost as if he's collapsing, the pain starting in his eyes and then moving inward, untying everything. Three months with someone might not seem like a long time, but a dog's life is short. Three months to a dog is like two years to a human being. Tuesday's experience was like giving a sensitive three-year-old a doting father, then taking that father away when the child turns five, never to be seen again.

He was devastated. I know him; he took the separation personally. What had he done? Why was he being rejected? I can almost see him standing at the cell door, staring down the cell block long after his raiser was gone, so long that his new raiser lost patience and started pulling on his leash, begging him to move. When he finally did, Tuesday walked away from his old life without complaint. He went into his new cell. Then he curled up under the man's bunk, put his head down, and pined.

That's the moment that makes Tuesday unique. I think of a young golden retriever heartbroken under a cot, refusing even to eat, and I think: only Tuesday. Only Tuesday would take separation so hard after just three months. Only Tuesday would feel the loss so profoundly. It was a rare and unfortunately confluence of events, a perfect storm of unintended consequences. Tuesday had been conditioned to leap enthusiastically into a human-dog bond. He had been trained through rewards to believe that all his master's actions were a response to his behavior. And he was a deeply, deeply sensitive dog. His moping wasn't an act. It was genuine pain and loneliness and regret. Dozens of other dogs went through similar experiences with only minor adjustments. Only Tuesday spiritually collapsed. Only Tuesday made you want to drop everything and throw your arms around him and say, *Come away with me, boy. I will give you what you need.*

The new raiser was high-strung. He wasn't prepared for this outward display of emotion, and he quickly grew frustrated with Tuesday's moping. I imagine him as a whiny Steve Buscemi type, tugging at the leash and saying, "C'mon, Tuesday, c'mon," then throwing up his hands and saying, "It's not my fault, man. Not my fault. It's the dog, man."

That wasn't going to work. Tuesday, more so than other dogs, sizes people up. He studies them, and he understands. He responds, as I have come to learn, to people he respects. As the begging from his new raiser turned to excuses, then complaining, I can imagine Tuesday sighing and wondering how he had fallen so far in the world. He went through his training, because that's what he was conditioned to do. But the moment it was over, he went back under the cot and didn't move. For almost a week, he lived with his head down and his spirit flagging, missing his friend.

Eventually, an inmate named Tom intervened. Tom was the oldest prisoner in the group, having served more than thirty years of a twenty-five-to-life sentence for second-degree murder. As a young man, he had read almost every book in the prison library. He had lifted weights and worked mess hall jobs and earned several college degrees. But when his first parole passed, he stopped trying so hard to improve himself and started to accept his fate. By the time Puppies Behind Bars came along, he was spending most of his time in his cell or watching television.

"In the prison system, you shut down your feelings," he said. "You gotta do that to survive, because it's hard. But the dogs brought me back, you know, to the human side."

By the time Tuesday came along, Tom had trained six dogs, all Labrador retrievers, and every single one of them had graduated to additional training. They were all out there in the world, making it a better place. This was rare. Lu Picard and East Coast Assistance Dogs had an 80 percent success rate, but many service dog training facilities graduate less than half their dogs. That's not a negative statement on them; it's just a reflection of the difficulty of the training. Service dogs must be elite in every aspect of their lives. So Tom was, understandably, proud of his perfect 6-0 record. There wasn't anyone else in his facility with that kind of record. In the closed prison world, success was his social currency, the reason other prisoners looked up to him and listened to him and, perhaps best of all, left him alone.

The other prisoners couldn't believe it when he offered to take Tuesday. "What do you want to risk your record for on that crazy dog?" they teased him. "That dog's no good." Tuesday was a washout. A bum. A broken-down six-month-old. None of the prisoners thought he was going to make it except Tom. And even he wasn't sure.

"It was more about timing than anything," he admitted. Tom's previous Labrador retriever had recently graduated to become an explosives-detection dog for Homeland Security, and he hated being without a dog.

The dogs brought it all back to, you know, to the human side.

Tom didn't cajole Tuesday. He didn't leash him. Instead, he climbed under Steve Buscemi's bunk and lay down beside him. Tuesday was about fifty pounds at the time, not the eighty he is today, so there was just enough room. Tom touched his paws and occasionally petted him behind the ears, but mostly he lay quietly, not saying a word. When he got up three hours later, Tuesday got up too and followed him back to their new home. He put his front paws on Tom's bunk, accepted a pat on the head and a "that's a good boy," then lay down in the kennel in the corner of the cell.

From then on, Tuesday was always at Tom's side. He leaned on him as they walked together, and he sat with his head drooped on Tom's lap in the television room. At night, he nuzzled Tom as he got into his bunk, then curled in the kennel to sleep. In the courtyard, when he was supposed to be training, he jumped on the bench and scrunched as close as he could to Tom's side. Nobody, not even Tom, had ever seen anything like it. Tuesday has such sad eyes, especially when he's wounded, that at seven months old he probably looked like exactly what he was: a lost kid. When I think of him then, I see a perfect picture of longing, of innocence at the moment it discovers there is pain in the world.

The other inmates started calling Tuesday soft. "What are you doing with that pansy, Tom?" they'd joke as they walked their hulking Labrador retrievers at their heel. "Get a real dog." They bet him the only things available, cigarettes and chocolate bars, that Tuesday would never make it.

Tom didn't mind. He believed in Tuesday. The dog was sensitive, sure, but he was also smart and intuitive. Tom was sixty years old, with thirty years in the joint, so he knew there was no need to rush. Heartbreak and crime are instantaneous. Transformation takes time, especially a transformation of the heart, so he was willing to shamble with Tuesday at his side, taking good-hearted abuse from the young guys and knowing from experience that the old dog always knows the best way to come out on top, even when his muscles are growing slack and his step isn't what it used to be.

Of course, Tuesday's obstinance could only go on for so long before he flunked out, so Tom drilled Tuesday on his commands. He didn't overwork him. He had seen guys in prison burn out dogs by working them too hard, and he'd seen them burn themselves out, too. He took it slow but steady, trying to make the training fun, but after a month there was still no progress. Tuesday watched, his eyebrows bobbing as he listened to the words, but his sad eyes stared up at Tom as if to ask, *Why? Why bother?*

"He knew everything," Tom said, "but would not respond. He just did not want to do it."

Any kind of training, whether to be a service dog, an accountant, or a soldier in the U.S. Army, takes desire. To learn a job well, you must want to succeed. This is the basis of Lu Picard's training methods: to make the task the connection to happiness. This work-reward relationship is inherent in dogs. As pack animals, they are conditioned to being judged on their contribution to a group.

Tuesday lost the connection. In his mind, he had followed commands for six months. He had been a good dog, and what had it gotten him? He had been passed from pack to pack, and when he finally found someone to accept him, he was kicked aside.

After a few weeks, Tom realized he wasn't going to be able to train Tuesday the traditional way. He was mulling this over, and possibly mourning all those lost cigarette bets, when he noticed the inflatable swimming pool in the prison yard. The pool had been brought in by Puppies Behind Bars as a training reward. The water was four feet deep and full of dogs, but Tom thought, *Why not? What's to lose?*

He rolled out of bed early the next morning, before any of the other dogs and trainers were out. As always, Tuesday jumped up immediately and followed him to the yard, where he watched intently as Tom lowered the water in the swimming pool to a few inches deep. It was already hot in the concrete prison yard, and Tuesday didn't hesitate. When Tom said, "In," he stepped into the pool.

"Out."

He stepped out.

"In."

He ran across the pool.

"Come back, Tuesday," Tom laughed.

Tuesday ran back across the pool. Tom's intention was to relax Tuesday, to take his mind off work and let him be a dog, but Tuesday was looking at him so enthusiastically from the water that Tom said, "Sit."

Tuesday did. Then he smiled that big doggy smile, with his tongue out and his lips curling into his eyes.

"Down."

Tuesday flattened himself in the water.

"Side."

Tuesday jumped up and loped to the side of the pool. Tom burst out laughing. "You sly dog," he said, bringing the hose over to the edge of the pool. "Do you want more water?"

Tuesday started to walk toward the hose.

"Stay," Tom said. Tuesday did.

"Side," Tom said, when the water was a foot deep. Tuesday stood to Tom's right, facing the same direction, with his collar beside his leg, exactly as he was supposed to.

"Let's go."

Tuesday didn't hesitate. He walked around the edge of the pool at Tom's side. By the time the other dogs arrived, Tuesday was rampaging through three feet of water to fetch his rattle ball, the tool Tom used to train his dogs to retrieve.

"What happened to Tuesday?"

"Candy bar," Tom said, holding out his hand for payment.

"Not yet, man. Not yet. He's still got a long way to go."

At first, Tuesday did most of his training in the pool, but after a few days he was trotting around the prison yard at Tom's heel, just as he had trotted beside his first raiser. The only problem was that whenever anything was thrown into the pool, Tuesday jumped in after it. The Labrador retrievers would step in to fetch, only to find Tuesday leaping past them, splashing water everywhere in his enthusiasm to reach the object first. The men who had been calling him pansy were now yelling at Tom, "Hey, man, control your dog!"

"He's not out of control," Tom replied with a smile. "That's just his pool. Maybe your dog shouldn't be so timid."

And that's how, with the help of a weathered-but-tender trainer, the pansy became King of the Pool, the prison yard alpha and ultimate fetcher of other dogs' toys.

"Once we broke the ice with the pool and we already had the bond between us, Tuesday would do anything. It was so simple to train him. It was actually no work at all."

That's right, *bonded*. And why not? "I bonded with every dog I've had," Tom said.

He was heartbroken when his first dog graduated, but he held himself in check, not wanting to make a scene in front of the guys. He trained his second dog, a guide dog, for sixteen months, and he broke down in tears when the dog left him. The other prisoners made fun of him, at least until they reached the point where they could cry themselves, but Tom didn't care. It was the first time he'd cried in twenty years, and it felt . . . human.

Tuesday was one of the hardest to leave, because he was such a loving dog. He was needy, but he was always there for you. That was important, because Tom hadn't adopted Tuesday on a whim. He needed a distraction, because five months after lying under Steve Buscemi's bunk with Tuesday he was eligible for parole. According to Tom, the months before a parole hearing were by far the worst time in a prisoner's life. Prison is monotony, a mind-numbing, soul-crushing nothing with freedom as the only reward. Most guys had an end date. Tom didn't. He was a lifer. He had parole, and with parole, there was no promise. And that's hard. Especially when, as Tom believed, making parole was the luck of the draw.

"I've seen guys going in there who just beat up a corrections officer and make parole," he said. "Other guys go in with recommendations and certificates from every program and not make parole." It's not about you. That's what the prisoners say. It about whether the parole board was made happy last night.

So prisoners up for parole nervously walked their cells. And worried. And started arguments because they were on edge. And worried that the arguments were undermining their cause. And started more arguments, because they couldn't let the last ones go. They tried to get their thoughts in order, both on paper and in their head, even though they didn't believe it would do any good, but the feeling of helplessness, of being nothing more than a number you can't even know, kept getting in the way. That behavior isn't just counterproductive—it can eat through your life, as I can attest from my long years of isolation and obsession in the depths of my wounds. Thinking and rethinking without the ability to act, and dwelling on your isolation in a faceless system, leads quickly to frustration, anger, and despair. Prisoners up for parole describe the last couple of months as agony—and the short, impersonal parole hearing as a letdown, no matter the result.

With Tuesday, though, Tom didn't just adopt a distraction. He adopted the perfect companion. When their owner gets nervous, most dogs mimic them, getting nervous themselves. Not Tuesday. He has the ability to act as ballast, to balance the relationship by going in the opposite direction. When Tom got nervous, Tuesday became calm. As Tom grew distracted by the hearing, Tuesday focused. He knew Tom needed him, and I suspect his desire to help, as much as the swimming pool, provided the push back into training. Tuesday was determined to succeed, in other words, not for himself, but for his friend.

He focused on his commands. He pulled less on the leash. He ignored the swimming pool, loping along instead at Tom's side. He jumped on the cot as the date approached and the nights grew long, and more and more often Tom let him stay. When Tuesday put his head on Tom's lap in the television room, Tom knew it was no longer just because the poor lonely dog wanted companionship; it was because he wanted Tom to know he had a friend.

The day arrived. The guards knocked. Tom gave Tuesday a last hug, stroked him under his chin, and went to meet his fate. He turned back to see Tuesday sitting in the jail cell, staring after him with those gentle, intelligent eyes, and he returned hours later to find Tuesday in the exact same place. When he received his parole notice, Tom broke down. He hugged Tuesday, who was of course at his side, and thanked him for his service. Even after almost thirty years inside, he was not a broken man, like so many other prisoners. He was not angry, at the system or himself. "The only way the prison system could win," Tom said, "was to get me to hate, and being around the dogs and everything, the hate was totally out of the picture." When Tom walked out the door and found his wife waiting for him, he had no problem giving her a hug, because he had been working on relationships for years. He was that rarity in the modern prison system: a totally free man.

Today, Tom owns his own business training dogs with his wife. He focuses on troubled dogs that others have given up on, especially pit bulls. He understands that everybody deserves a second chance, and with love and patience almost every animal can succeed. After all, he turned his life around. He spent a decade giving back to society by training service and explosives-detection dogs, and that, he said, "got my mind right and focused on the positives." When he walked out of prison, he knew he could succeed. He had a perfect 7-0 record, after all, and he had turned around Tuesday, the saddest dog in the yard.

And Tuesday?

He went back to ECAD. Alone. Again.

CHAPTER 3

THE LOST BOYS

Love is never lost. If not reciprocated,
it will flow back and soften and purify the heart.

—WASHINGTON IRVING

THE ECAD OFFICE AND TRAINING CENTER AREN'T A SHOW-piece. A low-lying building with a blue tin roof, it is almost ostentatious in its lack of decoration or architectural features. Inside, it is just as practical, composed primarily of a large open work space with a bare concrete floor. There are two long folding tables placed end to end in the center of the room (the brown particleboard kind you see in church dining halls), a circular yellow path outlined on the floor, and five or six green wooden platforms. Mostly, though, the room seems empty. Even the cinder block walls are spartan, painted pale gray and covered with checklists and behavioral diagrams. There are three modest, well-used offices along the right wall, and a steel door in the back that leads to a living area used by clients during their two-week training period. The windows on the left offer views of three enclosed outdoor play areas, two with those tiny plastic slides designed for two-year-olds and usually found in suburban basements. For an organization that survives on donations, in other words, ECAD doesn't waste much time or money catering to the rich and powerful.

Even the dogs don't live in luxury. When not being trained or exercised in the play areas, they are kept at the back of the large room in the kind of large kennels sold at the local pet store. The only training equipment, besides the yellow line on the floor, are the six green wooden boxes. They are used to teach the dogs to get up and down, and they are where the dogs sit attentively, with their handlers beside them, when taking a break. The rest of the training is done with the ordinary objects in the room: doorknobs, light switches, window blinds, chairs—things the future service dogs will encounter in their working lives.

The special thing about ECAD is the staff. This is a group of people, from Lu Picard down, who believe in their work. It's not just about the dogs, Lu always says. That was her old job, training puppies for wealthy families. ECAD is about the clients. Everything is done to provide the disabled with better lives.

It's hard to argue with that mission when you talk to a mother whose seven-year-old son has been falling down steps at school since having his brain tumor removed. "I just want him to be able to play like other kids," she says.

Or the young man in a wheelchair, able only to move his right arm. He did his own research and found ECAD when he was twelve, but his mother wasn't supportive. After three months, the boy gave the dog back, saying he couldn't handle the responsibility alone. Seven years later, he asked for another chance. He had finished high school. He was putting himself through college. He was going to succeed. A dog was the last tool he wanted before moving out on his own.

Or the mother whose son was struck by a hit-and-run driver at age twelve. The brain damage left him barely able to speak and, for four years, unable to walk. You can hear six years of exhaustion and anguish in her voice when she says, "He loves to read. He wants to walk to the library by himself. He's eighteen. It's only a few blocks away, but he has to walk past the place where the car hit him, and I can't do it. He gets so mad at me, but I just can't. This dog . . . it will give him his freedom. I think it will help me let him go."

That's why Lu Picard and the staff at ECAD work so hard. That's why they train the dogs so precisely, beginning on the third day of their lives, and nurture them so carefully. That's why they take less money to do more work, and endure frustrations and setbacks without complaints (or only a few). I don't think it's a sacrifice, any more than my life as a soldier was a sacrifice. We believe in what we do and we love it. What's monetary enrichment compared to personal accomplishment? What's a new car compared to the knowledge that you've bettered someone's life?

That's why Tuesday was a problem. Because their work was so important, the dogs at ECAD had to be the best. How can you give that young man in the wheelchair a dog that might ignore him? How can you give a brain-damaged child, who shuffles slowly and weakly when she walks, a dog that might pull her into the street?

Tuesday wasn't a bad dog. He just wasn't attentive to commands, and he sometimes refused to follow the two most basic: side and heel, the commands telling a dog to walk on your right or left side. In Lu's opinion, he was immature. I think he was wounded from losing Tom, as only a sensitive dog like Tuesday could be.

I know that ECAD dogs, when trained in the usual way, don't miss being bonded. How would they, as Lu argues, when they've never experienced a consistent relationship with a human being? Do you miss speaking Portuguese? Or seeing the sunset over the North Pole?

But what happens when a dog, especially an intuitive and emotional dog like Tuesday, experiences a strong human bond not once but twice, only to lose it both times? How does he feel then?

Lu saw the pitfalls. But she also saw the potential in Tuesday. He was warm and beautiful. He was mild-mannered. He was smart and sensitive and impossible not to love. And, Lu suspected with her fifteen years of intuition, she had the perfect trainer to reach him: Brendan.

It has long been known that training a service dog can be beneficial for the trainer as well as the dog. In fact, Green Chimneys Farms, one of Lu Picard's support organizations and a pioneer in the field since the 1940s, began training service dogs primarily as therapy for emotionally troubled children. For the past thirteen years, ECAD has performed that therapeutic role at Children's Village, a residential school for troubled teens in Dobbs Ferry, New York, about an hour north of New York City. Working at ECAD is a voluntary program for the students, so it is surprising, at first, that so many of the teenagers seem withdrawn, aggressive, or dismissive toward their work. But remember, these are some of the most troubled kids in the New York State foster care system. Like Tuesday, most have been passed through multiple caregivers and learned that hardening your heart—even to dogs—is the only way to survive.

Brendan's story is typical. Born in an impoverished area of Brooklyn, he bounced between a series of foster parents and his mother's house, never staying longer than a few months. He had always been quiet, but now he withdrew from the world around him. He stopped listening to his foster parents; he stopped trying to make friends. He was vulnerable, but even worse, he was large. He was always the huge new boy in a rough school. But he wasn't a fighter. This made him a target for hard boys and others trying to prove themselves. He got picked on and he got beaten up. He wanted nothing more than to go home to his mother, but she had younger children now. He never stayed for long.

Eventually, Brendan took to the streets. He stayed out as long as he wanted, whenever he wanted, and never worried about the consequences. No punishment could touch him, because he didn't care. He was angry, but more than that, he was hurt, and he was only a kid, so what did he know? All he wanted was his mother, and she wasn't going to take him back. So he fought. And argued. And stared at the wall and shrugged when they suspended him from school.

A social worker recommended Children's Village. The State of New York agreed. It was the ideal place for a lonely young boy, but the transition wasn't easy. He hated his old life, but he hated his new life even more. He wouldn't talk to anyone, even the other kids in his cottage. He wandered to class in a daze and ate his meals without enthusiasm. He was a young teenager, and he missed the city. He missed the action on the streets. He missed the hope, no matter how small, that his mother would take him back. Most of all, he missed his rottweiler, Bear, the only constant in his life. No matter what happened or where he lived, the dog had always been waiting.

Brendan knew dog training was an option at Children's Village. He heard the dogs were special. Golden retrievers that could turn on lights and open doors? He was intrigued, but he didn't admit that to anyone. He was too withdrawn; he didn't open himself up like that. Besides, it was probably a con, because everything in life turned out to be a con, just another way for adults to get what they wanted. But after the dogs performed for his class one day, he couldn't resist. It was no con. The dogs really could turn on lights with their noses, open doors, and walk right beside their trainers, who were kids from Children's Village just like him, except that with the dogs beside them, those kids weren't quite like him anymore.

I have to do that, he thought, despite himself. *I gotta be a part of that.*

He didn't thrive in the program. He liked the dogs, but he resented the rigidity of the training. He spent hours without talking, sullenly walking the dogs through their drills, but then, when he was alone with the other kids, he bullied and belittled them. He was a typical Children's Village student: afraid, resentful, and mistrusting—a bully when he felt bad but deep down, in his heart, a good kid. He was like Tuesday, in a way. He wanted affection, he wanted a task, but he felt abandoned by the person he loved. He was sixteen, but he acted like he was eight, and Lu wanted to wrap her arms around him even when he acted out, because she knew he was sensitive and wounded and needed a hug.

She gave him Tuesday instead, pulling him aside one day and telling him, "I have a special job for you, Brendan, okay?"

"What is it?"

"It's Tuesday. He's having trouble heeling. Can you help him?"

Brendan knew this was true. Everybody loved Tuesday, but everyone knew he was lagging behind the other dogs, too.

This is not to say Tuesday was a bad dog. His poor behavior was only a matter of degrees. The ECAD program sent the dogs out every few weekends to spend time as "normal dogs" at the homes of volunteers. One Sunday, Tuesday's foster mother took him to church. Not to sit in the car, but to sit under the pew and listen, without complaint, to an entire sermon. At communion, he followed his foster mother to the kneeler. Instead of sitting behind her as she expected, Tuesday sat beside her, with his paws on the altar rail. Everyone else had their hands there, so why not? When the priest came with the communion wafers, Tuesday quietly watched him pass, but his eyes said, *Hey, why didn't I get a treat?* The priest came back, placed his hands on Tuesday's head and blessed his future work. Tuesday waited quietly for a few seconds, then turned and walked back to his seat, the whole congregation chuckling behind him.

So he was not a poorly behaved dog—not by "normal dog" standards, anyway. In fact, he was probably the best-behaved dog you have ever met. He was just silly sometimes. He would lose his concentration and romp after the other dogs, or taunt his handlers by waving a toy in his mouth instead of handing it to them, or give them a goofy smile when they told him to sit on his box. If they asked him to fetch a sock, sometimes he'd grab two, then run around the room showing them to everyone. He was immature, as Lu put it. He'd stayed a fifteen-pound puppy, even as his body had grown into an eighty-pound dog.

Brendan knew Tuesday's history. He had seen Tuesday's behavior. He knew this wasn't another con by adults. Tuesday really needed special help. When Brendan turned and saw Tuesday watching him with those deep eyes and knotted eyebrows, I think he realized, for the first time, the connection between them.

You're a little broken, eh, Tuesday? Well, I understand. I'm a little broken, too.

It's amazing what focus can do. Training dogs is one thing, but to have a dog of your own? To watch him grow day after day, an increment at a time? To be able to say, even to yourself, *Tuesday turned on a light switch, and I taught him that?* That's different. That's taking responsibility and having pride.

Brendan was never frustrated when Tuesday jogged a few feet ahead or pulled on the leash. He never raised his voice when Tuesday botched the distraction test by stopping to eat the dog treats thrown onto the floor in his path. There was no failure for the children at ECAD. Lu didn't tell them, "Teach that dog to turn on a light switch in three hundred repetitions." She said, "Let's see how long it takes Blue to turn on that light." But the kids knew it usually took three hundred times to flip a light switch, so at five hundred or so most of them grew frustrated. They didn't understand why the dog wasn't performing, and they took it personally. Not Brendan. Not anymore. When Tuesday struggled with the multiple retrieve—picking specified objects out of a pile and bringing them back one at a time—Brendan just thought, *Tuesday's a little broken, but he means well. He'll get there.*

And when Brendan thought that about Tuesday, he started to think that about himself, too.

Tuesday, as always, responded to the attention. The leash goes both ways, and he could feel Brendan's confidence in him. But he also felt Brendan's lack of confidence in himself and his strong desire to succeed. I've met Brendan, and there is something about him that makes you want to help him. He's a good kid, but he is so vulnerable that if he ever asked for anything I can't imagine letting him down. Tuesday picked up on that vulnerability. When he asked himself, *Why? Why bother with this training?* he now had an answer: for Brendan. That answer was magic, because helping others was the only thing that ever seemed to matter to Tuesday.

It was a positive cycle. The more Brendan embraced Tuesday, and saw in Tuesday's success a reflection of his own, the more Tuesday wanted to please him. Soon, Brendan was excelling, but for the first time in his life he didn't need to brag. Instead, he took joy in his success, and he put that joy back into his affection for the dogs. After training, he stayed to clean their kennels and brush their coats. He came in on weekends. He became the morning feeder, waking up early and trudging across the Children's Village campus to give the dogs their breakfast. He was feeding and grooming all the dogs, of course, but he came for Tuesday. On Best Friend night, when the kids could come and watch a movie, Brendan and Tuesday always sought each other out. At the end of each training session, the children were given ten minutes to sit quietly with the dogs. Brendan and Tuesday didn't always train together, since rotating trainers was still ECAD's basic method, but no matter which child he had trained with that day Tuesday laid his head on Brendan's lap. Most of the time he fell asleep, while Brendan smiled and whispered, "Good boy, good boy, good boy."

They got along so well that the two of them, the former problem children, started going on regular outreach trips to local hospitals and nursing homes. Brendan became a demonstration handler for public events, and he appeared prominently in an ECAD promotional video still available online. When a new litter of puppies was born, Brendan was one of the children selected to name them. It was autumn, so there were several seasonal names like Harvest. Brendan, still just a kid at seventeen, chose Mac 'n Cheese.

Their parting was emotional, but not as difficult as Lu had feared. They had both grown accustomed to being passed off by this point, and they had each held something back. Tuesday respected and liked Brendan, but I don't think he was emotionally attached. Not like he had been to his first raiser in prison, or even to Tom. He had hardened himself against that kind of heartbreak.

And Brendan, while he loved Tuesday, had always known he was training him for someone else. The completion of that mission—the knowledge that for the first time in his life he had been trusted with an opportunity, and he had succeeded—was more valuable to him than keeping Tuesday. As Tom put it, knowing he was helping others "got his mind right and focused on the positives." By the time I arrived, both Brendan and Tuesday were ready to move on.

But that doesn't mean they forgot each other. A few months after being partnered with Tuesday, I returned to ECAD for a fundraising event. Tuesday was so excited, I decided to ignore Lu's advice and let him off his leash. He ran right to a group of kids, jumped on the biggest boy, and gave him a lick in the face. The boy laughed and hugged Tuesday, ruffled his fur, then pushed him off and told him to return to me.

"Would you look at that!" I said to a trainer standing nearby. "Tuesday is never that way."

"Yeah. Straight to Brendan," she said, as Tuesday came back to my side. When I looked at her with a puzzled expression, she smiled and said: "Brendan fixed your dog."

Later, I talked with Lu about Tuesday. He had been through so much. His heart was broken so many times. How was it, I wanted to know, that he had come out so perfect?

"Perfect?" Lu said with a laugh. "Tuesday's not perfect, Luis. Far from it. He's just perfect for you."

PART II

LUIS

CHAPTER 4

AL-WALEED

I am the enemy you killed, my friend.
I knew you in this dark: for so you frowned
Yesterday through me as you jabbed and killed.
I parried; but my hands were loath and cold.
Let us sleep now . . .

—1st Lieutenant Wilfred Owen,
"Strange Meeting"

THIS IS THE HARDEST PART OF THE STORY. THE PART THAT STARTS
the memories churning. The part that makes me sweat and keeps
me up for days at a time. A few years ago, I thought a probing NPR
interview about my combat service had only left me drained and
sick. When I listened to the broadcast later, I was surprised to hear

---

1st Lt. Wilfred Edward Salter Owen, a British soldier, was one of the leading
poets of World War I. Owen was injured in March 1917 when he "was blown
high into the air by a trench mortar, landing in the remains of a fellow officer."
Shortly thereafter, he became trapped for days in an old German dugout. After
these two events, Owen was diagnosed with "shell shock" and sent to Scotland
for treatment. After returning to the front, Owen led units to storm a number of
enemy strong points near the French village of Joncourt. On November 4, 1918,
just seven days before the Armistice, he was caught in a German machine-gun
attack and killed. For his courage and leadership he was awarded Britain's Military Cross.

myself stuttering and stopping, then getting up from my chair in the middle of the interview, limping to the bathroom, and throwing up. I listen to a recording of myself talking about Iraq last month, and I'm surprised to discover minutes of silence in the middle of sentences. Where did I go? What was I thinking about? And why don't I remember that?

I wouldn't put myself through this, of course, if I didn't think it would help. It's therapy for me, sort of pulling out the shrapnel and applying a field dressing, battlefield-style. More importantly, I think it will help other veterans, and especially their families. Post-traumatic stress disorder (PTSD) isn't something you just get over. You don't go back to being who you were. It's more like a snow globe. War shakes you up, and suddenly all those pieces of your life—muscles, bones, thoughts, beliefs, relationships, even your dreams—are floating in the air out of your grip. They'll come down. I'm here to tell you that, with hard work, you'll recover. But they'll never come down where they once were. You're a changed person after combat. Not better or worse, just different. Seeking or wishing for the old you is the worst thing you can do.

So I want to be precise. In the last section, I imagined much of Tuesday's early life. I had details, but I didn't have a mental picture, so I looked at his smiling mug sitting right here beside me and imagined him smaller, more needy, less sure of himself. I thought about what broke him and how special the people were who put him back together. I asked myself, why does this dog make such an impression on people? Why, no matter where he goes, does he change lives?

With Iraq, I have mental pictures. The emptiness of the desert. The terrible decimation of entire city blocks. A dead American private. The charred body of an Iraqi boy. The rows of Sunni men sitting quietly in a jail cell, staring blankly ahead like souls in purgatory, waiting to be cast into hell. I remember the smile of my Iraqi friend, Maher, only a few months before his death. The smell of his apple tobacco merging, like a bad dream, with the awful stench of the town of Hitt. I am haunted by the way a man stepped into an alley, and why I almost shot him, even though I didn't know him, and why that kind of experience, day after day, breaks you down.

I wish I could make you hear the whizzing of tracer rounds when Syrian soldiers ambushed us along the Iraqi border. It was four in the morning; there was nothing for miles but a flat line where the dark earth met the black sky. And then the Syrians were there, rising over the edge of the dirt berm that marked the border, firing machine guns and heavy munitions from a Soviet-made BTR tank. I was so outraged I just stood there and stared at them through my night-vision goggles. "I can't believe we're being fired on!" I yelled, watching their dismounts reload. "I can't believe we're being attacked by the Syrian Army!"

We returned fire. We pushed them back. I wish you could hear that sound, too, the steady *det-det-det-det-det* of Pfc. Tyson Carter's M240 machine gun and the hammering of our .50 caliber machine gun, because it was all instinct, all adrenaline and discipline, and that was our cadence. Luckily, we didn't take casualties, and when we returned to base later, just as the sun was burning off the night, we were flying. I mean, I was angry. I was pissed off that we'd been attacked from across the international border. But I was exhilarated, too. A firefight is one of the most intense feelings in the world. It was only later that the weight of the encounter hit me, when the high was followed by the low, like the cold ashes after a fire burns off.

And that's the contradiction of Iraq. For many of us, it was the greatest time of our lives. Iraq is the country where we found our purpose, where we did the work we are most proud of, and where we encountered people and places we can never leave behind.

But it was also a complete disgrace. The place where we lost our ideals; where the Army we loved sold us out for careerist brass, a war-porn-fixated media and military-industrial-complex corporate greed; where the only honor and integrity seemed to exist among the troops on the line. If I could give you one word to describe why I came back wounded from Iraq, it wouldn't be combat. Or fear. Or injury. Or death. It would be betrayal. Betrayal of our troops by their commanders. Betrayal of our ideals. Betrayal of our promise to the Iraqis and to the people back home. Where does incompetence become criminal? Where does selfishness become moral failure? How many lies can be told before it all becomes a lie? I don't know for sure, but in Iraq a line was crossed, and I'm outraged as hell. I can't get over it. Because good people died, and they're still dying for the same reasons today.

"Why do you want to tell that story?" Mamá asked me when she heard about this book. "Why do you want people to know you have problems? Who will ever hire you?"

I understand her concerns. I am very private, much more so since Iraq, and very ambivalent about sharing my life. But I don't want to tell her that. I don't want to admit to her that working on this book has already caused months of pain, but that I feel compelled to tell the truth nonetheless. Who in their right mind wants their mother to worry?

"I have to finish it," I tell her. "It's something I *have* to do." It's war and healing, I want to tell her. It's pain. It's triumph. "Don't worry, Mamá," I say finally. "It's just a book about Tuesday."

And to tell Tuesday's story, for better or worse, I have to tell my own. Because to understand Tuesday's impact on my life, and why he matters so much to me, you have to understand who I used to be and how far down I've been.

In 2003, when I arrived at Al-Waleed, Iraq, a tiny outpost three hundred miles from Baghdad and sixty miles beyond the nearest

American forward operating base, I was strong. I could bench press 350 pounds, do 95 push-ups, plow through an Army obstacle course, and run ten miles before breakfast with hardly any effort at all. But more than that I was confident, strong-willed, a leader of men in the U.S. Army. And I loved my job.

I wasn't raised in a military family. My father is a respected economist, my mother is a business executive, and they raised me in a comfortable, deeply intellectual environment. They expected me to attend college, like my sister and brother, but I grew up in the Reagan years, when optimism and nationalism were fundamental aspects of American ideology. I believed in "the Evil Empire," as Reagan famously called the Soviet Union, and wanted to do my part to topple it, even though I was only eight at the time of his speech. When the United States invaded Grenada in 1983, there was talk among my father and uncles, all Cuban refugees, that maybe Cuba was next. Not militarily, at least in my father's mind. He had been very much against the Vietnam War; he believed in economics and ideas, not blunt-force weapons. I believed sacrifice and hard work were required to change the world, and that meant action. So I defied my parents and enlisted in the Army on the day I turned seventeen. I spent the summer after my junior year in high school in boot camp. I was there when Saddam Hussein invaded Kuwait and the U.S. military, along with a broad coalition, drew a line in the sand. I was hoping to serve in the first Gulf War, but by the time I turned eighteen and graduated from high school in June 1991, the "100-hour war" was already over.

I spent the next decade in the Army as an enlisted grunt, graduating from college and getting married, training my body and mind. I knew we were going to go back to the desert. There was unfinished business, and Saddam was a wild joker in the Middle Eastern deck of cards. I just didn't know how we were going to get there. I was enrolled in the officer training corps at Georgetown

University in Washington, D.C., when the answer came in a cloud of smoke rising from the direction of the Pentagon. I called my infantry National Guard unit and told them, "I'm ready to go. Just tell me what to do."

It took two years, but when the fight arrived I was ready. More than ready, I was eager. I believed: in my country, my Army, my unit, and myself. Defending my country and securing freedom for the people of Iraq? That was my purpose in life. My task? That was Al-Waleed and Iraq's border with Syria.

Al-Waleed was the largest of only two functioning border crossings (known as ports of entry, or POEs) between Syria and Iraq and a notorious cesspool of corruption. For months, foreign fighters and weapons had been pouring across the border into Sunni-dominated Al-Anbar Province, which by the fall of 2003 was on the verge of revolt against the American occupation. So, in late September 2003, command sent my platoon—White Platoon, Grim Troop, Second Squadron, Third Armored Cavalry Regiment—to staunch the wound at Al-Waleed. Our job was to establish a forward operating base (FOB), secure the port of entry, and neutralize the flow of contraband and enemy fighters across more than one hundred linear kilometers of border and thousands of square miles of Anbar desert. To do the job right, it would take a few hundred troops. But the overstretched Third Armored Cavalry didn't have a few hundred men to spare. As platoon leader of White Platoon, I was given three Humvees and fifteen cavalrymen.

We tore into our assignment, working from the basics out. Our first task was to establish a base of operations, which meant commandeering a building at the Iraqi border compound, establishing a defensive perimeter, and jerry-rigging basic amenities like electricity. I had great men, like Staff Sgt. Brian Potter, Sgt. Carl Bishop, Pfc. Tyson Carter, and Pfc. Derek Martin, an indefatigable twenty-year-old who could hump more stone than most mules. But we had inadequate supplies. In the end, we strung our only roll of concertina wire, which we scavenged from an old Iraq Army outpost, and then spent weeks filling sandbags and wire mesh baskets with dirt and rocks so that suicide bombers wouldn't have unimpeded access to our post.

When we weren't improving our defensive perimeter, we patrolled the ramshackle villages and flat endless desert that surrounded us, usually nine men per patrol in three Humvees. It was like America's Wild West out there. When Saddam was in power, he had issued "shoot on sight" orders for anyone traveling or living within twenty-five miles of the border, so the small towns that had grown up near the POE in the fading years of his reign were 90 percent male, 60 percent smugglers and criminals, and 100 percent armed. There was a certain thrill in that, I can't deny. I remember my gunner, Spc. Eric Pearcy, sticking out of his turret yelling "Yee-haw, Carlos Montalván's Bedouin Assault Force rides again!" each time we went racing across the desert in pursuit of smugglers in pickup trucks. We discovered numerous small caches of weapons and ordnance, such as five brand-new AK-47s hidden under a haystack in a Bedouin camp, but ultimately the patrols were little more than a high-intensity, low-efficiency grind. The villagers, most of whom were members of criminal syndicates specializing in various smuggling schemes, were too sophisticated to hide weapons or anything else of value in their houses.

Our success or failure, I knew, depended on controlling the port of entry—a combination customs office, passport control center, and paramilitary base that straddled the main road just inside the Iraqi border. The port was in theory operated by our allies in the new Iraqi government, but in practice it was controlled by Sunni tribal leaders in Ramadi—the leaders who, almost assuredly, were supporting the burgeoning insurgency. The man in charge was a Ramadi-born official known as "Mr. Waleed"—that's what everyone called him, even me—and nearly all the police and border officials were his tribal members. They were little more than a mafia, operating more for monetary gain than ideology, but undermining the stability of Iraq nonetheless.

My goal, as a local American commander, was to shift the balance of power at the crossing: to send home or detain the corrupt officials, empower the honest ones, turn the Bedouins into our allies, and cripple the smuggling operations in the area. For this, we used a combination of hard and soft power. My men stopped trucks that had already been checked by Iraqi customs inspectors and police. When we found contraband, the officials were held responsible. We went on joint patrols and insisted on confiscations. We arrested Abu Meteab, known within the American military as the Tony Soprano of western Al-Anbar. He came quietly, despite his armed militia, but not before we searched the hundreds of U.S. Army–owned containerized housing units (CHUs) stacked behind his compound. The CHUs were supposed to provide comfortable housing for American troops across Iraq enduring the sweltering Mesopotamian heat. Abu Meteab was holding them until the United States paid a "toll fee" for their transportation from Al-Waleed.

We took on the benzene smugglers, the most brazenly corrupt aspect of Al-Waleed culture. Benzene, the Iraqi form of gasoline, is supposed to be free. It is given to government-sanctioned gas stations, including one in Al-Waleed, for distribution to the public. But the gas station in Al-Waleed was never open. Instead, the benzene was piped out the back of the station into barrels and sold for black market profit on the side of the road, often right in front of that very station.

If anything symbolized the depth of corruption at Al-Waleed, it was the benzene trade. So I refused to tolerate it. On my orders, anyone seen selling benzene was arrested. Their benzene was confiscated and their plastic barrels knifed. The offenders were then forced to stand outside the gates of the compound, where we could watch them, and pump free benzene to the thousands of trucks and cars that passed through Al-Waleed every day. We eventually had to requisition a giant tank to store the confiscated benzene, a symbol to both the criminals and the general population that we were serious about creating a legitimate, affordable economy for the Iraqi people.

The soft power was community outreach. White Platoon had been sent to Al-Waleed without a translator, a disastrous oversight in a strategically important place where trust was built on conversations over cups of hot chai. Fortunately, a customs inspector named Ali volunteered to translate for us soon after our arrival. Without him, we never would have succeeded. Ali allowed us to interact with the Iraqis at the POE, because I trusted what he said. Along with Spc. Pearcy, my gunner and right-hand man, Ali attended our nightly meetings with visiting dignitaries and local tribal leaders, a traditional honor important to gaining support. Formal yet relaxed, lasting well past midnight, and requiring the drinking of more chai and the smoking of more cigarettes than any person should endure, these meetings were our opportunity to reach compromises and bring rogue elements into our efforts. Often, I left the meetings to find dawn breaking over the desert, the morning call for prayer from the POE's mosque (the only decent structure for fifty miles) rolling beautifully across the vast desert, feeling utterly tired but as if we had accomplished more in eight hours of talking than we had on our last eight patrols.

Initially, I met with Mr. Waleed, who was as gregarious and friendly as he was corrupt. But when it became clear our intention wasn't to bandage the old corrupt system but to tear it down, Mr. Waleed became less interested in our chats. Instead, we met with other Iraqis, including Lt. Col. Emad, the incoming commander of the port's border police battalion, who had been a major in Saddam's

Army but was an honorable man. The sheiks in Ramadi didn't approve of his cooperation, especially after Lt. Col. Emad began to significantly curtail corruption, so they sent a steady stream of new commanders to replace him.

We were polite at first, but after a month we'd had enough. "Leave now," I told the new men, when they arrived with their "credentials" and politician's smiles, "or I'll have you arrested. You're not going to undermine Lt. Col. Emad's authority and destroy the good work that is happening here for Iraq and its people."

Our real find, though, was Maher Thieb Hamad, a junior officer in the local Iraqi Police Service (IPS) who had picked up passable English from American movies and often joked about moving to Las Vegas to live the good life. Maher wasn't from Ramadi, so he wasn't part of the mafia clan, and like many Iraqis, he saw the fall of Saddam as a chance to end the twenty years of corruption that, even more than Saddam's brutality, had destroyed the fabric of Iraq's more than one-thousand-year-old society. Once we gained his trust, Maher often invited my men over to smoke apple tobacco and discuss tactics, describing the habits of corrupt officials or telling us, "Don't worry, you can trust him, he's a good man." This was in the midst of the first wave of reprisal killings, before Saddam Hussein had been captured, and it took a great deal of courage to side so openly with the Americans. The first time Maher guided us on a desert patrol, in fact, he wore a *shemagh*—a traditional Arab scarf that covers the face—so that he couldn't be identified. He showed us a water culvert where foreign fighters and smugglers were known to store weapons. It was less than two kilometers from our compound but contained twenty-four rocket-propelled grenades, six fragmentary grenades, four AK-47s, three machine guns and eighteen hundred rounds of ammunition, enough to destroy our austere FOB and do serious damage to our small platoon.

Even with Maher's help—and with plenty of hilarious talk about juggling five girlfriends (Sgt. Willie T. Flores, a great soldier and ladies' man) and using Army hazardous-duty pay for a penis extension (name withheld, since I don't know if he actually got the operation)—the tour was a grind. During the day the temperature was often hotter than 110 degrees, and the sandstorms felt like they could eat through skin. Gunfire was commonly heard and more mentally draining, on a daily basis, than the Syrian ambush on November 3, which almost sparked an international incident. It's not the fear of death that damages the mind in the combat zone. I never thought about that. It's the constant state of watchfulness, the hypervigilance necessary to survive day after day as a small unit among thousands of possible enemies. After a while, my body stopped understanding that it was under stress and started thinking that watching for death, always, was simply the way to live. When you can laugh about gunfire and mortar rounds, instead of ducking them, your mind has changed.

Other American commanders, I know, tolerated corruption. By accepting gifts like lavish meals from corrupt officials—a huge temptation when American soldiers ate mostly cold military rations for months—they essentially condoned it. My men and I pushed against it, refusing to let any form of contraband or illegal activity slide. And it worked. When the Iraqis realized we weren't going to chisel meekly, but were going to stand our ground no matter how dangerous or difficult the situation, it gave the honest men courage to step up beside us. It gave ordinary Iraqis reason to believe in us. And when that happened, we started making progress against the smugglers. We were tipped off to hiding places and told how Bedouin guides use the extensive wadis, a complicated canyon system not well marked on any of our maps, to move valuable contraband like foreign fighters across the border. We learned about night movements and weapons caches. When the Iraqi Security Forces (ISF) started confiscating more contraband, we used it to make improvements to their woefully antiquated offices and systems, which helped them confiscate more contraband.

It took a tremendous effort. Tremendous. Everyone worked themselves ragged, seven days a week, in brutal conditions—spotty electricity, little running water, often no shower for days on end, not to mention the threat of enemy fighters, armed smugglers, and IEDs. I was pulling eighteen-hour days, easy, without a second thought. That's why they called me Terminator. Not because I could bench press 350 pounds while bellowing near-perfect imitations of Arnold Schwarzenegger, but because I never stopped, not even in our operations base. The main road passed straight through the compound at Al-Waleed, since it was more a border checkpoint than military installation, so trucks and cars had relatively easy access to our FOB. We had a gun position on our roof and razor wire on our perimeter, but beyond that the members of the unit relied on each other. Even in our living quarters, we were always on guard, because we knew we were outnumbered and susceptible to being overrun.

But it worked. I want to state that fact again, because I'm proud of it: our efforts in the Anbar desert worked. By December 2003, word had traveled up the American chain of command that Al-Waleed was coming under control. The Iraqi Border Police and its American partners were confiscating more contraband and weapons, and arresting more foreign fighters and smugglers, than any other port of entry in Iraq.

Word also traveled up the Iraq chain of command, through Ramadi to Baghdad. The sheiks were our allies, supposedly, but they were considerably less pleased with our success. Squeezing Al-Waleed meant squeezing a major source of funding for the struggling Sunni power base. That's why they tried to send more loyal—in other words, corrupt—officers to replace Lt. Col. Emad. That's why nobody seemed too pleased when Red Platoon joined us at Al-Waleed in early December, bringing our American troop level close to fifty men. When I informed Mr. Waleed soon after that 250 American-trained Iraqi border police were being sent to help him, he was clearly disturbed. The new border policemen, combined with Maher's hand-chosen men in the regular Iraqi police and two active American platoons, would destroy the old way of business at Al-Waleed.

Soon after, in mid-December 2003, Mr. Waleed was recalled suddenly to Ramadi. A week or so later, at nine thirty in the evening on December 21, 2003, I headed to the Iraqi border police headquarters for my nightly meeting over cigarettes and chai. The desert had turned cold with the coming of winter, and I could see my breath as Spc. David Page and I walked 250 yards down the wide road that ran through the complex toward the border. Outside the chain-link fence, the world was silent and black, a vast unpopulated emptiness; inside, a feeble yellow light threw shadows over the Iraq Ministry of Transportation office and the thirty or so tractor trailers still parked outside. Even from a hundred yards I could see the red tips of cigarettes, flaring and subsiding in the darkness, and the puffs of smoke from the drivers stuck in the compound, unable to complete their paperwork before the office closed for the night. I heard Page adjust his pistol as we approached the trucks, a reassuring gesture we often made unconsciously before walking up on Iraqi civilians. The scene was peaceful and monotonous, ominous and explosive. That was Iraq. You just never knew.

"Take the left," I said to Page, as I veered toward the men gathered in front of the trucks on the right. It was a nightly exercise. We had to push the truckers back into the desert; it was too dangerous

to let them stay overnight inside our defensive perimeter, waiting
for the customs office to open again after morning prayers. I spoke
to the first group of drivers in my limited Arabic, and they nodded, flicked out their cigarettes, and reluctantly climbed back into
their rigs.

Further on, however, a driver shook his head. "*Mushkila*," he said
("problem" in Arabic), and then in broken English: "No good." He
signaled toward his trailer hitch. I knew this game; it was a nightly
exercise, too. Nobody wanted to spend the night along the desolate
desert highway, where murders and kidnappings were common,
when they could stay inside the safety of the compound fence.

So I shook my head no.

"*Ta'al*," he said ("come here"), flicking his cigarette across the
concrete. He walked into the shadows between two trucks and
pointed to the rigging behind his cab. I should have sensed something then, I suppose, but I followed him. As soon as I bent to in-
spect the coupling, the man pushed me from behind, slamming me
into the metal hitch and wiring.

I turned immediately, instinctively raising my right arm to ward
off the next blow. That's when I noticed the second man approaching
on the run, a long knife in his hand. I remember a short barrage of
body punches and elbows in the confined space of the rigging before
the second man hit me full force, with his knife drawn viciously
above his head. His momentum carried him into me, an inch from
my face, and I tasted more than smelled his breath and felt more than
saw the hatred in his eyes as he stabbed downward toward my neck.
I shifted my weight, and the knife hit the top edge of the body armor
covering my left shoulder, deflected outward, then ripped through
my uniform and across the tricep of my left arm. I pushed off and, in
the second of space that followed, pulled the pistol from my thigh
holster and fired one shot center of mass into the first attacker, who
was charging from my right. A ghastly cry, a scream of primal pain

and loss, ripped across the emptiness, and then I was twisting and falling, the man with the knife on top of me, driving me downward. I fired two more shots before my spine hit the concrete, my head snapped backward, and the world, like the desert around me, went totally black.

CHAPTER 5

AN AMERICAN SOLDIER

———

I want to stand as close to the edge as I can without going over.
Out on the edge you see all the kinds of things you can't see
from the center.

—KURT VONNEGUT

IF I WANTED TO PINPOINT THE MOMENT MY LIFE CHANGED, IT was no doubt during the attack and the days that followed. I have spent years dwelling on the decisions I made then. I have dealt every day with the physical pain, both in my head and my back, and I have spent countless nights awakened by the faces of my attackers—the hatred in the eyes of the man with the knife, the wretched cry of the man I shot.

It has been a long road, filled mostly with downs, from there to Tuesday. I think of the quirks sometimes, the happenstance and detours. What if I hadn't tried to continue with my military career?

———

Kurt Vonnegut, one of the most influential American novelists of the twentieth century, was an infantryman with the 423rd Infantry Regiment, 106th Infantry Division, during World War II. He was wounded and, on December 19, 1944, he was captured during the Battle of the Bulge. As a prisoner, he witnessed the fire-bombing of Dresden. In 1984, he attempted suicide.

What if I hadn't seen the email to veterans announcing the service dog program? What if Tuesday hadn't been sent to prison? Because of his unorthodox upbringing, Tuesday spent three extra months at ECAD. What if we had missed each other and Tuesday had been matched with someone else?

The truth is, I was lucky. I was lucky to find Tuesday, and I was even more lucky in the hours after the attack. Spc. Page finished off the wounded attacker—the second man disappeared before Page arrived—and I was able to call for help into my radio. I was in and out of consciousness for the next twenty-four hours, so I remember bits and pieces: Staff Sgt. Len Danhouse bending over me saying, "It's all right, sir, it's all right, you're going home"; waking up nearly naked and freezing, strapped to a EMS spine board; the glowing night-vision goggles of the air medics as they worked in a dark Blackhawk Medevac; my buddy 1st Lt. Ernie Ambrose smiling widely as he gave me a *Playboy* and a Diana Krall CD when I woke up on a cot near an Army field hospital. I felt paralyzed from the waist down, and I was poundingly sore, but within a few hours I regained movement in my legs. By the third day, the worst visible wounds were the knife laceration and the bruise on my left arm, but the dried blood on the white bandage assured me it wasn't serious. No permanent damage, only a minor scar. I looked at the black blood and thought, *That's it? That's all I got? I thought I was dead.*

The real damage was inside: three cracked vertebrae in my back and a traumatic brain injury from the concussion that knocked me cold. Unfortunately, I wouldn't know about either for years. The medical team wanted to send me to Baghdad, since there were no X-ray machines at the field hospital, but I refused. I was in tremendous pain—just moving sent blinding flashes through my head—and I knew a trip to Baghdad meant the end of my tour. There was no way I was going home. Not after waiting thirteen years. Not with the job left unfinished at Al-Waleed. Not with my men in the middle of the desert without me, only a few days before Christmas. I had an obligation: to my platoon; to Iraqis like Lt. Col. Emad, Ali, and Maher who had risked their lives to help us; and to the nation that deployed me. I could leave Iraq having helped achieve a victory, or I could leave in a body bag, but I wasn't leaving for a sore back, a pounding headache, and a cut on my arm. So four days after the attack, on Christmas Day 2003, I arrived back at Al-Waleed to cheers from my men and a note on our platoon acetate mission board that read, "Grim Troop 1, Syria 0."

That's probably when my psychological issues started, although like my physical injuries I didn't notice the extent of them at the time. The soldier who left Al-Waleed on a stretcher was determined; the soldier who came back, I can see now, was angry and obsessed. That was no random attack. No way. That took planning and information. Maher told me later the order had come from somewhere in the Iraqi chain of command, possibly Ramadi, but that only confirmed what I already suspected: I was the target of an assassination, and it had been ordered by so-called allies that didn't like White Platoon's aggressive approach to combating corruption.

So we went after them. I didn't know who the perpetrators were, but I knew they had a vested interest in the smuggling operation at Al-Waleed, and I was determined to break it down, to prove that the cynical corruptors of the new Iraq had messed with the wrong Army, the wrong troop, and the wrong man. We pushed hard for the remaining three months of our tour. We pushed with extended patrols. We pushed with more stringent truck inspections. We pushed back when Iraqi officials tried to stop the American-trained border policemen from being sent, and we struck hard when Lt. Col. Emad's second-in-command, Major Fawzi, attempted an armed insurrection. The more the Ramadi boys squirmed, the harder we clamped down. I wasn't the Terminator anymore. I was no machine. This was personal. There was no way we were letting those bastards win.

My body started breaking down: searing pain, sleepless nights, and a malfunctioning digestive system that left me dehydrated and raw. My head and back hurt so bad I popped Motrin by the handful—we call them Ranger Candy in the Army, since so many soldiers self-medicate with them—but still the pain often made me grit my teeth and, when my men weren't looking, drop to my knees. I couldn't lie on my cot without discomfort, and when I did manage to drop off to sleep I had nightmares, wild mishmashes of the Syrian Army ambush, mortar fire, and the assassination attempt, always accompanied by shadowy figures and fire.

Meanwhile, my mind was racing so fast it left me with vertigo. (The vertigo was actually from the brain injury, but I didn't understand that at the time.) I had been cautious before, but now I was hypervigilant, acutely aware that one sloppy house inspection or patrol could be my last. I started sitting away from the door with my back to the wall, even in our FOB. I started questioning the look on every Iraqi's face, searching for the flicker of intention before the attack. I felt my finger above the trigger of my M4 carbine more often, and my mind snapping to judgment more quickly, calculating a long string of possible moves and countermoves. When I sat down for my nightly chai with the local sheiks, I chose my seat carefully, holding a knife by my side, calculating the best way to kill them all, if and when the need arose. My digestion got so bad I was ordered back to FOB Byers in Ar-Rutbah for treatment,* but I refused to stay for more than a day. Once again, I came back more

---

* FOB Byers was named after Capt. Joshua Byers, a twenty-nine-year-old cavalry officer and the former commander of F Troop, Second Squadron, Third Armored Cavalry Regiment. Capt. Byers was killed by an IED on July 23, 2003, when his convoy was ambushed near the town of Ramadi. While awaiting deployment to Iraq, I had the sacred honor of escorting the body of Capt. Byers from Dover Air Force Base to his home in South Carolina, where he now rests. It was a solemn journey, and one I shall never forget. Capt. Byers was beloved by many.

angry and determined. Al-Waleed was breaking me down, but it was my place, my war, and I wouldn't let it go.

When my tour ended in late March 2004, I didn't want to leave. I asked permission to stay for a few extra months and help with the transition to the Marine Corps, who were taking over responsibility for Al-Anbar Province. In fact, I begged for it, numerous times. If I could have, I would have dug in and not left until they dragged me out, my fingernails cracking as I clawed at the rocks and sand. When the traitors tried to kill me, they left a piece of my soul in Al-Waleed. I couldn't leave without knowing it was in good hands.

And I felt an obligation to my brothers. Everyone knows the Army never leaves a comrade behind, but I was leaving behind Iraqi allies like Ali, Lt. Col. Emad, and Maher. They had trusted me. They were as brave as any American. They were as important to our success as my own platoon. They were my brothers in arms, and they were in a fragile position. They weren't doing a tour in Iraq; they lived there. They had to be valued and protected. *Without them, I reminded myself, you'd be dead. And you're leaving them behind.*

My request was denied, and on March 15, 2004, I left Al-Waleed for the last time. Less than a month later, I was in Colorado Springs, Colorado. I stepped off the plane at Peterson Air Force Base, and I barely recognized my old world. I went to a restaurant and couldn't believe the portion size. For six months, I'd eaten almost nothing but meager Iraqi food and Army rations. I drove around Fort Carson and was shocked by the buildings, so elegant and clean. For months, I'd seen nothing but concrete and mud hovels, leaning into a ferocious desert wind. For days, I couldn't stop taking hot showers. I even called my mother to tell her how great they were. "Hot showers, Mamá! They're amazing!" She must have thought I was crazy.

In June, I was promoted to first lieutenant. I was also promoted in place, meaning I wasn't just given a new rank but also a coveted assignment as a scout platoon leader. When I read my evaluation from that summer—"Carlos Montalván is the best tank commander in my troop . . ."; "Montalván is an outstanding officer and has proved he is a leader . . ."; "promote him rapidly and assign him to positions of greater authority . . . [he] has almost unlimited potential"—it is clear I was a junior officer on the rise. I had performed well in Iraq; I was being rewarded. And it felt great. At my promotion ceremony, I turned to my men and enthusiastically recited from memory the Army's new Soldier's Creed:

I am an American Soldier.
I am a Warrior and a member of a team.
I serve the people of the United States
    and live the Army Values.
I will always place the mission first.

I will never accept defeat.
I will never quit.
I will never leave a fallen comrade.

I am disciplined, physically and mentally tough,
    trained and proficient in my warrior tasks and drills.
I always maintain my arms, my equipment and myself.
I am an expert and I am a professional.
I stand ready to deploy, engage, and destroy the enemies
    of the United States of America in close combat.
I am a guardian of freedom and the American way of life.
I am an American Soldier.

I didn't just recite it. I shouted it in front of the whole troop. I barked it like I would bark "Yes sir!" if a colonel asked me if my unit was ready to fight.

I added to the tattoo on my left arm. After September 11, I started having powerful dreams, all featuring a spiraling, burning sun. Before shipping to Iraq, I had the sun image tattooed on my left shoulder. At Al-Waleed, I dreamt of hawks. They were a constant in that miragelike world. They always flew above us on patrol, and every time I looked up they seemed to melt into the burning desert sun. So I had a hawk tattooed into the sun on my arm, for Al-Waleed, with an American flag draped around the edges for patriotism and honor. At that moment, I was the American soldier in that creed.

But even then, as I was pounding ahead, my injuries were pulling me back. For the first month, I slept like a baby in my comfortable bed near Fort Carson—after six months on a cot and in a sleeping bag. I drove to New York City to visit my infant niece, who had been born in November while I was patrolling the Anbar desert. Holding Lucia, feeling the warmth and purity of a newborn baby and family member, was cathartic. In that instant, the war was washed away, as if God smiled through Lucia's beautiful baby eyes. Afterward, I went home to Washington, D.C., where I gave a slide show presentation of my tour in Iraq to my parents and their friends. They smiled and patted me on the back, telling me sincerely how proud they were. It felt nice to be appreciated, but after that night, I couldn't sleep. I stayed awake for days, trying to shake the images, and when I finally did fall asleep I was troubled by dreams. I drove to Miami with an Army buddy but developed a splitting headache that kept me on edge. Silence descended; I felt separated from the world. When I recovered, I didn't want to talk. I didn't want to go out on the town. There were beautiful women walking around the pool at the Clevelander Hotel all day, but I was distracted by my thoughts. All I wanted to do was drink.

Back at Fort Carson, I continued to drink. I was sucking down half a bottle of Motrin a day, but it was no longer dulling the pain.

By the afternoon, I usually had a headache, and the migraines were sometimes so bad I threw up half of the night. Even on good nights, I only slept three or four hours, wracked by back spasms and vertigo. I started drinking at night, alone, trying to knock myself out, and waking up most mornings so sore and stiff I could barely get out of bed.

My marriage died. We had dated for two years and were married by a justice of the peace in a park near Fort Knox, Kentucky, shortly before I deployed overseas. Amy wanted to be there for me and I wanted to be there for her, but in the stress of preparing eighty soldiers to deploy to Iraq, I sent her away. She was hurt and lonely and soon, she told me, fell into depression. I was obsessed with my work, and in particular with a refugee crisis: ten starving Indian nationals who had been beaten and robbed by the Syrians, and I was ordered to deny aid to them. The U.S. Army didn't want to establish a precedent, but I was the one who had to look those men in the eye. I defied orders and saved the Indians by arresting and feeding them, but I couldn't save my marriage. I received one letter from my wife during the first half of my tour; when I was wounded, I didn't even call her. I called Mamá instead. I thought I could save my marriage when I returned to the United States. I spent the first few weeks in Colorado writing emails and calling. The day before the slide presentation with my parents, I traveled to Maryland, where my wife was living, and met her at the Applebee's near Arundel Mills Mall. I was desperate to reconcile, but within ten minutes I knew it was over, and we ended up drinking our sorrows instead. I drank those sorrows for weeks, sucking them down with Motrin and regret.

I wasn't the only one in trouble. When we learned the Third Cavalry was on short rotation stateside and we were going back to Iraq in the spring, soldiers scattered. I mean, they just disappeared. They left the Army, or they transferred to other units, anywhere they could find a place. A few were cowards or shirkers, but most realized they weren't in any condition to go back. There was no counseling in those days, no attempt to deal with the psychic wounds of war, and my troop was unraveling: fighting, drinking, splitting with wives and girlfriends, arguing about everything and nothing at all. There was a burst of thrill seeking—driving fast, jumping out of airplanes, rampant sex—anything to restart the adrenaline pumping. Pfc. Tyson Carter, one of my workhorses from Al-Waleed, lost a leg in a motorcycle accident. Another soldier was arrested in Colorado Springs; I drove there in the middle of the night to prevent him from being jailed. Being a leader of men in the Army is an honor, but also a responsibility. There's no nine-to-five, home to the family and forget about the office, like the civilian world. My life was intertwined with my men, and their off time was my responsibility too. We joked about bad dreams, about drinking too much, about how none of us could drive under a highway overpass without switching lanes, even in traffic, because we didn't want to give the bomber on the bridge an easy target. That's not normal, to worry about bombers in Colorado Springs. A lot of guys realized that, and they wanted me, as their superior officer, to help them. I never turned them down, no matter how late at night or how much I wanted to drink myself to sleep.

I am an American soldier. I am disciplined, physically and mentally tough, trained and proficient in my warrior tasks and drills.

I went to counseling, but I never mentioned the chronic pain, stress, or swirling anxiety that had settled over my life. Instead, I talked about my problems sleeping and my wife. I quit after two sessions, which was all the Army provided without authorization. I wasn't cured. I hadn't even figured out I was sick. But authorization for more sessions meant explaining myself to my troop commander, and back then that would have jeopardized my career.

I am an American soldier. I am disciplined, physically and mentally tough.

In late July, my physical problems started to outrun me. First, I pulled an abdominal muscle. A few weeks later, I pulled my hamstring. I had been unconsciously compensating for my cracked vertebrae for six months, and my body hit the wall. I stayed out of PT (physical training) with my platoon, rehabilitating myself in the swimming pool every morning, but my recovery was slow and my mind a jumble of contradictory thoughts. I was proud of my service. I had a bright future. I believed in Operation Iraqi Freedom and, especially, in the Iraqis themselves.

I am an American soldier. I am an expert and I am a professional.

But at the same time, I was coming unmoored, my mind dwelling on the hand-to-hand struggle for my life, the Syrian ambush, the sandstorms, the riots, and Ali, Emad, and Maher, the men left behind.

I am a guardian of freedom and the American way of life.

The wife of one of my best men from Al-Waleed had become pregnant during his midtour leave. The fetus was fatally deformed, but Tricare, the Army's health service, doesn't provide abortions under any circumstances, and she had no choice but to carry the child to term. *I will never accept defeat.* Little Layla was born without a nose and several internal organs. Her parents had no financial resources on a soldier's pay to provide her comfort. It was heartbreaking, absolutely heartbreaking, to hold baby Little Layla in my hands. *I will never quit.* Her life was pain, and it tore her parents apart. *I will never quit.* She lived eight weeks, and the difficulty of her life, and the inhumanity of forcing that existence not only on her but her parents too—*I will never leave a fallen comrade*—fueled my downward drive.

I was angry with the Army. Not on the surface, but underneath, in the depth of my mind. Why did Layla and her parents have to endure that pain, especially after everything they had already endured? Why were they forcing our regiment back to Iraq just ten months after our return? Why weren't they helping us cope with our pain? We were badly banged up. We were undermanned and underequipped. The Army didn't care. They were churning us through. They cared more about getting us back to Iraq and making the numbers than they did about our health and survival.

It was the summer of 2004. Victory was slipping away. Everyone could see that, but the media kept pounding the message: "The generals say there are enough men. The generals say there is enough equipment. The generals say everything is going well." It was a lie. The soldiers on the line knew it because we were the ones suffering. We were the ones who endured days of enemy mortar fire when we arrived in Iraq without weapons or ammunition, as my element of eighty troopers had in Balad in 2003; we were the ones going back in 2005 without adequate recovery time or armor for our Humvees. And that is the ultimate betrayal: when the commanding officers care more about the media and the bosses than about their soldiers on the ground.

In August, I informed my unit I was leaving the Third Armored Cav. I was an American soldier, a guardian of freedom, an expert, a professional, but I was physically and mentally worn out. I was pursued by pulled muscles and black thoughts, and I knew I could never get the treatment I needed in the Army. Not if I wanted to rise above my current rank, anyway. I wanted to be that junior officer with unlimited potential, I wanted to be that warrior who had barked the Soldier's Creed only two months before, but I couldn't run. I could barely stand the headaches. And I was drinking, in private and alone, almost every day. In short, I could no longer exceed the standard, something I had always pushed myself to do, so it was time for me to go.

One month later, in September 2004, I signed on for a second tour. *I am*, after all, *an American soldier.*

CHAPTER 6

ANYTHING
BUT STABLE

You are killing me, fish, the old man thought. But you have
a right to. Never have I seen a greater, or more beautiful,
or a calmer or more noble thing than you, brother.
Come on and kill me. I do not care who kills who.

—ERNEST HEMINGWAY,
THE OLD MAN AND THE SEA

IT'S TIMES LIKE THIS THAT I THANK GOD FOR TUESDAY. THE
last two chapters take me back to difficult times, to memories so
strong they blot out my present life. Instead of reading or writing

---

During World War I, Hemingway volunteered to be an ambulance driver in
Italy. On July 8, 1918, while stationed at Fossalta di Piave, he was seriously
wounded by mortar fire, sustaining shrapnel wounds to both legs. Despite his
wounds, Hemingway carried an Italian soldier to safety, for which he received
the Italian Silver Medal of Military Valor. Afterward, Hemingway spent five
days at a field hospital before being transferred to a hospital in Milan for six
months. In 1947, he was awarded a Bronze Star for his bravery during World
War II. He was recognized for his valor in having been "under fire in combat
areas in order to obtain an accurate picture of conditions," with the commendation that "through his talent of expression, Mr. Hemingway enabled readers to
obtain a vivid picture of the difficulties and triumphs of the front-line soldier
and his organization in combat." Ernest Hemingway was awarded the 1953
Pulitzer Prize for *The Old Man and the Sea*. On July 2, 1961, he committed suicide.

in the middle of my bed, for the last half hour I have been at Al-Waleed with the knife at my neck, or on a helicopter waking up to the sight of flight medics in night-vision goggles. I have felt the tension of sitting on my bed near Fort Carson in the summer of 2004 and acknowledging for the first time that something was seriously wrong, and I've been holding my breath against the long fall of the next three years.

And then . . . Tuesday sticks his chin over the edge of the bed. He has come to me from across the room, where he likes to lounge on the cool bathroom tiles. He has plopped his head beside me and stared at me so intently and lovingly that, even in my agitated state, I can't help but notice him. He was monitoring my breathing, scrutinizing my body language. He knew I was anxious, and he came to pull me back to the present.

When I see that look—or even better, when he climbs all the way up on the bed and puts his chin across my keyboard—I know it's Tuesday time. I never argue. Tuesday knows what I need more than I do, and besides, I love playing with him. When he interrupts my work, I know it's not because he's bored or lonely, but because I need him. So I'll slip on his vest, the one that announces he is a working dog, and go out with him for a walk. Other times, I'll toss the tennis ball. My Manhattan apartment is a tiny room, too small for an eighty-pound dog to chase anything, so we usually go into the narrow hallway and bounce balls off the wall.

Right now, though, it's the middle of the night and neither option is available. So I close down the document and give Tuesday what he really loves: YouTube. He loves dog videos: dogs popping balloons, dogs riding skateboards, and best of all dogs running around with each other having a good time. He follows the action with his head, twitching in crazy patterns and letting out a soft bark for the good stuff. He's not as crazy about cats or hamsters, but frenetic squirrels make him lurch to attention and horses put him in an excited mood. He likes to put his head down, a boozy smile on his face, and watch them run.

Tonight, I click a bookmarked favorite, then say, "Jump on, Tuesday," to tell him to climb on the bed and watch. He's big enough to lie side by side, or I can prop myself on his belly and drift off, using his body as a pillow. This time, I sit and watch him stare at the screen, aware that I might write this moment into the book because it's so perfectly emblematic of what Tuesday does for me. As if reading my thoughts, Tuesday turns to look at me, a twinkle of love and thanks in his eyes, then turns back to the screen.

"No . . . thank *you*," I say, giving him a rough shake. "Thank you, Tuesday, for being my boy." He rolls over slightly, allowing me to pet his belly, but he doesn't take his eyes from the two dogs who are jumping back and forth over each other in front of a glass sliding door. I laugh, give him another shake, then walk over to refill his water and grab a glass for myself. In the cabinet is my knife. I carried a bigger one in Iraq, never putting it down after the assault at Al-Waleed. I carried this one, with a blade one millimeter shorter than three inches, the average legal limit, for three years after returning from my second tour. I put it down for the first time a few months after adopting Tuesday. It reminds me how much difference he's made in my life.

It's also a reminder of why I went back to Iraq for a second tour. Even now, I don't question that decision. I had to do it. Al-Anbar Province was in revolt. Abu Ghraib had hit the national news. Iraq was disintegrating and my friends, both American and Iraqi, were in danger. We had shaken hands with the Iraqis, eaten with them, fought and died with them. I couldn't have lived with walking away at that point; I would have felt empty and disloyal for the rest of my life.

I wouldn't have gone back, though, if I hadn't believed in success—not that it was inevitable, or even probable, but that it was possible. One man made me believe: Col. H. R. McMaster, the new regimental commander of the Third Armored Cavalry. He didn't try to convince me to stay; instead, he sat down with me and showed me what I could accomplish. Col. McMaster rarely gave orders, I soon found out; instead, he inspired you to lead. He made me believe I could make a difference. In short, he restored my faith. Then he offered me a position on his regimental staff as Iraqi Security Forces (ISF) liaison officer. How could I refuse?

We deployed in March 2005 to south Baghdad, part of the so-called Triangle of Death, and it was everything you'd expect from a war zone: broken and abandoned buildings, shattered glass, charred rubble swept into piles; snipers, bombers, militiamen, spies, and men I had no idea whether to shoot, arrest, or congratulate for their fortitude. We drove through the street, scanning the buildings, and it was like Mogadishu or Saigon or Berlin or any of the other fractured places Americans had held in their grasp over the last sixty years.

As the liaison officer, my responsibility was to embed with and advise Iraqi units in the area. Even in those surroundings, I was astounded by the Iraqi Army's disarray. There were hundreds of men on the roster, and therefore the American payroll, who never showed up and might never have existed. Most of the troops had insufficient weaponry, and those with decent weapons often lacked ammunition, even though the level of violence was extraordinarily high. A day never passed without an attack, and often it was three or four incidents per patrol. Car bombs. IEDs. Snipers and armed gangs. Suicide attacks on living quarters, traffic checkpoints, and payroll lines, threats against wives and children, firefights in crowded streets. The Iraqi Fourth Brigade had been losing men for more than a year, and if they ever had any discipline, it had long since broken down. Men were deserting en masse. Others had the thousand-yard stare of the shell-shocked; still others looked like they wanted to hunt down every suspected "insurgent"—in this case, Sunnis—and beat them to death with their bare hands.

It was an impossible situation, especially for a group of poorly trained men fighting not for their screwed-up government but mainly for pay. South Baghdad was a major ethnic and sectarian fault line, with a population split almost evenly between Sunni and Shia, but the local Iraqi Army was almost entirely Shia and it was impossible, after a while, to determine who was in the right. One day, there was a suicide bombing at a Shiite mosque, complete with mothers screaming, bloody children, and innocent vendors dead in the street. Two days later, we raided a different Shiite mosque and found a cache of weapons large enough to arm a battalion. In a back room, we found photographs of Sunni men being tortured, beheaded, and bound in chairs with their eyes burned out.

I was leading a patrol in downtown Mahmudiyah, accompanied by *New York Times* reporter Sabrina Tavernise, when I received word over the radio that a major clearing operation by the Iraqi Army was degenerating into sectarian aggression, with soldiers grabbing Sunni men out of buildings and beating them in the streets. I managed to keep those facts from the reporter, telling her instead when she asked: "These Iraqi troops aren't ready for combat operations—they shouldn't even be out here."

When that quote made the front pages of the *New York Times*, the commander of the 2-70th Armor Battalion demanded to speak with me. "We don't need that kind of publicity," he told me. "Keep it positive from now on." I wasn't sure what to think. I had asked Colonel McMaster for two extra months in south Baghdad to create a basic level of organization for the Iraqi soldiers and the next American advisers. I had believed in the American mission, even after discovering the depths of the problems in our "allied" Iraqi Army. But by the day of the street beatings, it was clear that there was civil war in south Baghdad. The Iraqi government, through the Iraqi Army, was engaged in a campaign of tribal and sectarian cleansing against the Sunnis, and the U.S. Army was aiding and abetting that effort. Didn't the commanders know that? Or did they simply not care about combat readiness and morality among the Iraqis as long as the promised trained troop numbers were met? What, pray tell, did they want me to say?

By the time I joined the rest of Colonel McMaster's regimental staff in Nineveh Province, northwest of Baghdad, I was drained, mentally and physically. The regiment was taking significant casualties, and I could no longer understand what those men were fighting and dying for. Were we helping the Iraqis? Were we making the world more secure? Were we saving lives over the long term— the ultimate job of an army, not the killing soft-hearted liberals suppose? Violence was surging. American troops had never been held in lower esteem by the local population. The ultimate goals of the war had never been less clear. And yet the message from the top was the same: We have the right strategy. We have enough men. We're winning this war.

As the Third Armored Cavalry's lead operations officer for our border region, I was high enough up, despite my relatively low rank, to travel to the Red Zone (the Iraqi government area next to the Green Zone) to participate in high-level meetings with General Petraeus's key staff, as well as briefings with General Abizaid in Mosul and General Casey in Tal Afar. After returning home, in April 2006, I accompanied Colonel McMaster to the Pentagon for meetings with General Odierno and Secretary Rumsfeld, among others. By then, it had long been clear that the top officers in Baghdad, CENTCOM, and Washington weren't asking combat officers what they needed; they were telling us what they wanted. And they wanted successes to back up their claims. Not real success on the ground—the brass had long since lost contact with the actual soldiers fighting the war. They were fixated on metrics, like the

number of detainees captured and "enemy" KIAs, even if that
meant taking time away from more important work or angering
the local population. They wanted me to report a certain number
of Iraqi security forces trained, even if I knew half those soldiers
were "ghosts" who either never existed or never showed up—but
still got checks from the American taxpayer. And, especially, they
wanted us to say we had enough soldiers. Several times, I heard Colonel McMaster tell superior officers he didn't have the manpower
necessary for the mission. The next week, I'd hear those same generals telling the media, "The commanders have assured me we have
enough soldiers for the operation."

When you're a leader on the line (in a combat position), your responsibility is to the men and women beneath and beside you. You
do everything you can for those troops, because they are your brothers and sisters and if you let them down, some of them might die.

For the senior officers in Iraq, at least in 2005–2006, the responsibility was to the men at the top, the media, the message, the
public back home—anything and everything, it seemed, but the
soldiers under their command. And that's the ultimate betrayal of
Iraq, the one that disillusioned me in Baghdad and Nineveh and
keeps me outraged today.

I can't vouch for the other regimental staff officers in the Third
Armored Cav, but by the second half of my second tour I didn't
feel like I was working for the U.S. Army or implementing a
higher plan. I was working for the men below me, both Iraqi and
American, to keep them alive. I was a military attaché, spending
most of my time at forward operating bases, but I had served recently as a combat leader and advisor, and I was close to the troops.
I knew Pfc. Joseph Knott, who was killed by a roadside bomb.
Our Regimental Command, Sgt. Maj. John Caldwell, whose skull
was shattered by an IED, was a friend and the first person to shake
my hand when I arrived in-country in 2003. The soldier I bailed

out in Colorado Springs the previous summer suffered a devastating combat injury. We lost three officers in a Blackhawk helicopter crash, and I knew them all. Death wasn't a number; it was something that crept up in quiet moments and stabbed at my neck, then reared back to strike again. It had a face, and a hot salty breath. I felt a tremendous responsibility to the troops of the Third Armored Calvary. Tremendous. I felt my work might save their lives, and I felt guilty whenever I took an hour off. So I didn't drink. I didn't socialize. I didn't watch television or play video games. I don't believe in being too tired to feel pain, but I believe in being hurt to the point that giving in to the pain, even for a day, will drag you down for good. So for six months I dragged my cracked back and throbbing head through twenty-hour days with the help of nothing more than a fistful of Motrin, then collapsed every night into a dreamless sleep.

Eventually, I was promoted to Colonel McMaster's adjutant, a unique position for a junior officer. The colonel worked from 7:00 a.m. until 1:00 a.m., seven days a week, and I was always with him. When he went to bed, I worked an additional four hours making sure the regimental headquarters was organized and efficient, and that every operational component that Colonel McMaster needed for the next day was ready. I was relentlessly driven, sleeping less than two hours a night, and I wasn't surprised when the official assessment of my PTSD, compiled by a doctor I worked and roomed with in Nineveh, stated that I had "unrealistic expectations of others." Nobody could work that hard for an extended period of time. Nobody could meet my high expectations. Including me.

When my tour was up, I didn't ask to stay. I had volunteered twice for extended duty, once in Al-Waleed and once in south Baghdad. This time, I was ready to leave. I had been, for as long as I could remember, just hanging on, trying to make it through the day without a breakdown, sort of like the American operations in

Iraq. By the time I touched ground in Colorado in February 2006, I was burnt toast. That's the image that always comes to mind when I think of myself then: a blackened, smoking hunk of bread, still jammed between the heated wires.

Four months later, in June 2006, Colonel McMaster completed his command with the Third Armored Cavalry. As his adjutant, it was my honor to sprint across a field at his change-of-command ceremony. I hadn't run for more than a year because of my injuries, but I figured one short run couldn't hurt. Fortunately, there was a rehearsal the day before. I sprinted one hundred yards before stepping in a sprinkler hole, slamming my head to the ground (another concussion), and ripping the patellar tendon from my right knee. My kneecap was floating six inches up my thigh as they loaded me into a truck, wincing in pain. We were heading to Evans Army Hospital at fifty miles an hour when a fire extinguisher exploded and started whipping around the truck, spraying foam in all directions. The driver swerved violently, shouting "I can't see!"

"Pull over! Pull over!"

"I can't see to pull over!"

"Do it anyway!" I yelled.

When we finally careened to the side of the road, the two soldiers tumbled out, coughing and puking, leaving me lying in the back yelling, "Get me out! Get me out! I can't breathe in here." By the time I found the door handle and threw myself onto the street, my lungs were burning and my skin and uniform were toxic-white. I could taste the fire retardant in my mouth, and believe me, it was worse than Tuesday's toothpaste. And more relentless. The more I tried to spit it out, the more it clung to my throat, choking me. It would have been funny, really, if it hadn't been my life.

CHAPTER 7

HARD DECISIONS

The most hateful grief of all human griefs is this, to have
knowledge of the truth but no power over the event.

—HERODOTUS, *THE HISTORIES*

THE REALITY OF WAR WOUNDS IS THAT THEY'RE WORSE WHEN you're out of the combat zone. That's why so many psychologically scarred service members end up back for second and third tours, telling people they "couldn't adjust" to civilian life. That's probably why I volunteered to spend extra months embedded with Iraqi troops in south Baghdad, the point of the Triangle of Death. I had almost been killed by traitorous Iraqi allies, and yet I put myself back in Iraqi hands, in one of the most dangerous sections of Baghdad, partly out of responsibility and guilt but mostly to quiet my mind. I ignored my physical injuries, engaging in combat clearing operations and raids despite debilitating pain. I needed the adrenaline rush, the distraction of action, more than I needed personal security.

The worst thing you can experience is time to think, and that's exactly what I had during the two months I was bedridden while recovering from patellar tendon surgery. My body was a mess. My knee was immobilized. My fractured vertebrae had, in two years without treatment, developed "wedge deformities" that threw off my alignment and rubbed nerves, causing numbness, soreness, and shooting pain. Headaches from my multiple concussions developed suddenly and lasted for days. Sometimes I was afraid to move. Even opening my eyes in a lighted room could bring on stabbing pains.

My mind was worse. Flashbacks, black thoughts, bad dreams. I woke up almost every night in a sweat, convinced I was back on the ground at Al-Waleed, awaiting the assassin's knife. During the day, without duties to distract me, I dwelled on the war. I walked step-by-step through battlefields and relived my anniversaries: my first combat, my first dead body, my first kill the day I escaped death, and all the other dates that never leave a soldier's mind. Eventually, I started researching. I was unable to turn away from the war, so I started reading everything I could about the war planning and objectives, from soulless Department of Defense (DOD) documents to combat reports to soldiers' blogs from the battlefield. I was driving myself crazy, but there was no way I could stop. The search for answers was keeping me sane.

After my two-month recovery, the Army sent me to Fort Benning as the executive officer of B Company, First Battalion, Eleventh Infantry. It was a recovery assignment, because it was clear by then to everyone that I was in bad shape, but like everything else in the Army, B Company was undermanned and the operations tempo too high. My job was to help train 650 newly commissioned officers for combat tours, but there were too few instructors to properly train that many leaders. I was hurting, most notably with a serious limp, and I needed to take care of myself, but it would have been irresponsible not to kill myself for those men and women bound for war, even though I no longer believed in the U.S. Army.

No, that's not right. I believed in the Army. I loved the Army more than ever, and I respected and cared about the men and women who fought for it. But I didn't believe in the men running the Army or the civilians running the war effort. These junior officers were being sent to an undermanned and badly planned war; the least I could do was try my best to prepare them.

I was angry. Looking back, that emotion probably defined that year of my life. PTSD is a dwelling disorder; it makes a person psychologically incapable of moving beyond the traumas of his or her past. The mess hall, the uniforms, the training exercises: they all triggered memories of my worst moments in Iraq. When I wasn't distracted by work, I was lost in the past, trying to shift through the details and figure out where I had gone wrong. Betrayal and anger were my watchwords, feelings that never really left me, even in my best moments. But I also wheeled through cycles of outrage, frustration, helplessness, sadness at the loss of friends, guilt, shame, grief at the loss of my life's work, and an ever-present bone-deep loneliness that seemed to entomb me like a ceremonial cloth.

Alienated and haunted, I moved thirty miles away from my fellow soldiers to a trailer surrounded by a seven-foot-high barbed-wire-topped fence (it was already in place; the landlady had trouble with her convict ex-boyfriend). I was trying to wall myself off from the world, I suppose, but the present was already lost, and even in Salem, Alabama, the memories of Iraq came to bury me, triggered by everything from the smell of my dinner to a bird flying across the sun to the knife I kept always at my side.

I didn't run from the memories. Instead, I delved deep, continuing the research I'd started in Colorado, spending twelve hours a day training officers and eight hours a night studying government documents, a beer in my hand or a bottle of Bacardi on the desk beside me. Slowly, page after page, I turned my anger into righteous indignation, and then a call to arms to fight for justice and truth. I had been a warrior for sixteen years; this was a survival instinct. With a cause I believed in, a hidden part of me realized, I would never give in to hopelessness and despair. So I read thousands of pages of State Department and DOD reports, crunched thousands of numbers, and wrote out my thoughts, night after night, trying to figure out why the war I experienced in Iraq was so different than the one portrayed in the media—and so different than the victory we might have achieved.

In January 2007, two days after George Bush announced the surge, a twenty-page condensed version of my assessment of what I had seen in Iraq ran in the *New York Times* as an op-ed entitled "Losing Iraq, One Truckload at a Time." The essay focused on two things— tolerance of corruption within the American and Iraqi armies and lack of accountability by high-ranking officials—and caused quite a stir in the military hierarchy. I heard from dozens of active-duty officers who supported my conclusions, including several high-ranking officers I had served with. A faculty member at West Point suggested I apply for a professorship. I was invited to the American Enterprise Institute, the conservative think tank "unofficially" developing the strategy for implementing Bush's surge, where I participated in serious discussions with scholars and strategists like retired generals John Keene and David Barno and Gen. William Caldwell, currently in charge of the NATO training mission in Afghanistan.

Most of my superior officers at Fort Benning were less supportive, however, and as my articles kept appearing in places like the *Washington Times*, the *Fort Worth Star-Telegram*, and the *Atlanta Journal-Constitution*, they expressed a strong interest in seeing me muzzled . . . or gone. And so that summer, by mutual consent, the American military and I officially ended our relationship. My honorable discharge date was September 11, 2007, six years after the terrorist attacks, seventeen years after I joined the Army at seventeen, and only a few days after Tuesday was released from his own period of exile at a prison in upstate New York. Even on my worst days, I can't help but smile at that parallel in our lives.

By then, I had accepted a position at the New York Office of Emergency Management. Within a month, I moved straight from a small trailer outside Salem, Alabama, to a small apartment in Sunset Park, Brooklyn, a bustling immigrant neighborhood far from the yuppie enclaves to the north. I had no furniture; I had no more clothes than would fit in a small closet and a rucksack; I sat on the floor to use my laptop and slept on the carpet with only one blanket for warmth, much as I had slept in my sleeping bag at Al-Waleed. I looked into the closet days before I was to start my new job, saw the two new suits hanging from their wooden hangers, and knew it wasn't going to work.

It wasn't the responsibility. I knew planning. I knew implementation in life-or-death situations. At Fort Benning, I had been responsible for hundreds of people and millions of dollars of equipment, and my evaluations had praised my "extraordinary performance" and suggested a promotion to major. I was a leader; I would rise to the occasion in an emergency. That was when I thrived.

But the daily grind? I wasn't in any condition for that. I limped; I used a cane; I experienced frequent bouts of vertigo that resulted in falls; I was in near constant pain. As I looked at those suits, I realized a job meant riding a subway during rush hour, walking into rooms full of people, and making small talk with the receptionist. The fact was, I hadn't made small talk with anyone in a year. At Fort Benning, I had withdrawn, both physically and mentally, ignoring social obligations and invitations. In Brooklyn, I barely left my apartment. When I did, it was usually late at night, to buy necessities like packaged food. I wasn't an alcoholic, but I drank every day to calm my anxiety and most of the night to put myself to sleep. There wasn't any one thing I could point to—no recurring dreams or angry outbursts, no paranoid voices in my head. I just wasn't myself. Some nights, it took me an hour to work up the courage to walk one block to the liquor store.

Turning down the position at Emergency Management was the right thing to do, but it was also the hardest. The night I paced my apartment before making the call was one of the most difficult of my life. I wanted the position. It paid well, it was interesting, and it was a great career opportunity. Turning it down felt like failure. I wasn't sure I'd ever get another chance.

But when I made the call, I felt free. I felt more liberated, in fact, than I ever had in my life. For almost four years, I had ignored my problems. I had worked too hard, pushing myself too far, so that I wouldn't have to deal with them. I had almost done that with Emergency Management, too. But I had stopped. I had been honest. I had summoned the courage to stop pretending and accept the reality of my life. Now, finally, I was going to get help.

My parents didn't see it that way. Mamá shook her head, then walked out of the room. My papá got in my face—I had traveled to Washington by train to tell them, a harrowing journey in my agoraphobic state—and said, "You are not going to be one of those broken veterans."

It wasn't a threat. It was a statement of fact. My father thought I was doing this to myself, and he wasn't going to allow it. He knew I was wounded in Iraq; my parents had received that horrible call from the Army in the middle of the night, telling them I was hurt. He didn't realize those wounds were still with me, a poison in my life. He thought I was wallowing in misery, and if I was a real man I'd pull myself out of it. He thought my diagnosis with PTSD, which I received before my honorable discharge, was some kind of excuse.

I wanted to curse him right there, right to his face, but I wasn't raised that way. And truth be told, I was too angry. It was, in many ways, the lowest moment of my life. The betrayal of the Army cut my heart; losing the respect of my papá ran a saber through my soul. It was the moment when anger took over and my memories of

Iraq consumed me. I had been isolated from the world long before Alabama, but that night, for the first time, I felt terminally alone.

I spiraled downward, becoming anxious and paranoid. Without my family, there was nothing to keep me moored. I clung to my righteous indignation, but without my parents I lost hope. I scanned the computer nightly for war news, and I wrote frequently— sometimes obsessively—about my condition, but I essentially stopped going outside except to the liquor store, where I would buy a large bottle of rum and four liters of Diet Coke. I'd drink them to the bottom over the next few hours or days, then head back to the liquor store, numbed against the world. I skipped Thanksgiving, bottoming out alone in my apartment with Bacardi. There was no turkey, no mashed potatoes or stuffing, just a bottle of amber liquor quickly descending toward the bottom and a single lonely string of Christmas lights twinkling dimly in the dark.

Sometime early in the morning, blitzed on rum and sadness, I wrote an essay for NPR's *This I Believe*. It talked about my feelings of abandonment, of betrayal, of being denied even basic medical assistance. It ended, "I hope I get help before it's too late."

I look at that essay now, and I don't know what I meant. I wasn't suicidal, that I know for sure. But I was, as I can see now, hurtling toward an end. Sometimes, as I lay on my bed after three days awake, having consumed too much alcohol for too long to be truly drunk, I thought, *Wouldn't it be nice if I could fall asleep? And wouldn't it be even better if I never woke up?*

I trudged on, too indignant to give in. Despite my official diagnosis with multiple injuries, there was a delay in receiving disability benefits, and my meager savings from seventeen years in the Army were running out. Still, I took a car service (like a taxi, but I could call and ask for the same driver) several times a week to my only standing obligation: the Brooklyn Veterans Affairs Medical

Center. It cost $11 one way versus $2 for the bus, something I couldn't really afford, but I had to do it, because I couldn't ride the bus. The faces, the smells, the enclosed space. I tried, but I couldn't do it. I had to step off. I needed to be somewhat coherent, after all, when I reached the VA, because they were running me through the usual routine, making me fill out endless paperwork, making me wait for hours, making me see a different medical intern every visit who would walk in with a smile and say, "So what's wrong with you today?"

I didn't like talking about my condition. I didn't like talking about Iraq. I didn't like strangers. I was, in other words, a typical wounded veteran. What did the VA not understand? Why couldn't they give me medicine or treatment instead of the runaround? They were understaffed and underfunded, probably because the government didn't want to acknowledge the damage being done in Iraq and Afghanistan, but for me, in my state, it felt personal. They didn't want to help me. They wanted me to just go away. They wanted to pretend I didn't exist. It was a betrayal, just another betrayal by the U.S. Army I had loved and served.

That fall, I had been accepted to graduate school at Columbia University. I had told my parents I was applying when I turned down the job at Emergency Management, but I knew they didn't believe me. So I sent the acceptance letter home without a word of explanation. For months, I had been stewing in anger, mixing my father's betrayal with that of the Army, seeing in his face as he dressed me down the face of the assassin who came for my life. Sending him the acceptance letter was, to me, an elegant "Fuck you."

I started classes in January. Columbia was on the upper west side of Manhattan, more than an hour away from Sunset Park, but moving closer was far beyond my financial or psychological means. The subway was a teeth-jangling, stomach-clenching experience, one that often left me with massive headaches or throwing up into trash cans on subway platforms. It wasn't that I wanted to turn back to my apartment some mornings; I was desperate to turn back *every* morning. But I forced myself to endure. I may have been a broken soldier—and I say that now with pride, not shame—but I was not a failure. Columbia was my way out of Sunset Park and my truncated life. If I didn't have graduate school, I realized somewhere in the back of my mind, I didn't have anything to live for, and then I really would end up alone in my bed, dead and undiscovered for days.

I admit that I sometimes went to class drunk, and that I always went with a few drinks in me at least. I often walked out in the middle of class, looked in the bathroom mirror, and was surprised to find my eyes bulging and my face covered with sweat. Presentations for my seminar left me paranoid and anxious, and I cursed my own foolishness. I had given presentations to Colonel McMaster and his superior officers. I had stood before generals at the American Enterprise Institute and advised them on the war. I had held the lives of a thousand men in my hands. And I aced it every time. Why was I terrified now to present a graduate school project in front of fifteen of my peers?

Outside of class, I hardly spoke. My neighbors in Sunset Park, I found out later, were vaguely frightened of me. I still don't really know what my classmates thought. I showed up; I sweated through class; I left and went straight to a bar or a convenience store, where I bought tall-boy Budweisers in a paper bag. Between classes, I was spending thirty hours a week at the Brooklyn VA hospital, fighting for a thirty-minute doctor's appointment, a therapy session or two, and a few prescriptions. My back ached. My ruptured knee ached. My mind cracked and spun. I fell down a flight of concrete subway stairs, knocking myself out. The migraines crippled me. I was making progress, I was passing classes, but the effort was wearing me down.

It all came to a head on May 7, 2008, near the end of my first semester at Columbia. At the invitation of the Wounded Warrior Project, a support organization for veterans, I traveled to New Jersey that night for a Bruce Springsteen concert. Despite drinking rum-and-Cokes at the lobby bar to calm my nerves, I suffered a panic attack halfway through the show and, hyperventilating and physically sick, took a bus and then a subway back toward my apartment. It was miserable, absolutely miserable. I huddled in my coat, my hand on the knife in my pocket, wondering what had made me think I could endure such an event. A Bruce Springsteen concert? An hour from home? In my condition? It was absurd.

At least the subway was mercifully empty, even though it was not yet midnight. By the time we reached Brooklyn, there was only me, an elderly Asian couple, and one other passenger in the subway car. Then two young Latinos entered. They were looking for trouble, I could tell right away, and sure enough one finished off whatever he was eating and threw his trash right on the elderly woman's lap. Then he started cursing at her in Spanish. I couldn't stand that type of disrespect.

"That's enough," I said.

"What's that, *hombre*?" the young man said, walking toward me.

"I said, pick up your trash and sit down."

"You want to start something?"

"I think you already have."

He came at me, but I knew he was going to, so I stood up and easily swept him past me into the back of the car. Then I lost my balance, either as the train lurched or my cane slipped or my back gave way, and with a blinding pain everything went black.

They found me later, unconscious on the F train platform at Fourth Avenue and Ninth Street with a broken ankle and blood pooling around my head. I woke up in Lutheran Hospital the next day. Another brain injury. Another bloody mess. I can't think of a better image of my life at that moment. And this time, there was nothing funny about it.

Less than two months later, I heard about the dogs.

CHAPTER 8

THE THOUGHT
OF DOGS

---

*You are passing through a darkness in which I myself in my
ignorance see nothing but that you have been made wretchedly
ill by it; but it is only a darkness, it is not an end, or the end.*

—HENRY JAMES, LETTER TO GRACE NORTON

I CAN'T BEGIN TO TELL YOU HOW MUCH MY LIFE CHANGED
when I read the email on July 1, 2008. (A Tuesday, I just realized.
I'll have to add that to my list of fake reasons for Tuesday's name.)
The Wounded Warrior Project, the veteran service organization I
went with to the Bruce Springsteen concert, forwarded the message. They forwarded messages every day, actually, but I usually
didn't read them. This tagline intrigued me: "WWP and Puppies
Behind Bars." Puppies behind bars?

The message was almost as simple: "Dear Warriors, please note
below. Puppies Behind Bars has 30 dogs a year to place, free of
charge, with veterans from Iraq or Afghanistan who are suffering
from PTSD, traumatic brain injuries or physical injuries. I've attached the Dog Tags brochure, which explains the program, as well
as the Dog Tags application."

As soon as I read the attached description, I knew the program was for me. I suffered from debilitating social anxiety, and the dogs were trained to understand and soothe emotional distress. I suffered from vertigo and frequent falls, and a dog could keep me stable. Because of my back I could barely tie my own shoes, and a dog could retrieve and pick things up for me. I was the perfect candidate. I was down, but I was working toward a future. I was a leader, so I could handle responsibility. I was a worker, so I would never give up. And I was lonely. Terribly, terribly lonely.

Most importantly, I loved dogs. At Al-Waleed, one of the most heartbreaking duties our troop performed was euthanizing dogs. There was a large loose pack of them roaming the area, and it was as if they'd been visited by a pestilence: thin, mangy, covered with boils, sick with tumors, and throwing up blood. It wasn't safe, either to the local population or the healthy dogs. And it wasn't humane to let the animals suffer. So we culled the most diseased and, with a heavy heart, shot them in the head. It was brutally dehumanizing work, made acceptable mostly by the continued trust and affection of Bruce, a white and gray former member of the pack adopted by Staff Sergeant Snyder, our hilarious and kindhearted mortar section leader. Bruce became our unit's mascot, a cool alpha male that always appeared just in time for MRE handouts and naps in the cool midafternoon shade of the FOB. We were too busy defending Iraq to take care of him like a pet, so Bruce took care of us. His presence lifted our morale. After the assassination attempt, it soothed me to see Bruce standing guard or napping carelessly on our front walk. He was the only living thing I really trusted to alert me to danger. And it just felt better—more like a regular life—to have a dog around.

Then there was Max, the giant schnauzer I owned as a child. Like many Latinos, my parents were very achievement-oriented and strict. Mamá gave me lessons on manners; Papá told me to be tough and never quit. They were caring and kind, but I soon realized their affection was most available when I succeeded, and there weren't too many arms to comfort me when I failed. I don't blame them. They loved their three children; they wanted us to embrace our opportunities. They had each grown up without fathers, watching their mothers struggle, and they didn't want that for us. We moved often, as my brilliant and driven papá worked his way toward the top of the Organization of American States (OAS), so I developed a work ethic, but I never forged many close friendships.

In junior high, I was badly bullied. Once a week, three boys waited to beat me up on my walk to the tennis courts, where I played for the school team. I think they first chose me because I was the new kid. They kept at me because I never told on them, and although it wasn't a fair fight, I never backed down. I took my licks every day and kept swinging. Mamá would shake her head when I walked in the door and say sadly, "You got beat up again?" Then she'd go back to her chores. Papá never seemed to notice, until I borrowed his car when I was sixteen and the bullies slashed all four of the tires. He stopped it cold after that, but by then I had been beaten up for years.

My comfort, during all those hard days, was Max. I never hugged him or cried with him or anything like that. For most of my childhood, Max was simply my best friend, the dog that always wanted to play. As soon as I walked out the door after changing out of my school clothes, he came running. We went everywhere together, out in the park and around the neighborhood and tromping through the drainage ditches. Mamá hated having him in the house because he was filthy, or so she said, but Max and I didn't care. We just played outside, even in the rain.

When Max disappeared in my teens, after eight years together, I was devastated. I put posters on lampposts; I made my papá drive me around the local streets every night for a week. I took a beating from my bullies, then rushed home to scour the neighborhood for my lost dog. For months, I thought I heard Max barking in the nearby Watts Branch Park in the middle of the night, and I tromped through the deep forest for miles in search of him. He never came back, but I never forgot, even twenty years later in my Brooklyn apartment, how important his companionship had been to me.

Twenty years later, I wanted that companionship in my life again. No, I *needed* that in my life, more even than I needed physical therapy and a steady job. As soon as I received the assistance dog email, I wrote to everyone I knew for recommendations: my professors, my old friends, my priest, my therapist. I compiled a record of my achievements and my medical evaluations. I called the Wounded Warrior Project and expressed my enthusiasm, asking if there was anything else I could do. Even before the first interview, I knew I would be chosen. That happens sometimes. I knew I would get into Columbia, so I didn't apply anywhere else. I knew I would write a book. I know I will eventually live out west on a spread of land with a view of the mountains and a few horses in the back pasture. It's not just that I set a goal. I know it will happen, then I work to achieve it. That, I suppose, is called faith.

I had faith in the assistance dog program. When I met Lu Picard at my second interview in the late summer of 2008, I knew she was going to change my life. I knew it. The training was supposed to start in September, and when the date was pushed back to November I was disappointed, but not disheartened. I wanted my dog. I wanted a new lease on life. I wanted it right now. But I didn't *need* it now. The anticipation of a service dog had already saved me.

It wasn't just the thought of Tuesday, though. I had made other changes, too. After eight months of battling for adequate care in Brooklyn, I switched to the Manhattan VA hospital. The subway ride was longer, but I finally found a great primary-care physician, a medical regimen that addressed all my physical wounds and PTSD symptoms, and a female former Marine and therapist who listened to me and understood what I was going through. Instead of reading only depressing news about the war, I spent that summer searching the Internet for information on service dogs and staring at photographs of golden retrievers. That's how far gone I was: I stayed up night after night watching YouTube videos of dogs. By the fall, as the presidential campaign of 2008 ratcheted into high gear, I was feeling better than I had in years. "Hope and Change" was Barack Obama's message that fall, and if you don't understand why those words would mean so much to me at that time, then you don't understand the previous five years of my life.

I arrived at East Coast Assistance Dogs on the night of November 3, 2008, the day before the presidential election. That first day, for many veterans, is not an easy experience. My friend Kim, for instance, whom I met at a wounded veterans retreat as I was departing the Army in August 2007, had been badly affected by her time in the Air Force. We kept in touch by email, often touching on the subject lightly, and at my urging she applied to ECAD and was accepted a year after me. When she arrived at the facility in Dobbs Ferry, though, she couldn't walk through the door. She waited outside in the parking lot, pacing back and forth, almost in tears.

Finally, she poked her head in and whispered to Lu Picard, "Are those puppies?" There were young golden retrievers, little miniatures of Tuesday and his littermates, in the kennels at the back of the room.

Lu nodded. "Would you like to see them?"

Kim walked to the kennels and, without a word, lay down with the puppies. She stayed on the floor for an hour, by herself, crying and holding onto the dogs.

"I'm ready," she finally said.

I had similar psychological problems, but my experience at ECAD was markedly different. Even on my way, on the commuter train, I was flying. There were three other wounded veterans in the program, and we would be living together in small quarters at the back of the training facility while we developed a relationship with our dogs. That usually would have scared the hell out of me. After all, I had never met these people, and in many ways we couldn't have been more different. Army Sgt. Mary Dague, a young woman from Montana, had lost both her arms above the elbow to an IED. Army Spc. (Ret.) Andrew Hanson, a quiet soldier from Minnesota, had lost his legs to an IED. Army Staff Sgt. (Ret.) Ricky Boone, a gregarious African American from Yonkers, was a spinal (someone with a debilitating spinal cord condition) with PTSD, a mohawk, and two arm braces to help him walk.

And yet, as soon as I met them, I felt more comfortable with these strangers than I had with anyone in a long, long time. Maybe it was the proximity of the dogs. Maybe it was the camaraderie of combat. Maybe it was the election, about which we passionately disagreed (Mary and Andrew on one side, Ricky and I on the other). Maybe it was just hope. And change.

I stayed up until 4:00 a.m. that night, long after the others had gone to bed, watching election coverage. Nobody was saying anything of value, but I couldn't sleep. Tomorrow, whoever won, George Bush, the primary architect of and cheerleader for the debacle in Iraq, would be on his way out. The long nightmare, for the country and myself, would be over. And I would meet my dog.

Hope and change indeed.

If only it were that simple.

PART III

TUESDAY
AND LUIS

CHAPTER 9

THE FIRST CHOICE

But after the fires and the wrath,
But after searching and pain,
His Mercy opens us a path
To live with ourselves again.

—RUDYARD KIPLING,
"THE CHOICE"

THESE WEREN'T ORDINARY DOGS. THAT WAS CLEAR THE MO-
ment Tuesday and the other ECAD dogs walked into the room.
Their coats were radiant; their eyes were bright; their posture was
perfect, like contestants at a kennel club. When they came through
the door, everything seemed to stop: the noise, the chatter, time
itself. I had been thinking about this moment for six months,
dreaming about the dog that would change my life, but this was
more than I had anticipated. A door opened, a dog walked in with
a teenager at its side, and I couldn't take my eyes off it. There was
nothing hurried or unsure about this dog. It made everything
seem easy. A second later, another dog walked in exactly the same
way. Then another. And another. I sat at the table in the middle
of ECAD's main room with the other veterans, the instruction
sheet we had been studying still in my hand, and watched in awe
as the dogs walked calmly around us and then, with a two-word

command, "Jump on," stepped onto their green boxes. When they sat down, nobody said a word.

There were four golden retrievers, one black lab, and one yellow lab. They were wearing vests and enormous instruction harnesses, but they didn't seem to notice. They sat casually on their boxes, waiting for their next command, as if this parade around strangers was the most ordinary thing in the world. They had walked out for training at the same hour every day for the last three months, and for them today was really no different. But for Ricky, Andrew, Mary, and me, the world stopped when those dogs entered the room. It was like seeing your bride walking down the aisle on your wedding day. The moment stretches out, and part of you wants it to last forever so that you can admire every detail of the woman who will be your partner for life. Part of you wants to run down the aisle and throw your arms around her and say, "Let's forget all this. Let's get out of here right now, just you and me."

The yellow lab had been trained for Mary. Since she had lost her arms above the elbows, Mary needed a docile dog that would follow voice commands and didn't need to be controlled with pressure on the leash. Remy was a shy female, small and sweet. She had been trained to work on a leash attached to Mary's belt, and she had been drilled hard on retrieval skills. Remy clearly wanted a partner, and she and Mary bonded instantly. From the moment they were introduced, that dog was at Mary's side, looking toward her with loving eyes.

I wanted that with my dog. I wanted special moments of togetherness. I wanted instant affection and companionship. But I didn't want a docile dog like Remy. I'm a headstrong, opinionated, type A personality, and that's what I was looking for in a dog. I wanted an outgoing leader, one that projected energy and commanded respect. I wanted people to look at my dog and see the embodiment of what I wanted to be: a confident individual destined to succeed.

But more than that, I wanted enthusiasm. I had withdrawn emotionally even before my move to New York. I had withheld my affection even from my family and turned inward on myself. For more than a year, I hadn't physically touched another living thing. I wanted to throw my arms around a dog, to hold it against my chest and feel my love coming back to me a hundredfold. It was all I could do that first morning to keep from throwing myself on the dogs and hugging them. That's all any of us wanted—to play and touch and feel that animal connection.

Tuesday wasn't that dog. Of all the dogs that morning, in fact, he seemed the most reserved. We were only with the dogs for two hours the first day, a half hour with each dog with instruction from Lu in between. Mary was bonded, but the other three of us were free-floating. On the fourth day, after Lu had watched us together, we'd be matched with our dogs. The first day was about getting used to having a leash in our hands and practicing the basic twenty commands.

It may have been the same old training routine, but these dogs were attuned. They sensed something special. They had new trainers, and these trainers were showering them with affection—we couldn't help it, even if we wanted to—and most of the dogs responded with enthusiasm. By the afternoon, they were nudging us and licking our hands, and when we used my favorite basic command, "Snuggle," they would rise up excitedly so that we could give them a hug.

Not Tuesday. When I trained with him that afternoon, he wagged his tail and looked happy, but there wasn't any overflow of emotion. The other dogs had been focused on me, waiting for my commands, but Tuesday glanced around the room and strayed carelessly from my side. He seemed more interested in what the other dogs were doing, especially his alpha brother Blue, with whom he had a friendly sibling rivalry. I couldn't see it at the time, but I now understand that he was going through the motions that first morning, just doing what he was supposed to do until it was time, once again, to curl up in his crate and ease off to sleep.

After the first day, I had my eye on Tuesday's other brother, Linus. Tuesday and Blue were energetic, but they seemed more interested in themselves. Linus was the social dog. He trotted beside me with his head up, as if he enjoyed my company and wasn't worried about anything in the world. His confidence made me feel confident, and his joyful presence made the exercises fun. When we missed the mark, he looked into my face, as if encouraging me to try again. His bouncy energy and eternal optimism made everything seem easy, and after months of darkness that was exactly what I wanted from my service dog: an easier life.

Instead of Linus, though, I was paired with Tuesday for the morning session on the second day. The thing I remember most about him that morning was watching his back waving from side to side as he walked two steps in front of me. He was supposed to walk beside me, but I didn't mind. What I had taken for carelessness the day before now seemed like eagerness, a desire to go places and see the next thing, even if we were only walking in a circle.

We were working on the second set of commands that morning, which included "Shake" and "Kiss." These are highlight reel accomplishments for a standard pet, but for Tuesday they were easy, so he was still distracted when he put his paw into my hand. When we moved on to the kiss, though, he was forced to focus on my face. And when he did, suddenly, I saw a sincerity in his dark brown eyes I hadn't suspected. This dog was handsome. He was intelligent. But he was also deep and emotional and hurting at the core. When he sat back on his haunches and bobbed those eyebrows at me, I almost burst out laughing, not just from amusement, but from happiness, too. This wasn't a machine. This was a *dog*, and he both ran on and gave off kindness, dedication, and love.

We stared at each other for a few seconds, and I could tell Tuesday was checking me out, assessing the situation. He wasn't timid. And he wasn't selfish. Something about the softness in his eyes told me Tuesday craved a relationship, but he was too smart to fawn just because somebody handed me his leash. I didn't know why he was wary. I didn't know he was sensitive. And needy. And that he had lost so much confidence in himself, because of his multiple abandonments, that I would have to slowly build back the intelligent, caring dog I glimpsed in those pleading eyes. But I knew that if I wanted his affection, I was going to have to earn it, and when I did, it would be deeper and more meaningful than anything I would ever feel with another dog.

The last ten minutes of the training session were like walking on air. Tuesday and I were totally botching the commands, but that didn't bother me. We were a team, and Tuesday was a partner I could grow with. Every time we bumped into each other because I told Tuesday "Heel" (stand on my left) when I meant "Side" (stand on my right), I laughed with childlike glee. Tuesday wasn't perfect, but he was a dog I could respect.

"I'm choosing Tuesday," I told Lu at the end of the session.

"Not yet, Luis," Lu laughed. "It's only the second day. You have Linus this afternoon."

"No, I'm working with Tuesday this afternoon. He's the one."

"We'll see," she said.

But she didn't stop me when, after our lesson on cues and commands, I went directly to Tuesday. That's how I know I made the right choice. Each dog is different, a bundle of personality and behavioral quirks no training can totally shape, and therefore each dog is best suited to a particular client. Training a dog isn't worth much, really, if you don't have the insight to match them with the right owner. Lu was a master at matching, and she never would have allowed me to work exclusively with Tuesday if she didn't know we were a good fit. There was too much—an entire life for both me and Tuesday—at stake.

From that moment, Tuesday and I were inseparable. We worked on drills together for the rest of the afternoon, and when the session was over I spent ten minutes grooming him while he lay with his head on my lap. Afterward, we walked together to the living area behind the training room, our first social interaction. I spent most of the afternoon on the couch resting my back or cooking dinner in the small kitchen, and Tuesday stayed at my side. He seemed to have realized, without being told, that he was with me now, and he followed me with an enthusiastic sense of duty I recognized from my days in the Army.

When we went to my bedroom that night, I expected Tuesday to sleep on the floor. Instead, he followed me into bed. Instinctively, I wrapped an arm around him and pulled him close. There really wasn't much choice. We were a 215-pound man and an 80-pound dog sharing a twin bed, so the only thing we could do was spoon. But even if we'd been on a king-size bed, I would have wrapped my arm around Tuesday, because it felt good to have him there beside me.

"Easy, Tuesday," I whispered as he squirmed, pushing against me with his back, trying to hog the bed. "Easy, boy." I could tell this wasn't the first time he'd slept with someone, but it had been a long time, and he was restless and unsure.

It had been a long time for both us. It had been longer than I cared to remember since anything besides a bottle of rum had lain with me in bed. But I wasn't hesitant. I knew this was right. I felt safer already with Tuesday beside me, as if the present were closer and the past further away. So I held him, listening to his soft breathing and the sound of his heart until, with my head pushed awkwardly between a pillow and the wall by Tuesday's big shoulders, I fell asleep.

During "Operation Brush Back" in South Baghdad, I stop to take a photo with some precious Iraqi children. Despite coping with physical and psychological issues, my return to Iraq in April 2005 was spotted with moments of beauty like this one.

Resting in my HMMWV, completely fatigued, after "Operation Squeeze Play" in South Baghdad. Culminating in June 2005, Squeeze Play was the largest Coalition and Iraqi Security Forces combined military operation conducted since the initial invasion in 2003.

White Team (my platoon) shortly after reaching Al-Waleed, a port of entry on the Syrian-Iraqi border, in October 2003. We established a forward operating base (FOB) and then began area reconnaissance, counter-smuggling, customs, security, and reconstruction operations.

A Sunni gentleman pours me a glass of chai. It was humbling to be asked to spend a few moments with this family, despite having just searched their home. (Photo by Craig Walker—*Denver Post*)

Tuesday as a puppy.

Army Sgt. Mary Dague receives a kiss from her new service dog, Remy.

Lu Picard, Founder and Director of ECAD, talks with Army Staff Sgt. (Ret.) Rick Boone about how to brush his service dog Raeburn's teeth.

Four wounded Army veterans of Iraq—Ricky (*left*), me, Mary, and Andrew—and their newly partnered service dogs proudly capture a moment near the end of ECAD's "Project HEAL" in November 2008.

Giving thanks to Puppies Behind Bars inmate dog trainers in November 2008. Tuesday is visible resting at my feet.

(Photo courtesy of Timothy Lamorte)

Tuesday sneaks a kiss at a charity event to help provide wounded veterans with service dogs. While anniversaries of 9-11, like this one in 2010, conjure a lot of painful memories, Tuesday and I feel compelled to leave home to help other veterans in need.

Tuesday and I make our way to a graduation ceremony at Educated Canines Assisting with Disabilities (ECAD). A year later, in November 2009, we proudly attended the second graduating class of ECAD's Project HEAL.

(Photo courtesy of Leslie Granda-Hill)

Senator Al Franken plays with Tuesday at a party to celebrate his election to Congress, while I look on. The August 3, 2009, celebration was made even more festive by the Senate's passage of Franken's first piece of legislation, the Service Dogs for Veterans Act (SDVA), the day before.

Tuesday and I carefully descend the steps to Sunset Park in Brooklyn in early 2009. (Photo courtesy of Leslie Granda-Hill)

Tuesday and I pose in our caps and gowns on May 18, 2010, the day we graduated from Columbia University's School of Journalism.

Tuesday and I walk down a block in Sunset Park, Brooklyn, in March 2009.

(Photo courtesy of Leslie Granda-Hill)

CHAPTER 10

COMPANY

It is better to be in chains with friends
than to be in a garden with strangers.

—PERSIAN PROVERB

IT FELT GOOD TO BE AT ECAD WITH RICKY, ANDREW, AND
Mary, far better than it ever felt in my small Brooklyn apartment.
These were fellow soldiers. My people. My blood. They understood what I had gone through overseas and in the VA bureaucracy,
and they had suffered life-changing injuries, too. Amputations,
spinals, PTSD: we were all brothers at ECAD, even Mary, who, I
suppose, was technically a sister.

I had always, even during my worst periods, felt most comfortable around combat veterans, and my few attempts at social interaction since moving to New York had always involved them. For
New Year's Eve 2007, the Wounded Warrior Project invited its
members to a front-row seat (courtesy of the NYPD) to watch the
apple drop in Times Square. I had always wanted to do that, so I
asked and was given a pass to attend. As the date approached,
though, the event starting eating away at my mind. I was so worried about the crowd, and the logistics, that I started drinking the
day before to alleviate the stress. Not December 31, but the morning of December 30. I had been so hammered for so long by the

time the police arrived to escort us to Times Square that the whole evening was like a city at sea, shimmering on a floating horizon you're never quite sure is real.

I visited a veteran in the hospital with the Wounded Warrior Project. I remember that for sure, but I can't remember how he was wounded. I saw the first half of the Bruce Springsteen concert, with disastrous results. I attended a Mets baseball game or possibly two, again with the Wounded Warrior Project, again plastered on booze so I could deal with the crowd. Please forgive my imprecision. I realize I should know how many Mets games I've been to, but there are large chunks of my life, especially in the year before meeting Tuesday, that I seem to have lost.

I remember other events with crystalline clarity: the burned-out suicide car in Sinjar, the call to prayer at the Al-Waleed mosque, the taste of the apple tobacco I smoked with my Iraqi friend Maher. I hear the sound of the Syrian tracer rounds in my sleep, but I can't remember the date my grandmother died. My brother, my sister, and I spent time every week at her house growing up, and she was my childhood hero. By sheer force of will, as a young widow, she got her son (my papá) and daughter (my aunt) out of Cuba in the madness after Castro took over. She worked for decades as a nurse before returning to school for a master's degree in education at age fifty-five and then working for the U.S. Department of Education. Cut off from my relatives still on the island, Granny was a big part of my history. She told me stories; she taught me our family traditions; she showed me, by example, how to build a life on hard work, without bitterness but also without forgetting the tragedies in your past. She died during my second tour in Iraq, in May 2005. I missed the funeral and the gathering in honor of her life, and now I can't even remember the day Granny died, and it makes me so angry, so very angry at myself.

But things were different at ECAD. This wasn't a forced outing. I didn't tell myself, *Hey, you sorry sack, get yourself up and out of this stinking apartment and prove you're still a man,* like I did for New Year's Eve or the Mets games. I told myself, *Be strong. This is it. This is your life.*

In the days leading up to ECAD, I must have put the bottle down untouched a hundred times, steeling myself for the unknown. But when I met the other veterans, my apprehension vanished because I recognized them. No arms, no legs, a pair of braces, and wary eyes. These soldiers were hurting. They needed help. It was my duty as an officer to display leadership and self-control. Suddenly, I was Captain Montalván again, a soldier in the company of soldiers, and it felt good. Very good. I took the responsibility so seriously that by the second morning I was licking my classmate, Staff Sgt. (Ret.) Ricky Boone, on his mohawked black head.

I was pretending to be a dog, by the way. That was part of our training—ordering each other around like dogs so that we could learn the feel of issuing commands. Ricky put me through my paces, and when he finally ordered "Up," the command for the dog to place its front paws on the object in front of it, I thought, *What the heck, do what a dog would do,* and licked a big stripe right across his head.

That started it. Ricky was five-feet-four—all right, Ricky, I know you're reading; five-feet-four *and a half*—and shaped like a beefed-up bowling ball. He'd been a bail bondsman and an infantryman; he dreamed of being a bounty hunter; there was no way he was letting me get away with that foolishness. So he did what any hardened foot soldier would do—he laughed out loud, then plotted his revenge. Ricky had a mohawk and a weakness for gold jewelry (and a lovely wife named Tammy, who tolerated them both, if you can believe it), and he'd snap into a hilarious Mr. T act before belting me down to size.

"I pity the fool, Luis, and that fool is you!"

It was easy, amazingly easy, for all of us to get along. But for the first few days, that familiarity was little more than a cover for our nervousness. We were all here to start rebuilding shattered lives, and we were well aware of the consequences of failure. It didn't start to feel natural until we were matched with our dogs. With Tuesday at my side—and after my insistence on training with him on the second day, we were rarely apart—things started to slow down. That's the best way I can describe the calm that came over my life. My mind had been racing for years, dragging my worn-out body with it, but Tuesday kept me firmly in the moment, since I was always touching him, talking to him, fidgeting with his collar or leash. The training was physically demanding, especially in my compromised state, and I spent a lot of time on the sofa near the kitchen resting my back. Tuesday always sat beside me, watching the room with an almost lethargic interest or lounging across my lap. By the second day, I developed the habit of touching him whenever I spoke. Even then, it wasn't a conscious movement. There was a trigger in my brain that, since coming home from Iraq, caused me to tense up when my mouth opened, and touching Tuesday released it somehow.

So I'd playfully insult Ricky. Ricky would respond with his Mr. T impersonation. His dog, Raeburn, would stare at him in complete confusion and Tuesday, seeing Raeburn's look, would turn to me as if wondering what was going on. So Rick and I would laugh at both our dogs and ourselves, both of us with our hands on our dogs for comfort, and Mary would come walking in with Remy tied to her belt. "If you guys don't stop it," she'd say with a smile, "I'm going to beat you to death with my stumps."

That was big for her. I don't think Mary had ever joked about losing her arms before. Losing a limb in combat is not a tidy thing. It's sudden, bloody, and extremely violent, but it's also a long and painful process of surgeries and rehab. Mary had lost her arms less than six months before. She was still in the middle of a series of surgeries; she was in a lot of pain. She was trying to figure out how to put her life back together, and she was so young, not more than twenty-one and looking more like sixteen. Jared, her husband, also a soldier, was with her at ECAD. He was a wholesome guy, very quiet but polite. They were just a couple of kids from a small town in Montana, unfailingly friendly, ordinary people, and I swear I spent hours wanting to throw my arms around them and protect them from the world. We all did. Even Tuesday.

But she was tough as nails, too. As Mary wrote of her experiences in a bomb disposal unit in Iraq: "I was shot at, sniped, stabbed, smashed, run over, blown up four times, rocketed, mortared, had to clear sites that my friends were just killed at, had an Iraqi man try to buy me and had an ovarian cyst rupture, all before having an IED go off while holding it, taking off my arms." It was a litany of trauma, wounds, and pride that only a soldier could understand, and only the strong could endure. You don't give up easily after experiences like that. You don't talk much about them either.

And then, on the fourth or fifth day at ECAD, Mary came waltzing in with Remy and threatened to beat Ricky and me to death . . . with her stumps! Her word: stumps. That's the fighting spirit of an American soldier. That's a testament to the power of service dogs. They're psychological bodyguards. They make you feel secure and comfortable, merely by their presence. Especially in the honeymoon period, when you first get them, they are the embodiment of your new and better life. They give you confidence, when there was little but doubt and anxiety before.

That is not to say my days at ECAD with Tuesday were easy. I had classes at Columbia most days, so the schedule was grueling. Drill, drill, drill, then off to class, take a break, then drill some more. Tuesday was trained, but I was not, and I had only two weeks to learn the basics of a new life. It was hours of frustration, punctuated by short bursts of accomplishment and joy. Tuesday knew eighty commands, and that's a lot to remember—for a human being. Especially one with PTSD. And especially when Lu kept raising the bar for success.

When I finally learned "Heel" and "Side" and we became competent at walking together, Lu added other commands. "Tell him to climb onto the box."

"Stop, Tuesday. Good boy. Jump on."

"He knows the box. You can say box. Now tell him to look out the window."

"Let's go, Tuesday. Good boy. Heel. Heel. Window."

"He doesn't know 'window.' What do you think we teach him here, Luis?"

"Up, Tuesday. That's a window. Win-dow. Good boy."

"Now try your cane."

"Look, Tuesday. Get my cane. That's it. Get it! That's right. Bring it here. Good boy!"

Lu and her staff tried their best to disrupt us. They opened doors as we walked past or dropped treats in Tuesday's path that he was supposed to ignore. We were told to use the "Go" command, which tells Tuesday the next commands will be given from a distance, then distracted him with wheelchairs, chew toys, the mailman (she wanted to see how Tuesday would react to a stranger), other dogs, and umbrellas. The world is a complicated place; out there, an umbrella suddenly opening was the least of the distractions.

On the fourth day, when Ricky and Andrew were matched with their dogs, we started walking around the campus at Children's Village. The next day, we took a van to a local mall for public practice, then returned to walk around the table in the big room at ECAD, following the ever-present painted yellow line. It was a topsy-turvy time, both highly stressful and blissfully freeing. Sometimes it felt like Tuesday and I were making progress. Other times it seemed we were losing the basic commands we had mastered three days before. Ricky bought a blinged-out gold collar for Raeburn, and I went around for two days saying, in my best Mr. T impersonation (which unfortunately sounded more like Hulk Hogan), "I pity the dog that has to be seen with Ricky Boone." The next day, my hand shook when I reached out to touch Tuesday, and I knew that contact with him was the only thing keeping me nailed to the ground.

I didn't realize how far we'd progressed until we took the train to a nearby town for our first long outing, a morning in the park. It sounds easy, I know, but it's not. Parks are crowded, distracting Tuesday and me for entirely different reasons. I was hypervigilant and nervous; Tuesday was fascinated by the squirrels. My failure to reach him, combined with the pressure of being in public for several hours, had a strong effect on my mood. I had left my medicine back at ECAD, and as noon approached my back began to hurt and my head to swim. I could feel the drugs leaving my bloodstream, and by the time we headed for the train station for our return to Dobbs Ferry, I was so anxious and unnerved I had almost forgotten Tuesday was at my side.

By the time the train approached, I was on the edge. I could feel the emptiness in my veins, and my brain was pounding against my skull. I needed to get on that train so I could get to my medicine, but Ricky was having trouble with Raeburn. They weren't going to make it to the platform in time, and with the complexity of the midday schedules on the Metro-North Railroad nobody was even sure if this was the right train. As the train slowed to a stop, the sound around me grew into a buzzing, then a throbbing, then a confused cacophony as everyone blathered about whether we should get on the train or wait for Ricky or go and patrol that house or bomb that building or . . . or . . . or . . .

In the past, the situation would have overwhelmed me, leading to a migraine and, more often than not, a round of violent vomiting. But this time, instead of spiraling, I looked down at Tuesday. He was standing calmly against my right leg, looking up at me. He knew I was agitated, but he wasn't discouraged. In fact, he was more focused than he'd been all day. He wasn't encouraging me; the relationship doesn't work that way. He was simply expecting me to make a decision that he could follow. So I did. I got on the train, leaving the rest of the group behind. As I settled into my seat, Tuesday looked at me again. There was no doubt about it, he was giving me an *Atta-boy*. My dog was proud of me, and that made me proud of myself. By the time the others arrived, I was lounging in the kitchen at ECAD with Tuesday at my side, the medicines racing through my system.

"What took you so long?" I said with a smile.

"I oughta whack you," Mary said, raising her stump.

"Why don't you grab a chair," I joked, "and sit down!"

And then, like she so often did, Mary smiled.

CHAPTER 11

THE RIGHT DOG

———

Nothing can dim the light that shines from within.

—MAYA ANGELOU

AFTER THE TRAIN, I FELT CONFIDENT. THAT WAS A MAJOR TEST, but I faced down my anxiety and, with Tuesday's help, quieted my mind. I could tell Tuesday respected me more after that, or maybe he just felt more comfortable with me as his alpha dog, and with comfort came more responsiveness to my commands. By the second week together, we were knocking our training out. Walk around the block. No problem. Turn on the lights. No problem. Walk, stop, step onto a chair, back down, pick up the cane, switch sides . . . that's all you've got? We could do that in our sleep, even in our tiny bunk bed with our roommates Andrew and Blue snoring ten feet away.

Sure, Tuesday wasn't the best-behaved dog. He was good at commands, but he still tended to get distracted. Instead of staring at the road ahead, he'd wag his head from side to side, his tongue hanging out when he saw someone he wanted to impress. We practiced drills where Lu piled ten or twelve objects together and I told Tuesday to fetch one in particular.

"Get the ball, Tuesday. Good boy. Now get the sock."

He didn't have trouble identifying the right object, but after a few runs he couldn't help taking a victory lap around all the dogs and people in the room, the object bobbing in his mouth while his ears and long leg hair flowed beautifully behind him.

"You can't let him do that, Luis," Lu told me. "You've got to be the boss."

There was never any doubt of the leader between Tuesday and me. Lu always says: "A service dog should be more enthusiastic and less assertive than its owner." That's her mantra. Well, Tuesday wasn't more enthusiastic than me, but that wasn't his fault. No dog could have been as enthusiastic as I was for those two weeks. We were a perfect match, though, on assertiveness. I had a leader's mentality from my years as an officer, plus I was a stubborn, hard-headed soldier, and Tuesday was a natural wingman. He liked to have fun, to be the jokester in our pack, and I like that about him. I took the training seriously, and I always listened to Lu, but I could also see Tuesday's smile behind that sock in his mouth, and I didn't put much heart into disciplining him. He was a happy-go-lucky dog, making everyone smile. Didn't I want him to be himself? Wasn't that one of the reasons I chose him?

It was impossible for me, blinded by joy as I was, to see the problem. Tuesday followed all my commands. He was attentive, at my side, and always snuggled tightly against me in bed, although I must admit that might have been to keep from falling off. Compared to even the most loving, devoted, and affectionate "normal" dog, Tuesday was an octopus impaled to my face with its tentacles wrapped tightly around my head. I couldn't get away from that dog, even if I had wanted to. I couldn't look around without seeing Tuesday in my peripheral vision. I couldn't take a step without feeling the tug on the leash as Tuesday stood up and followed. He was with me in the bathroom, for Christ's sake! (Fortunately, the Army had destroyed my need for comfort and privacy.) Whenever

I needed a reassuring touch, Tuesday was there. He was my miracle dog. I already loved him and depended on him more than any other animal I'd ever known—and most other people, too.

So how was I to know we weren't connecting, that there was more to a service dog relationship than following orders and standing side by side? I had been told that the leash, not the voice, was the ultimate connection. Tuesday, Lu told me, felt everything I communicated down the leash: fear, anxiety, distrust, hesitation, pride, power, respect, and love. Eventually, when the leash became an umbilical cord between us rather than a means of control, I would feel Tuesday's emotions, too. I heard that, but I didn't understand it. When I held the leash, I felt slackness and pulling. I felt when Tuesday wanted to go in a different direction, when he was impatient to walk faster, when he wanted to stop and rest, and I thought that was how it worked.

If I had been able to read the leash, I would have felt . . . apathy. Well, not apathy, exactly. Tuesday liked me, I have no doubt of that. He enjoyed being there for me, because he knew that made me happy. But he didn't have a connection with me. Not really. It's so easy to overanalyze the moment on our second day together when I saw potential in Tuesday's eyes. It's easy to imagine it had all been planned. Tuesday had been watching me. He knew I was the one. He was testing me, opening up to me alone, saying, *This is who I am. I am loving but wounded, and I need someone to take me as I am.*

But that wasn't how it worked. To Tuesday, I was just another special trainer, like Brendan or Tom. I was a great trainer, mind you, and he appreciated that. After all, he got to stay with me all the time, even at night. When he did something well, I gave him treats, which he hadn't received much of in the past year. I was extremely affectionate. Every ten minutes, I knelt down and gave him a big burly two-armed hug, roughhousing with his head and neck and saying in that enthusiastic, almost raspy talking-to-a-dog voice, "You're a good boy, Tuesday. I love you, Tuesday. You're a good, good dog." He ate that up. He puffed out his chest, lifted his head, and curled his lips into a smile. When I was finished, he'd spring up and look at me, ready for his next command. I was using classic touch-talk affirmation, but I was using it with an enthusiasm he'd never experienced. How was Tuesday to know I wasn't using a training technique, that I was petting him from the heart?

I could see the difference in the other dogs. Mary and Remy, for instance, were bonded from the start. Remy didn't need a reward; she would have done anything for her friend. Mary improvised a system anyway. She had her husband wrap two-sided duct tape around each of her upper arms, then pressed them against a pile of dog treats until she had ten or twelve stuck to each piece. When she wanted to give Remy a reward, Mary bit a dog treat off the tape and held it in her teeth. Remy slowly stretched up and, with a gentleness I've never seen in any other dog, grasped the treat in her own teeth. For a long moment, they would linger with their lips together until Mary pulled away with a smile. Remy was even happier, judging by the way her tail whapped the floor. She was exactly the kind of dog Lu intended to provide: a well-trained obedient animal salivating for a loving bond. If Remy threw her arms enthusiastically around Mary from the moment they met, then Mary was no less enthusiastic in return. I know, I know, Mary didn't have arms. Neither did Remy. When I say arms, I mean heart. The thing war can break, even mangle, but never destroy.

Tuesday and I didn't have that relationship. Not to put those guys down, but we were both more complicated—or wounded, if you prefer—than that. We were more like Ricky and Raeburn, who, despite their Wonder Twins–style matching gold jewelry, were feeling their way toward a relationship.

We were tighter, though, than Andrew and Blue, who were clearly working hard to reach an understanding. Andrew was funny, but he was also quiet, a laid-back small-town Minnesota kind of guy, never caused any trouble. Between his *Hogan's Heroes* DVDs and his nightly dose of *South Park*, he was pretty much set. I needed a go-getter, a dog that liked getting out of the house and stretching his world; Andrew needed a chill partner. He also needed a patient dog, because he was a double amputee recently fitted with prosthetic legs, and he wasn't too good at getting around on them yet.

Blue wasn't that dog. He was the alpha of Tuesday's litter, and he liked being in charge. That's fine for a type A owner, but that wasn't so good for laid-back, physically awkward Andrew. Several times, I saw Blue almost pull Andrew off balance, and there was a certain lack of enthusiasm when it came to commands. But Andrew stood by Blue, even when it became clear that trying to corral the headstrong dog was stressing him out, and for a few days Lu let the relationship ride.

"I've got no patience," Lu told me once, but that's just the New Yorker talking. Lu Picard has more patience, and a bigger heart, than anyone I know. It takes patience, after all, to train a dog. And it takes patience to lead hurt and scared people through the training they need to change their lives. Imagine all the disabled people who have come through her doors, desperate for a better life but barely able to hold a leash. She helped them. Think of all the mothers who cried themselves to sleep for years, praying for a way to empower their sick children. She relieved their pain.

Think of the people like me. I was all in for Tuesday. If it didn't work out, I don't think I could have gone back to living on my own. I had pinned so many hopes on finding a partner that returning to Brooklyn without a dog would have sent my life into an irreversible spin. At best, I'd probably be a broken veteran, as my father feared. At worst, I'd be homeless or dead. Lu understood that when she took me into the program. She knew this was my chance. She understood that with all of us, which is why she kept asking, "Are you all right with that dog, Andrew?"

"Yes, ma'am."

There were times I wondered if she was pressuring him. There were times I thought she was wrong to keep asking, "Are you sure you're all right, Andrew? Are you sure?"

"I'm sure," Andrew kept saying. He didn't like to cause a fuss. And he hated the attention. I think he just wanted Lu to leave him alone.

Near the beginning of the second week, we took our dogs to the movies. It was a treat, but also a challenge—two hours together in a dark, cramped space. Before we left, Lu pulled Andrew aside.

"I want you to take Jackie instead of Blue."

"No, Lu. I'm fine. Really."

"It's a movie, Andrew. It's not a commitment."

He hesitated. "All right."

By the time the lights came on at the end of the movie, it was a love affair. For a week, Andrew and Blue had waged a war of the leash, trying to figure out who was boss. Within two hours, Andrew and Jackie were hugging and rubbing noses like teenagers in love. "Feel her ears, Luis," he said in a dreamy voice. "They're so soft."

Andrew had never been like that with Blue (although I admit he was right, Jackie's ears were ridiculously soft). I don't think he'd ever been like that in his whole life. I swear, I think he and Jackie spent the whole movie making out. Metaphorically speaking, of course.

Lu had known Andrew's relationship with Blue wasn't right, but Puppies Behind Bars, the sponsor of the veterans program, had limited her choices to dogs they had trained. She waited patiently and hoped for the best, but in the end she ignored the limitation and chose another animal. She risked her funding, and possibly the program, to give Andrew the dog he needed.

"I can't promise you a Ferrari, then give you a Volkswagen," she told me later. "That's not how I work." It was a typically un-romantic image from Lu, but the next sentence is the one I re-member. "I can't tell you I'm going to make your life better, then not do everything I can to make that come true."

Shortly after the switch, we were riding in the ECAD van to an outdoor training session when I felt something jiggling my hair. I looked over and Andrew, whose prosthetics often rubbed him the wrong way, had his leg bent backward and was scratching under his artificial knee. "Get your foot out of my face, man," I said, knock-ing his toes away. He looked at me and smiled. I'm not saying he came out of his shell—he was a quiet guy by nature—but after that, you never knew when you were going to get a metal foot in the face.

I appreciated Tuesday more, I think, after seeing Andrew struggle with Blue. Even at ECAD, I realized the relationship won't work with the wrong dog. Not a bad dog, mind you, just the wrong dog for that particular person. Andrew wasn't an alpha by nature, so he needed a dog that would chill with him while he played video games, not butt heads with him over control. I must have given Tuesday a dozen hugs after that, thinking how lucky I was to have a dog I could love.

That doesn't mean we didn't struggle. I had intentionally cho-sen the complicated dog, after all. The smart one. The goofball. The one that figured out after sitting between my last row seat and the back wall of the movie theater that the space was too small for me to come in and get him out. So what did he do? He ran back and forth behind the seats while I grabbed for him, refusing to come out. Occasionally he stopped, and I don't even want to think about what he was finding to eat back there, but he loped off again as soon as my fingers grazed his collar. Eventually, we had people guarding each end of the row and four of us reaching over the seats trying to grab him. It took several minutes for Tuesday to tire of that game. He finally trotted out with an insouciant air and a giant grin, as if that was the most fun he'd had all week.

That behavior was fine at ECAD, I suppose (although Lu would hasten to disagree with me), but the closer we came to the end of class, the more anxious I became about Tuesday's attention lapses and playful episodes, as minor as they were. My frustration culminated, finally, on a trip to downtown Dobbs Ferry. A photographer from the local newspaper wanted to document the first class of wounded veterans to receive service dogs, so the four of us paraded up and down in front of the store windows of Dobbs Ferry's quaint downtown with our dogs. The rest of the dogs walked calmly, as instructed, but Tuesday was . . . well, being Tuesday. He was showing off, bouncing around, and focusing on the other dogs and the photographer instead of me.

One of the trainers, perhaps out of embarrassment at Tuesday's foibles, started barking suggestions. I was determined, though, to solve this problem on my own. I had a whole toolbox of motivational tricks, from a sharp command to repeatedly telling Tuesday to heel until I focused his concentration, but the trainer (who is no longer at ECAD) was a real drill sergeant, and she kept insisting I jerk hard on his leash to regain his attention. Well, I'd had enough of drill sergeants, and Tuesday had too. I didn't have any interest in choking him, but with Tuesday refusing to behave, and the trainer chirping at me, and the photographer waiting, my pulse began to pound and I felt a familiar PTSD-like anxiety creeping into my mind.

So I took a time-out. I got down on one knee, right in the middle of the sidewalk in downtown Dobbs Ferry, grabbed Tuesday around the neck, and put my forehead against his. I waited until he stopped glancing around, then started talking to him in a calm, quiet voice. I don't know what I said exactly, but I was telling him that he was my dog, that I was his person, and that we were a team. I wasn't going to hurt him, but he had to listen to me. And if he listened to me, I would love him for the rest of his life.

After a few seconds, I knew Tuesday was listening. He locked into my eyes, and a calm came over him that I had never seen before. Maybe the part of him that wanted love opened up. Maybe he realized, finally, that this wasn't like any relationship he'd had before. He had been on a treadmill, racing toward each new handler but always ending up in the exact same spot: alone. He didn't know I was the mission he'd been training for, but at that moment, at the very least, he realized I needed him. And maybe I realized, in my heart and in my head, that this was a two-way relationship and he needed me too. All I know for sure is that when I looked up, everybody was staring at us. Staff, dogs, veterans, everybody. Even the photographer had lowered his camera. Lu Picard told me later we were together for five minutes, although I could have sworn it was thirty seconds at the most.

"What was that about?" she asked, as Tuesday and I walked past, side by side.

"We're okay now," I told her. "We reached an understanding."

Two days later, Tuesday and I rode the Metro-North Railroad together to our new lives in the city. I cannot describe the elation I felt that day, the ease with which I handled every step of the process, and the optimism I felt about the future. Everything was different. Everything. And it was all because of Tuesday. He had a little trouble with the turnstile into the subway—so low and loud, such menacing arms—but for more than two hours he sat or walked beside me like a perfectly trained service dog, calmly assessing the world around him. But I could feel his excitement, too. I could feel his joy. This was what he had been training for his whole life; New York City was his Al-Waleed. I knew I wasn't supposed to distract him when he was on duty, but I couldn't help myself. At Grand Central Terminal, I reached over and hugged him.

"It's just you and me now, buddy," I told him. "We're free."

CHAPTER 12

THE FIRST TEST

I understand a fury in your words. But not the words.

—WILLIAM SHAKESPEARE, *OTHELLO*

LIFE WAS BETTER WITH TUESDAY, THERE WAS NO DOUBT ABOUT that. It was nice just having someone with me in my apartment. Lu had stressed many times the importance of bonding with our dogs, which meant not letting anyone touch Tuesday or interact with him for the first two months we were together. This was far from a hardship; in fact, it was ideal. I didn't feel comfortable leaving my apartment anyway, and now I had the perfect excuse. Instead of going out, Tuesday and I practiced commands. Whenever either of us grew restless, whether it was noon or the middle of the night, we'd work on sitting, heeling, retrieving, carrying, snuggling, fronting, speaking—everything but "Get busy," which meant now was a good time for Tuesday to relieve himself—until I wound up on the floor hugging Tuesday and telling him what a good boy he was. For the first week, it was the primary way we interacted. If it was my choice, I would have lived in that cocoon for months.

Unfortunately, the real world was still out there and I still had to interact with it. The trips to the VA were significantly better since I had changed to the Manhattan hospital and found a good primary-care physician, psychiatrist, and therapist, but classes at Columbia were still a grind, especially Reporting and Writing 1.

There were a number of reasons for my dissatisfaction with that particular class, and in true PTSD fashion I obsessed about them all. The assignments were glorified crime blotters, I muttered, not journalism. The professors were too focused on local New York news. The planning was muddled and contradictory. The objectives were unclear. The two-hour-long discussions weren't worth the heart-pounding, claustrophobia-inducing three-hour round-trip subway ride.

Those were all true, but I'd also put myself in a difficult spot by essentially refusing to follow the course syllabus. For two years, I had been obsessively immersed in foreign affairs and defense policy. In the last year alone, I had written editorials and opinion pieces for major newspapers like the *Denver Post*, the *New York Times*, and the *San Francisco Chronicle* on war issues and veterans affairs, and with such big things on my mind I found it difficult to switch to local zoning laws and disputes over how much car horn honking was too much. My god, I wondered, don't these people understand we are at war?

The war had also, once again, become deeply personal. After I left Al-Waleed, Al-Anbar Province had collapsed into sectarian violence, and I had lost track of my Iraqi friends there. I heard a few times from Ali: short notes to say the border was in chaos and Iraqis I had known were dying. In 2005, he wrote that his life was being threatened, but I had no way to contact him and lost touch after my official Army email was shut down. In the spring of 2008, he resurfaced again with a desperate plea. Under constant threat and fearing for their lives, he and his family had fled Iraq. Since 2006, they had been living in squalor in a slum area of Amman, the capital of Jordan. Jordan issued six-month work visas to Iraqi refugees, but they refused to extend them, and Ali's visa had long since expired. He was scrounging day labor to feed his family while the United States repeatedly denied his request for immigration. I hadn't filled out the required paperwork, officials told him, so there was no proof he had ever worked for Coalition forces. It's true I never filled out paperwork for Ali. He wasn't a paid consultant; he worked for free because he believed in us.

All through the summer, I wrote letters and made phone calls on Ali's behalf, calling in every favor I had earned in seventeen years of military service. I received letters for Ali from Col. Christopher M. Hickey, my squadron commander in western Al-Anbar, and Sgt. Eric Pearcy, my Humvee gunner. I won support for Ali's petition from Gene Dewey, assistant U.S. secretary of state for the Bureau of Population, Refugees and Migration during President Bush's first term, and from Fred Schieck, a friend of my father and former deputy director of the U.S. Agency for International Development (USAID), the government organization that provides U.S. economic and humanitarian assistance around the world.

With former U.S. Marine Capt. Tyler Boudreau, a friend from my work on behalf of veterans, I established a nonprofit organization to aid Ali and other Iraqi refugees. That August, a few months before meeting Tuesday, and while my classmates were writing reports on neighborhood issues in New York, I flew with Captain Boudreau and two professional journalists to meet with Ali and highlight the refugees' plight. I was stunned by the number of refugees—750,000 people scattered in substandard squats in the worst parts of Amman, forced into scavenging, prostitution, and sex slavery on a massive scale by a lack of work papers and basic human rights—but I was more stunned by the American officials who lacked any coherent plan to deal with the crisis.

Ali was lucky. Thanks in part to our efforts, his special visa and request for asylum had been approved. By the time I arrived, he was awaiting his final paperwork. He was so magnanimous and gracious, so thankful for our efforts. It had been a difficult four and a half years since we parted, filled with terror and deprivation, but he was getting out. The invasion of Iraq had not turned out as he had hoped, but he had no regrets. He still believed in America. He still appreciated the effort, even after our reckless failures.

I wasn't as magnanimous. Ali was receiving his reward, after several years' delay, but there were many thousands of others who worked with us still suffering. They had risked their lives and the lives of their spouses, children, parents, siblings, cousins, nieces, and nephews (yes, the revenge killings went that far) to help us. Their efforts had been vital. We welcomed them, until we needed to reciprocate. Then America turned its back. What I saw in Jordan wasn't just a betrayal of a friend but of the American way. We had made promises to the Iraqis—explicit promises. Help us, and we will stand by you. Now our goal as a nation was to break those promises and keep our Muslim brothers out.

My multimedia presentation on Iraqi refugees, titled *Saving Ali,* is still available at Flypmedia.com. I watch it now, and I can see the strain of those times. Ali's face is obscured in his interview because he was still a target of reprisal. In my interview, I am clearly in the grips of PTSD, stuttering and looking away from the camera, unable to collect my thoughts. My eyes are popping, glazed, and unfocused, and I am sweating profusely, even in an air-conditioned room.

It wasn't just Ali's plight. During our conversations in Jordan, I learned that Maher, my brother-in-arms in the Iraqi Border Police at Al-Waleed, was dead. He was my best friend among the Iraqis, a funny guy who loved to tell a joke, and in my opinion the U.S. Army's most valuable intelligence source in the western Anbar desert. He went on patrol with us all the time, since he understood the tribal and ethnic fault lines in that part of the world; he showed us dozens of caches of arms and ammunitions. It was a stressful existence, especially away from the base, but Maher always made us laugh. I remember an Enrique Iglesias song coming from a radio in our Humvee one afternoon, and Maher and I singing together like two college buddies on our way to the beach. Fifteen minutes later, we were holding guns on a roomful of men while we confiscated their weapons cache.

Maher got married in 2004, just before I left. He wanted me to attend the wedding, but the Army wouldn't have allowed me to leave my post. He showed me the pictures. Shuruq (which means "shining" in Arabic) was a beautiful girl from Ar-Rutbah, his hometown, and they looked incredibly happy. They were young, they were in love, they were planning to start a family. A few weeks later, someone threw hand grenades into their house, collapsing the roof and blowing the walls apart. It was an assassination. Retribution for helping us at Al-Waleed. Both Maher and Shuruq were killed.

Every time I went to that investigative journalism class, I was reminded of that fact. Every time I was given an assignment to explore a local issue in some inward-looking New York neighborhood, I was reminded of the big stories, the suffering and betrayals that were being ignored. Oh, your co-op board isn't happy about the schedule of garbage removal? Well, we're at war! A society is collapsing. Thousands are dead and 750,000 Iraqis are living in Jordan without garbage removal . . . or houses . . . or visas that would allow them to work.

And Maher is dead.

So needless to say, I wasn't in the best frame of mind for my investigative journalism class that fall, and especially for the last gathering of the semester, a party at the professor's apartment with food, drinks, and the presentation of our final group projects. It was exactly the kind of event I dreaded: social, claustrophobic, requiring a public presentation. Before Tuesday, it would have left me a quivering mess. I would have drunk for two days to work up the courage to attend, and even then I doubt I would have gone. With Tuesday, I was apprehensive, but I was confident I could make it through. We had been together only a few weeks, but already my mental outlook had changed.

Tuesday and I were the first to arrive. This was intentional, so that I could case the apartment and choose a safe location to hole up for the night. I was completely sober and, with Tuesday at my side and my knife tucked in my trousers, reasonably secure. The second person to arrive was a cute girl in a red tube skirt and, to my complete horror, the first thing Tuesday did was stick his nose up her skirt. I mean, we really need to hold it together, the two of us, not make unprofessional moves. Plus, it was embarrassing, especially after I pulled Tuesday aside and told him to behave, only to have him stick his snout straight back up her skirt, his face flailing wildly as Kristina blushed as red as her skirt.

We laughed about that. She was a good sport, thank god, and Tuesday is such a charmer with those sensitive brown eyes. I even talked to her for a minute, I think, and felt strengthened by surviving Tuesday's gaffe. Unfortunately, the night went downhill from there. As I watched in horror, the apartment filled with people I barely recognized, even though I had spent a semester in class with them. I could feel the heat rising by the minute, and the chatter buzzed in my ears, making it impossible to focus.

Even worse, two of my classmates brought dogs. I guess the thinking was, *If Luis gets to bring Tuesday, then everyone should be allowed to bring their dogs.* I hate that. Absolutely hate it. That's like saying that if someone is coming in a wheelchair, than everyone else gets to ride motorcycles. I don't care how well-behaved a pet dog is, or how loved; it's not the same as Tuesday and me. Don't get me wrong, I know how much dogs mean, but a pet dog's presence is a luxury. You may want them to attend a party with you, but it isn't a necessity. I require Tuesday. I cannot survive without him.

The dogs were a disaster. They were clearly agitated by the noise and the crowd—what untrained dog wouldn't be?—and they kept barking and nipping at Tuesday. He had grown up around dogs, of course, but those were exquisitely trained golden retrievers, and these little nippers completely disoriented him. He didn't know what to do with them. He kept turning and giving them looks, but they followed him around the apartment, even after he started pushing at them with his head, trying to make them go away. I needed Tuesday to be calm and focus on me, because I was panicking in that crowded room, but he was anything but calm.

By my group's presentation, I was gone. Anyone could have looked at my eyes and seen it. They were bulging and glassy, unable to focus on anything in the room. Think of it as being bombed on alcohol, although my wine consumption had nothing to do with it. I was so overwhelmed, I experienced near blackouts, and my mind was so consumed with anxiety that the apartment was reeling wildly around me as thoughts pancaked in my mind: yippy dogs and Ali and hot apartments and Iraqi assassins and unruly Baghdad crowds and suicide bombs and our dumb presentation and Maher dead, and for some reason, when I got up to give the first part of my group's report, I started into a stumbling explanation of how our presentation wasn't that good because we hadn't been given enough time to prepare.

Someone in my group yelled, "That's not true."

That's when the stack of pancakes hit the skids and my thoughts flew everywhere. Not true? Not true? I understand why he did it. I was undermining his grade. But not true? That kid doesn't know how close he came to being punched, because at that moment everything since 2003 was linked in my mind and it was true, all of it, including the fact that the teacher hadn't given us enough time to create an in-depth and meaningful presentation. Denial of any one of those facts, at that moment, felt like a betrayal of everything.

I'm not sure exactly what happened next. In fact, for more than a year I didn't remember the evening at all, so the actual sequence of events is fuzzy. There was an argument, I know that, and Tuesday and I left. I guess the presentation went on. I passed the class, but I left the investigative journalism program a few days later, when I had my head straight again, and switched to print and magazine journalism.

I didn't hold it against Tuesday. If anything, I blamed the professors for forcing me into an impossible situation. And I blamed myself for not being smarter about my surroundings. And I blamed those two yippy dogs, *especially* those two damn yippy dogs, because they had thrown Tuesday and me off our routine. Hot apartment, big crowd, bad dogs. It was too much, really, to expect, especially only a few weeks into our relationship. As long as we kept it simple, I told myself between hyperventilating breaths on the long subway home, Tuesday and I would be fine.

CHAPTER 13

THANKSGIVING

And I will put my father to the test,
See if the old man knows me now, on sight,
or fails to, after twenty years apart.

—HOMER, *THE ODYSSEY*

I BURIED THE EVENING IN MY MIND. THIS WASN'T EASY TO DO with PTSD, but something told me I needed to rid myself of the bad thoughts to survive. My mind was full enough with the memories of Iraq and our betrayal of Ali, Maher, and so many others, and that fall I was becoming increasingly anxious about Afghanistan, even publishing a piece on "endless Army mission creep" there. The piece noted that the Marshall Plan, the Allied effort to rebuild Europe after World War II, had been run by the State Department. The rebuilding effort in Iraq, because of State Department deference and incompetence, was being run by the military and staffed by soldiers. With so much of my time focused on military disaster, both real and surmised, I needed stability in my life.

And besides, Tuesday and I had a far more important mission to prepare for than a college class. That Thanksgiving, we were going home to spend time with my family.

Family had always been the bedrock of my life. I didn't join the Army because of family issues or even as a means of escape. Ronald Reagan, and his vision of a society founded on morality and hard work, made me want to enter public service. When the nation needed us, Bush told us to shop for washing machines; Reagan, like Kennedy before him, challenged us to set a personal example. I chose the Army as my means of service, perhaps as an answer to my papá. He was an economist, and he fought the Cuban dictatorship with words and numbers. As a teenager, I joined street rallies against Castro and supported Hermanos al Rescate (Brothers to the Rescue), which supported "the efforts of the Cuban people to free themselves from dictatorship through the use of active nonviolence." If I challenged my papá's methods, though, I never questioned his integrity, intelligence, or honor. He was the man I admired. I grew up wanting to be like him, but in my own way.

When I returned from my first tour in Iraq, the only people I wanted to see were my parents. For me, they were life in America. But they weren't at the armory at Fort Carson to greet me like all the other families. This was my fault. I told them it wasn't necessary to fly all that way, that it would be fine to see them in a few weeks in Washington, D.C. I was wrong. Stepping off the transport plane after a combat tour was a profound experience, simultaneously exhilarating and disorienting. It was impossible not to be overcome with relief and joy. Everyone was rushing to hug their wives, husbands, children, girlfriends, parents, but as I moved alone through the crowd I felt that joy turn into disillusionment. I was cut off from the world I had known in Iraq, but without someone to welcome me home I didn't feel a part of this world either. At the end of the crowd, I just kept walking, alone, out of the armory and into the bright Colorado sun.

At the end of my second tour, I didn't ask my parents to meet me. I can't even say why. I just didn't feel like seeing anybody, I guess, not even them. By then, I was a different person. Isolated. Anxious. Obsessed with the war . . . and with the past. In a way, I suppose I hadn't come all the way back, and that made me reluctant to meet the people I had always loved. No matter how much I wanted to keep my scars from my parents, though, they knew. Parents always know. That's why my papá demanded, in a moment of weakness, "You're not going to be another broken soldier." He didn't recognize me anymore, and he was afraid.

A few weeks later, he sent me an email urging me to change my mind. Among other things, he wrote:

I'm shocked, saddened, and dismayed (and a few other things along that line). . . . I have to tell you from the bottom of my heart that I firmly believe you have made a wrong decision [in not taking the Emergency Management job], one that may affect you greatly in the future, and not positively. Certain signals were worrisome, among which, in my opinion (I stress this!) is your joining groups of disabled vets. There are two reasons this was worrisome to me: (a) I believe many of the members of those groups, while presumably supporting each other, essentially fall into the trap (vicious circle) of helping each other take maximum advantage of disability benefits, thereby deepening their own disability and strengthening their desire to live "on the dole" rather than on overcoming disability; and (b) I also believe that the members of those groups tend to drag each other down to the "lowest common denominator," similar to the weakest link in a chain.

I responded eight hours later, at one thirty in the morning, with a message I still think sums up my life path since Iraq better than any other:

Papá:
I understand your points and appreciate your candor, concern and love.
    Much of what you say is sound and very reasonable. I certainly do not aim to descend to the lowest common denominator of the living.

That being said, I have neglected some issues that are fundamentally weakening my ability and the possibility to thrive and live a happy life.

I am, in fact, committed to being honest with myself so that I can overcome this situation. This includes not succumbing to the path of least resistance (denial) but rather the path of hardship which I know will lead to my evolution.

Despite the path that I have now embarked on which includes some elements of fear, I feel more at peace and consequently a greater sense of assurance that I can move forward in the fashion that is truly in keeping with what I am about and where I will end up.

I don't expect you to fully realize what I'm saying as my experiences are but personal stories to you. To me, they are blood, sweat and tears that consume my being. . . .

I sounded reasonable, I think, but I was reeling. I don't think my father can ever realize how painful it was for me to lose his respect. I went down the rabbit hole after that. Except for thumbing my nose at my parents by sending them my acceptance letter to Columbia, I didn't speak to them for months. I didn't tell them I wasn't coming home for Thanksgiving, I just didn't show up. This was unprecedented in the Montalván family, and it was probably one of the primary reasons I spent that weekend blasted on Bacardi, contemplating the idea of falling asleep and never waking up.

A few weeks later, on December 15, 2007, I received another email from my father that said in part:

I went to a recommended psychiatrist to try to understand what's happened between us. We talked for an hour, he recommended some readings and a couple of websites, which I've been reading.

While my level of understanding is still in initial stages, I now understand that I should not have sent you that email, and I

apologize. I respect your decision [not to speak to me anymore], but if
you want to help me understand, I'll be here for you anytime.

This was a major concession. Latino men of my father's generation don't go to therapists. They never say, "I don't understand.
Please help me." And they rarely apologize. We talked on the phone
the next day, and although I don't remember what we said, I remember the relief at hearing his voice. "Just count on me—we're
in this together," he wrote me the next night. I sat in my furniture-
less apartment and cried when I read that line.

I was deeply confused. I was still angry at my father, but he had
reached out to me, and I missed my parents terribly. I couldn't bear
the thought of missing our family Christmas, and not only because I feared spending another holiday alone, except for alcohol,
in my empty apartment. So two days before Christmas, I did what
I always did when I needed help: I called Father Tim.

Father Tim was a Jesuit priest in California, and I had met him,
by phone, after my second tour ended in the spring of 2006. He
was not affiliated with the armed forces at that time, but I was
given his name by a friend and fellow soldier. It was one of those
informal suggestions. "Hey, I know what you're going through,
man. This guy can help."

I grew up a practicing Catholic, so I can say this without hesitation: Father Tim was the ideal priest. He knew the military, having
been a chaplain for collegiate ROTC, and he was highly educated.
He had five advanced degrees, including a PhD in neurobiology, so
he understood how my traumatic brain injury affected my thoughts,
actions, and impulse control. He was a former alcoholic. He had
worked the twelve steps hard for thirty years, and he still worked
them every day because an alcoholic, like a PTSD sufferer, is never
healed. He was very compassionate. He was very patient and con-
siderate. Perhaps because of his past, he never condemned my

choices or mistakes. He listened. He made suggestions, but he also guided me toward my own solutions. He was deeply religious, and he shared with me his beliefs, but he never forced me to agree with them as a condition of receiving his solace. I don't know how many soldiers he was talking with at that time. It must have been dozens, maybe more, and yet he was available at any time, day or night. I called him at my lowest moments, often at four in the morning, but he never turned away a request to talk. There were months when Father Tim and I talked every day, but he never complained.

When I told him about Papá's letter, he told me simply, "Go home."

I arrived unannounced in the middle of Noche Buena, our traditional Christmas Eve dinner. Mamá threw her arms around me, her cheeks glistening with tears. It was hard to see the hurt and fear in her face, and to know how much suffering my condition had caused her. When Papá hugged me, I saw that he was crying, too. That's when I broke down, because I had never seen my father in tears. That's something else Latino men of his generation never do.

"I'm sorry," he said, but I didn't need the words. We held each other, two big men over six feet tall, crying on each other's shoulders, and that was more than enough.

I won't say it was easy after that. It wasn't. I was still deep in the grip of PTSD, and social interactions, even with my mother and father, were mentally grinding. So I rarely spoke to my parents over the next year. Between classes at Columbia and the Brooklyn VA hospital, I didn't have the energy. But I no longer hated them. I no longer thought that they were working against me, like the Army and society at large. I no longer felt betrayed by my father's words. In early May 2008, around the time of the subway attack, I bottomed out. Unable to navigate the VA bureaucracy and desperate for decent medical care, I called my papá. He traveled to New York and sat with me during a difficult meeting with the hospital board. I didn't get the proper care I needed, even after the meeting, but having my father there kept me sane. He understood. He was on my side.

So the trip to Washington, D.C., for Thanksgiving 2008 was not perilous, but it was important to me nonetheless. My parents were my primary emotional support, and I wanted them to like Tuesday. Even more than that, I wanted them to be impressed with him. I knew they were skeptical. When I told Papá about Tuesday, and that he knew eighty commands, he played it off with a laugh. "Wow," he said. "That's more than you know."

Mamá didn't say anything. Even more than my father, she understood the seriousness of my situation, because she knew me better than anyone. She had watched me trying to readjust to life in the United States; she had read my writings and knew I spent my last Thanksgiving drunk on rum, wondering if the government would make good on its promises before it was too late. She saw the changes in me, and she was terrified. Truly terrified.

She didn't believe Tuesday was the answer. Her son was suffering from mental and physical illness. He was alone. He was possibly suicidal. The thought that a dog—a dog!—could solve those problems seemed ludicrous to her. She didn't understand what Tuesday could do, in terms of physical assistance. Unless you've seen a service dog balancing, stabilizing, and doing chores for a disabled person, you can't understand how much it affects that person's life. It is an extraordinary daily change.

But more than that, my mother wasn't a dog person. I mean, she never even liked my giant schnauzer Max. She never saw how much he meant to me; she only saw the hair and the dirt. She didn't understand how much animal companionship can affect your psychology and moods . . . or ease your loneliness and pain.

I wanted to convince her that Tuesday was a good idea. I didn't want her to worry about me, and I didn't want her to think I was forgoing better options because of my faith in him. I was attending therapy, both one-on-one counseling and group counseling with other veterans, and regularly taking more than twenty different medicines for my various conditions. Tuesday was an addition to those treatments, and he was making a difference. If I could convince a skeptic like Mamá of that, then, frankly, I'd feel more confident of my chances for success. And confidence matters.

Nothing proved Tuesday's worth to me more than the trip to Washington, D.C. Tuesday, you see, loves trains. He loves them so much, he must have been a conductor in a previous life. This was vital to me, since I was forced by my economic situation to ride the subway every time I went to Columbia. The subway was a horror for my PTSD-addled brain, a nail-gripping, muscle-tensing ride in a claustrophobic tube full of faces my mind compulsively studied for signs of malicious intent. For Tuesday, they were fascinating. I hate going underground, but Tuesday bounced along the platform, eager for the show. I could tell when a train was approaching because Tuesday perked up, then wandered a few steps away to stare into the tunnel, excited and alert. As soon as the first car passed, Tuesday whiplashed his head in pursuit, his tongue hanging out as he wandered a few steps down the platform, as if pulled along in the train's wake. He loved the express trains that didn't stop at the station, especially the ones that barely slowed down and went barreling past with a mad clanging. He always watched until the last car was out of sight, then turned to me with a look of wonder, like he'd just seen a rocket to the moon.

Actually riding on a subway car wasn't quite as much fun. They were smelly, they were crowded, the cars lurched and banged in no discernible pattern, and the brakes squealed maniacally at every stop. It's wise that no pets are allowed, because I doubt most dogs could handle it. A veteran I know once took his cat on the subway in a carrying kennel. When he got off after a short ride, the terrified animal was covered in its own urine. Which may explain, now that I think about it, the horrible odor down there. It's the odor I imagine Tuesday smells whenever we pass that great dog restroom commonly known as a fire hydrant. Of course, Tuesday likes it.

He likes everything. That's what's so amazing about him. Even on the subway, where he had to deal with urine, crowds, rude New Yorkers, and my rampaging anxiety, Tuesday seemed to enjoy himself. Most of the time, I made him sit right in front of me on the floor, upright and alert, with his shoulders between my knees. He was a physical barrier, and I could grab him at a moment's notice if necessary. He never seemed to mind; the more agitated I was, the calmer Tuesday became, and nowhere was he quite as calm as on the subway. He could sit for twenty minutes without moving, if that's what I needed. The subway ride to Columbia was more than an hour long, though, and the position ultimately wore him down. When the crowd was light, I often let him lie on the floor, or I would let him turn around to rest his head on my lap between stops, when no one would step on his tail. When the crowd was heavy, I usually pinned him between my knees and sat hunched forward with an arm wrapped around his neck, whispering in his ear. It looked like I was restraining him to protect other passengers; in fact, I was holding Tuesday to keep myself calm.

The train to Washington, D.C., was different. As soon as Tuesday saw it, gleaming in the station and dozens of cars long, his tongue dropped out and his whole back half started to wag. He may have thought we were going back to ECAD, because that was the only time we'd ridden a real train, but he didn't express any disappointment when he figured out that wasn't the case. He just lay calmly under the large double seats, lifting his head every time someone walked by. He loved the conductor, watching with his eyebrows bobbing as the man came through punching tickets. Eventually, somewhere in southern New Jersey, the gentle rocking of the train put him to sleep. Every so often, he climbed up to make sure I was okay, and more often than not he stayed with me on the seat for a minute or two, both of us staring out the window as the trees and power lines and small houses of New Jersey and Maryland sped past. It was a nice feeling, having my big dog beside me, leaning his warm body against my arm, but I didn't need it. Just knowing he was resting beneath me calmed my mind.

It was amazing how comfortable and natural my parents' house felt, both for Tuesday and me. It had a fenced backyard, so I let him run and fetch whenever we had a few spare minutes. He loved sleeping with me in the big upstairs bedroom, and like the rest of us, he loved the smell of Mamá's cooking. He hit it off instantly with Papá, who can be a pretty stern judge of character. On the first afternoon, while my father read his newspaper, Tuesday snuck up behind him and jammed his head through the crook in his arm.

"Don't pet him," I warned, as my dad laughed out loud.

It was an odd request, I know, but Lu had hammered into my head that for the first month at least, no one was to interact with my service dog. No petting, no bumping, no talking to or distracting Tuesday while he worked, which of course was all the time. Rick and Mary, my old classmates from ECAD, weren't even supposed to let their spouses touch their service animals. These were not our pets; they were our life support systems. Our bond was essential, and Lu didn't want anything to interfere with the "pack of two" mentality we needed to thrive.

So that was the refrain of the weekend.

"Don't pet Tuesday."

"Don't pet Tuesday."

"I'm sorry, but you can't pet Tuesday."

My sister was down from New York City with her two dog-loving children, and I must have told them that fifty times. Christina and I lived a subway ride away, but we never visited each other. She had a family, I told myself, and I didn't want to intrude. In reality, I didn't want to face her. She didn't understand me, and I suspected she was disappointed. She might even have been scared of me. And now here I was, completely confusing her kids.

"Why can't we pet Tuesday, Tío Luis?"

"Because he's not a regular dog. He's my service dog. He works for me. That's why he wears this red vest, see? He's really smart. He brings my shoes and supports me on the stairs and reminds me to take my medicine."

They must have thought I was totally out of my mind.

Mamá was the more complicated problem, but I didn't push her to accept Tuesday. Sure, I had Tuesday turn on and off the light switches the first night. I had him open the kitchen cabinets ("Open"), retrieve his bowl ("Get it") and then place it on the kitchen counter (three commands: "Up," "Reach," and "Drop it"). I didn't try to convince her, I just wanted her to see what an extraordinary dog Tuesday was. He was well-groomed. He never barked, unless I commanded him to speak. He sat quietly under the table for our entire Thanksgiving dinner, only occasionally sticking his nose up into my lap to ask politely for a bite of turkey. After being told once, he never again walked on Mamá's favorite rug, which for her may have been his most important trick.

He had produced a profound change in my life, something I knew my mother comprehended. I was more focused on the present and less apt to spiral into damaging thoughts. I slept better. I was more social. I was more confident in my body. And, as my mamá no doubt appreciated, I drank less. Much less. Sure, I drank a healthy quantity of wine at my parents' that Thanksgiving, but it wasn't out of necessity. I wasn't trying to drown my problems or quiet my mind. It was social drinking, taken a sip at a time, and for my mother, I think, that was reason enough to give thanks for Tuesday. And to hope.

"He's a well-behaved dog," Mamá said as we left. It wasn't love, and not quite respect, but from the woman who had given me countless manners lessons when I was a child, it was a start.

"Thanks, Tuesday," I told him on the train ride home, throwing my arm over his shoulder like an old friend. You never know how much you want your parents' approval, even in your thirties, until it's gone.

CHAPTER 14

SMOKED

Every dog must have his day.

—JONATHAN SWIFT

BACK IN BROOKLYN FOR THE LONG WINTER SCHOOL BREAK, I settled into my New York–sized apartment with my suburbs-sized dog. In a burst of credit-wrecking optimism, I had purchased a queen-sized bed for the two of us to sleep in together. It took up one entire room of my two-room apartment, so I started using the bed as my desk when I researched the war and, in particular, the inefficiency and corruption of the New York City Veterans Benefits Administration (VBA) regional office (which led to a shake-up in top management), of which I and thousands of other veterans had been victims. As part of our daily training, I taught Tuesday to stay off the bed while I was working, and then immediately got in the habit of slapping the comforter and telling him, "Jump on, Tuesday. Jump on, big boy." He jumped right up and snuggled beside me. When I finally turned off the computer several hours after turning off the lights, he lay down next to me, his hot breath in my face. I always put my arm around him and talked to him. He nuzzled me gently in return until I fell asleep. Then he left my bed and curled up on his bed on the floor.

I missed his warmth, but otherwise the sleeping arrangement didn't bother me. I knew Tuesday was only a few feet away, and I knew he was watching and listening to me. Every time I woke up from a nightmare, disoriented and wondering whether I was in Sunset Park or Al-Waleed or a bombed room somewhere in south Baghdad, Tuesday was standing beside the bed, waiting for me to reach out for him. When I lay awake staring at the ceiling, I listened to his breathing, and I let it be a quiet rhythm for my thoughts. After a few minutes, I'd hear Tuesday stir, followed by the pressure of two paws on the bed and then, finally, the warmth of his breath. Tuesday always knew when I was awake.

I bought him dog toys and rubber balls to keep him entertained. I wasn't ready for the world outside, and besides, it was winter and the nearest park was fifteen blocks away. So when Tuesday and I weren't working on commands, I sat on the couch and bounced tennis balls against the wall of my living room. Tuesday loved the chase, but the room was so small it took him only four steps to cross it. He was a smart dog, though, and he soon figured out that the best technique was to romp two steps for momentum and then, with a small leap, slide into the wall, turning over and slamming his rear into the plaster before scrambling back to me on clicking paws. He could easily do this thirty, forty, fifty times in a row without getting bored. It wasn't great exercise, but Tuesday always came back with his tail up and a tennis ball—or a sock—stuck between his teeth. Tuesday brought my shoes and socks to me every morning so I wouldn't have to bend over and put pressure my back. I can't tell you how many days were ruined, before Tuesday, because I wrenched my back bending over for my shoes, but it was far too many. Now Tuesday ruined my socks instead of my day. He loved to wrestle with them on the way back from retrieving them, and half the time I delicately slid slobber-covered socks into my desert combat boots.

When I went out for anything other than class and the VA, it was usually at night. Most people in Sunset Park avoided going out after midnight, because the crime rate in the neighborhood was high. Muggings and burglaries weren't common, but the groups of loitering young men on Fifth Avenue and the other commercial streets felt more intimidating and aggressive late at night. It was commonly assumed among the regular Joes that the people out late in Sunset Park were not the type you wanted to run into.

I didn't mind the nights. The threat of attack didn't worry me—after all, I was trained for that, and what could be worse than Baghdad?—and I liked the streets being deserted. The biggest challenge for me was navigating the streets during the day, when people were everywhere.

The defining state of PTSD is not fear. That's a complete misunderstanding. The defining state of PTSD is hypervigilance. Psychologists describe it as the flight-or-fight syndrome, because PTSD is essentially the superaroused state normal people enter when they are suddenly in danger, the one where the blood rushes to your head, your muscles coil, and your breathing slows. You are in survival mode, ready to fight or flee for your life. For ordinary people, it only lasts a few seconds, but for combat-scarred veterans like me, hyperarousal was a near permanent state.

In *Achilles in Vietnam*, a groundbreaking book about PTSD, a veteran scolded his therapist, who is also the author, for being oblivious to the world. They had walked on the same street many times, but the therapist never noticed. The veteran, on the other hand, had not only watched the therapist but knew all his habits and quirks.

In Sunset Park, I felt exactly the same way. Most people walked down the street oblivious to the world around them. I could see it in their eyes, and I was both jealous of their mindless sense of security and appalled by their carelessness. I analyzed everybody I passed, watching the expression on their faces, their body language, the way they held their hands. I took note of the way they dressed and the places they looked. If a person glanced at me twice, I locked onto them as a potential threat, and I remembered that not just for the next five minutes but for days and weeks as well.

It wasn't just people. In my hypervigilant state, I was acutely aware of the environment around me. I was seeing things in sharper detail, hearing individual sounds more clearly, picking individual scents out of the thick New York air. The smell of gasoline and sewer sludge, the tang of Middle Eastern cooking spices, took me right back to Iraq. I wouldn't *see* Iraq. Most veterans like me don't suddenly think we're in combat or have visual flashbacks like movie scenes. I experienced the *feeling* of being there: the adrenaline, the hyperarousal, the awareness of imminent danger. My mind jumped at every movement in an upstairs window, calculating the probabilities, while my eyes scanned doorways, parked cars, and garbage bins. Especially garbage bins. They were always overflowing with bottles and wrappers, the perfect place for an improvised bomb.

Most people hate rats. Tuesday loved them. He'd strain way out over the edge of the subway platform for a better view of a rat. They were a close third on his excitement meter after trains and squirrels. I didn't mind the live ones; they were harmless. The dead ones, though, made me nervous. In Iraq, insurgents hid IEDs in animal carcasses, so I never went near a dead animal.

Or a soda can. Insurgents could place enough explosives in a soda can to blow off your arms and half your face. They did it all the time. In Sunset Park, my mind was constantly searching for soda cans. I didn't avoid them—that would have been crazy, right, to cross the street to avoid a soda can?—but I knew exactly where they were, and I wasn't going too near them.

None of this was a conscious effort. It took place in millisecond bursts deep in my mind, but instead of staying in the subconscious as it does for ordinary people, the warnings were being sent in a constant churn into my conscious thoughts. My mind was wheeling in a dozen different directions at a thousand miles an hour every time I stepped onto a crowded street. That's what brought on the anxiety, the constant checking, checking, checking to determine if I needed to act.

Medicine helped. The right prescription drugs took the edge off my mind even better than alcohol. But nothing soothed me like Tuesday. There was something about seeing him a few feet in front of me, walking calmly, that eased my mind. He was trained to recognize the unusual, after all, and to alert me at the slightest hint of danger. When I jumped at shadows, I saw him out of the corner of my eye and thought, *Tuesday's calm so there's nothing there, everything is fine.*

Of course, Tuesday wasn't always calm. He never panicked, but he was occasionally distracted, especially in those early months. This was understandable. How could a dog, even one as well-trained as Tuesday, not be distracted by the blaring music, flashing lights, passing cars, and crowds on Sunset Park's Fifth Avenue? Many service dogs could never make it in New York City. There is too much stimulus. Too much concrete instead of grass. It's a unique assignment, to say the least.

But knowing the difficulties didn't make Tuesday's lack of focus easier for me. When Tuesday was distracted, I felt unsure. In the years ahead, I learned to read his reactions. I knew when his mind was wandering, when he was merely interested in something (Squirrel! Urine-smelling tree!), and when he was alert to possible danger. Knowing Tuesday's mood calmed my mind, because I could trust his vigilance. Today, I can walk down the street distracted and carefree because I have faith Tuesday will alert me to danger. In those early months, before I'd learned to trust his instincts, Tuesday's greatest contribution was his presence. He was my point man, walking slightly ahead of me, symbolically leading the way. He was a buffer against the world, but also a diversion. If they were going to look at me, most people looked at Tuesday first, and that was a relief.

Still, I preferred the night, especially in the winter, when it was too cold for anyone to stand outside for long. That December, I bundled myself up many nights, slipped the service dog vest on Tuesday, and headed out to the convenience store or the all-night liquor shop, where the bulletproof glass partition meant I never had to come in contact with another human being. It felt good to be outside, where the air was fresh and where Tuesday bounced along beside me, happy to stretch his legs after long hours inside. The streets, I suppose, held a vague menace, the spindly trees along my block throwing shadows over rusted iron railings, the streetlight buzzing yellow at the end of the block. The houses where women sat on folding chairs during the day leaned darkly, the paint peeling, music thumping softly from an open window.

At the bottom of the block was Fifth Avenue—Brooklyn, not Manhattan—the main commercial strip. The night opened up here, with a wider street and sidewalks, and although most of the buildings were shuttered, the streetlights kept the shadows back against the walls. It was one block to the liquor store, two blocks to the all-night convenience store, and even in winter groups of young men loitered on the sidewalk, leaning against cars or storefronts. They were punks, mostly, young guys with too much time on their hands, but they never worried me. Sure, I limped, but I leaned on a big wooden cane known as a Bubba Stik. And in my hypervigilant state, I was studying them from a block away. By the time I was close enough for trouble, I knew their group dynamic, their mood, and their intentions. There was no way they could take me by surprise.

And they never tried. I was more than six feet tall and muscular, even slouched in my black coat. I had long dark hair, full stubble, and a grim expression, so I didn't look like someone to mess with, especially not with a large dog at my side. Tuesday may have been a tenderhearted golden retriever, but he was three feet tall and eighty pounds of muscle, and there weren't many street punks who wanted to mess with a dog like that. Besides, neither one of us showed any hesitation. We never made eye contact, but they were wise enough to know it wasn't out of fear. I was coiled and, in some subconscious part of my mind, ready for a fight. Sometimes, I think, I was hoping for it. I kept my knife deep in my pocket for that reason. I didn't want it to be too easy to reach.

After the liquor store, we often walked a few extra blocks down Fifth Avenue, then up a side street to Sixth Avenue, then back down to my block. At the corner, there was a small park. It was called Rainbow Park, according to a small green sign, but it was nothing more than a concrete slab containing a basketball court with no nets and two handball courts separated by a concrete wall and surrounded by a twenty-foot chain-link fence. Tuesday always gave the leash a little tug and glanced at me as we passed the park. I knew what he wanted, but I didn't like the idea. The park closed at nightfall. Cops regularly drove down Sixth Avenue, and they would question someone out late. It was that kind of neighborhood. I wanted to indulge Tuesday, but I didn't like to think about that kind of scrutiny.

Then I realized the back handball court, behind the concrete wall, wasn't that visible from the street. I thought about that fact for a few weeks, ignoring Tuesday's tug on the leash, until one night, just after the New Year, Tuesday and I ducked out of the house and headed up the hill to Sixth Avenue. It was after midnight. I could see our breath like white clouds, but the tapping of my Bubba Stik was the only sound. Tuesday was walking a few steps ahead of me, pulling slightly on the leash. He wasn't wearing his service dog vest, so he knew something was up, and I could feel his excitement. When he saw the park, he shifted toward it, a move so imperceptible only someone with a leash in hand would notice. Despite his polite suggestion, he expected me to turn down Sixth Avenue, as always, but this time we crossed over to the fence. There was no lock on the gate. I pushed it open and led Tuesday to the back handball court. The streetlights were on along the side street, but the concrete wall between the courts cast a dark shadow. Slowly, I knelt and unhooked the leash, bending from the knees to preserve my back. Tuesday stared at me with his natural smile, reading my face. He was excited, but he waited, silently, a perfectly behaved service dog. I shifted my cane to my left hand and pulled a tennis ball from my pocket.

"Do you want to play, Tuesday?"

He stood up, ready to run but not breaking eye contact until I winged the ball against the concrete wall. As it went bouncing over his head, Tuesday leapt, turning in midair as it sailed past his teeth. I laughed as he took off running, tracking the ball down in the corner then jogging back to me with it clenched in his teeth.

"Another throw, Tuesday?" I said, slinging the spit-covered ball.

He missed again, then sprinted after it. By the time he reached me with the slobberball, he was already a little winded.

I threw it again. Tuesday chased, the ball bouncing wildly off the concrete court. I threw odd angles and high hard ones, trying to bounce it past him each time. I expected him to get tired, but the more Tuesday chased that ball, the more he wanted to run. In the Army, we have an expression: "getting smoked." We worked out in the early morning, pushing ourselves until the sweat poured down our skin. As the day heated up, the sweat evaporated until, on really punishing days, a cloud of water vapor rose off our shoulders like smoke. By the time I was tired of throwing tennis balls, Tuesday was smoked. It wasn't sweat, since dogs don't sweat, but heat was rising from his core and right off the top of his head. He stood looking at me through a pale cloud, huffing giant breaths of smoke, his tongue dangling and a look on his face I recognized from my own time getting smoked, back before my injuries: exhaustion and joy. He could have run for days.

For the rest of the winter, we went to Rainbow Park. We went between midnight and five in the morning, when the world was quiet. The streetlights buzzed, and every few minutes there was the soft whoosh of a car, but otherwise there was nothing but the thump of a tennis ball against a concrete wall and an occasional word of encouragement as a sleepless veteran leaned on his cane in the shadows and his dog got smoked.

CHAPTER 15

CATS AND DOGS

Love must be learned, and learned again; there is no end to it.

—KATHERINE ANNE PORTER

TWO MONTHS INTO OUR LIVES TOGETHER, TUESDAY AND I were getting along great. We were building a healthy respect for each other, working on our bond, and Tuesday was beginning to realize this was more than a fleeting relationship. Some service dogs sit around watching television, because that's what their owners do. Tuesday traveled to Washington, D.C., played in Rainbow Park, and rode the subway every few days to Columbia and the Manhattan VA hospital. He was an active dog, and he liked it. He liked it even more that I was affectionate and attentive to him. It was never a matter of him deferring to me, because I was the "pack leader" from the moment we met, but I think he started to appreciate me as a partner after Rainbow Park.

Still, there were a few bumps, especially in social situations. I had trouble, I am ashamed to admit, with Middle Easterners. If a person appeared Middle Eastern, my mind went into overdrive, searching for signs of danger. That's racist, I understand, but it wasn't hatred. Not at all. I love my Iraqi friends and I respect the Muslim world. It's just that 100 percent of the people who had ever tried to kill me were Middle Eastern, and there had been plenty of them. I spent the better part of two years studying faces in Al-Anbar, Baghdad, and Nineveh provinces trying to determine who would next attack, and I couldn't stop doing that in America, too. That's a symptom of PTSD, the inability to act differently in ordinary society than you did in combat. My mind told me it didn't matter if the young Middle Eastern men were well dressed and on their way to work in Manhattan; that could be a diversion. It didn't matter if they were women, especially if they were wearing head scarves. Enemy fighters often dressed as women and besides, women had been known to blow themselves to smithereens. All those virgins in heaven were a smoke screen; the real reasons for suicide bombings, like most of the other atrocities committed in the world, were poverty, propaganda, stupidity, and anger, and those reasons weren't confined to the male sex.

Tuesday, meanwhile, had a problem with cats. He wasn't afraid of them, but he didn't trust them. He thought they were crazy, and their lack of logical actions and intentions, at least from his point of view, completely freaked him out. Lu had told me, jokingly, about Tuesday's cautious relationship with a cat that lived near ECAD, but I don't think he really made up his mind about cats until the incident in Sunset Park.

It was about eight thirty at night, a difficult time for Tuesday and me because the streets were still crowded. We were passing George's Restaurant on Fifth Avenue when, out of nowhere, a mangy alley cat jumped out of the bushes and landed on Tuesday's back. I mean, it leapt in full attack mode, with claws out, hissing and tearing. I was so surprised, I almost fell down. All my hypervigilance, and I never saw the cat coming. And it was coming for blood. Fortunately, it landed on Tuesday's vest, but it dug so far into the fabric that Tuesday couldn't shake it off. He was twisting and growling, trying to snap at it, but the cat was in that place on your back where you can't reach, and it wasn't letting go. I started swinging at the cat with my cane, but Tuesday was moving so much that I missed him two or three times. Finally Tuesday twisted like a rodeo bull and the cat went flying, landing on all four feet by the bushes. It hunched its shoulders, collected itself for a moment, then turned and lunged at Tuesday again.

"Are you kidding me?" I said.

The cat was a foot from Tuesday, hissing and swiping at him. Tuesday had his head lowered, growling to warn it away. I was pulling on the leash, trying to keep Tuesday from hurting the crazy animal, and leaning on my cane to keep my balance. I kept saying, "Get lost, you stupid cat. Get out of here!" waving my cane as much as I could, and I guess it was a show because soon a little crowd gathered around us. They were all saying, *Shoo cat, shoo,* half of them in a foreign language and most of the rest in broken English. An Asian man showed up with a broom, and between the cat's circling, Tuesday's growling, the swinging broom, and my cane, it was a three-ring circus. Finally, the cat retreated to the bushes, completely unharmed, and Tuesday and I retreated to our apartment, where he gave me a look as if to say, *See, I told you—cats are crazy.*

So it wasn't an auspicious moment when I walked into the pet store a few weeks later and saw a woman wearing a hijab in one of the two aisles. I admit I panicked, just a little. "That way, Tuesday, that way," I said, pushing him toward the other aisle.

Around the corner, Tuesday froze. There was a cat in the middle of the aisle. Oh crap. What now? Tuesday wasn't going any farther. I wasn't going back. The cat stared at us lazily, with no intention of leaving. So Tuesday and I stood there, cowering in the corner by the canned meats display, until the perfectly nice woman in the hijab left, which I swear, in my state, seemed to take three weeks. It would be an embarrassing story if it weren't so emblematic of how Tuesday and I lived back then. We had our little problems, like everyone else.

On balance, though, Tuesday was a social dog. Much more social than me. He didn't want anything to do with cats, but he had an innate curiosity about everything else, especially squirrels. There was a section of the Columbia campus that was swarming with squirrels, and with the start of the new semester I started walking Tuesday past so that he could stop and stare at them. He wanted to run. He was almost trembling with the excitement of it—which often made him pee, by the way, although I don't know if that was biological, coincidence, or an intentional marking of this majestic squirrel-chasing sanctuary—but I couldn't let him off the leash. He was my working dog; daydreams of romping were the most I could offer.

Still, I knew by January that change was coming to our tidy cocoon. For weeks, whenever Tuesday and I arrived home, we heard little feet inside the apartment of my landlord, Mike Chung, whose first-floor apartment was across from the front door. The footsteps started slowly, then built to a fast clicking on the linoleum floor, then ended with a sudden thump against the door that always made Tuesday startle backward. After a short silence, which involved much sniffing from Tuesday, the scrambling would begin, accompanied by a high whining and the scratching of claws on the floor, as the creature on the other side tried to dig its way under the door.

"Come on, Tuesday," I'd say, pulling him toward the narrow staircase. He always held back, staring at the opening under the door, but as soon as his attention broke he was the old Tuesday again, walking slowly beside me so that I could use him to brace myself on the stairs.

One day, while I was working at my desk, I noticed Tuesday pop up from a drowsy afternoon sprawl, flip his ears to attention,

then stare at the door. A few seconds later, I heard quick little footsteps on the staircase followed by heavy panting at the door.

This was it. The creature was outside.

But nothing came of it, much to Tuesday's disappointment.
When it happened again, Tuesday looked at me pleadingly, but I
shook my head no. The animal scratched, then whimpered, and I
heard heavier footsteps on the stairs.

Don't knock, I thought. *Don't knock.*

It wasn't that Tuesday couldn't have friends. We were past our
two-month bonding period, and I knew he accepted me as his alpha
dog. My hesitation was more personal. I felt comfortable having
Tuesday with me, just the two of us, and I didn't want to be disturbed. I wanted to keep our exclusive time together, and our safe
haven in the building, intact. I knew eventually I would reconnect
with the larger world, and that Tuesday would be my guide back,
but I wasn't ready yet.

Tuesday seemed so genuinely excited, though, that I knew I
couldn't keep him cooped up for long. I loved him too much for
that. So with less and less reluctance, I listened for the little feet on
the staircase, the soft whimper, and the heavy tread. Sometimes I
felt glad when I heard a female voice say, "Come on, Welly. Let's
go." Other times, I felt disappointed. I wasn't going to initiate contact, but I was ready to open the door.

So it was with some relief that I finally heard the knock. It was
Huang, my landlord Mike's wife. "Can Tuesday play with Wellington?" she asked.

I looked down. Standing beside her was a muscular little French
bulldog no more than a third the size of Tuesday. It was mostly
white, with a few brown patches, bowlegs, and a classic bulldog
face: smushed snout, bugged-out eyes, floppy jowls, and the most
determined low-lip scowl I had ever seen. I've got to admit, the dog
had personality.

"Sure," I said, trying not to laugh. My Cambodian landlord had a French bulldog with a British name and a big city attitude—very New York. "Tuesday," I said, turning to him, "meet Welli . . ."

Boom. Before I even finished the introduction, Tuesday was out the door. He didn't stop for the traditional butt-sniff of friendship, either. He bolted straight out and bowled Wellington right over onto his backside. Welly jumped up with a quick bark, stuck his lower lip out, then jumped on Tuesday who, three times his size, enthusiastically pushed him back onto his rear. They wrestled their way along the landing, little Welly trying to jump on big Tuesday, and Tuesday always managing to push him back until, suddenly, they disappeared down the stairs in a bundle of legs, fur, and snouts.

By the time Huang and I reached the stairs, Tuesday was on his feet and leaping back up the staircase four steps at a time. Wellington was right behind him, hopping on each step with his little bowlegs, but what he lacked in size he made up for in determination. Tuesday took one look at me from the top of the stairs, his tongue out and his eyebrows bobbing, before Wellington hit him in the side, knocking him back into the wall. Immediately, they were at it again, rolling and snapping at each other, Tuesday on his back and Wellington bouncing around his head. Welly got an ear in his teeth; Tuesday threw a paw over Welly's shoulder. They snorted and chortled and pushed each other back and forth, and then, suddenly, they were rolling down the stairs again. I looked down to the bottom and Tuesday was sitting there, panting, a big goofy grin on his face.

"Where's Welly, Tuesday?"

Tuesday stood up and there was crazy-eyed Wellington sprawled out beneath him. The little dog was already breathing hard through that smushed nose of his, but he was a gamer. He sprang to his feet and sprinted up the stairs, with Tuesday right behind, chomping at his tail.

Huang started to laugh. So did I. It was hilarious, really, watching this muscular little dog run circles around Tuesday. Wellington had the energy, but Tuesday had the smarts, boxing him playfully into a corner and then battering him with his head while Welly tried to grab Tuesday's ears and jam them into his mouth.

"I think they like each other," Huang said.

"I think you're right."

After that, it was on like Donkey Kong. Every time we walked into the building, it seemed, Mike and Huang's door would fly open and Welly would come tearing out. Tuesday would brace for the impact and then throw the little bulldog to the ground, nipping at his belly. Wellington would shoot up the stairs with Tuesday chugging after him, then both of them would come racing down again while Mike and I, and occasionally Huang, stood at the bottom of the stairs laughing.

One time, Tuesday came rolling down the stairs covered in white dust and bits of plaster. Even from the bottom of the stairs, I could see the dent where he had hit the wall. Mike laughed it off.

"Don't worry," he said. "I'll fix it."

I was a good tenant. I was extremely quiet—never had a single guest over, didn't play music or own a television, rarely talked to myself in more than a mutter, pathologically neat, and always paid the rent on time. Mike liked me for those reasons, but until Welly and Tuesday starting playing we hadn't exchanged more than a few words. After the roughhousing started, we often hung out in the hallway, chatting. He was a nice guy, a survivor of the Cambodian killing fields, and the father of two grown children, and I'm sure he'd be surprised to hear that, for a few months, he was my best friend in New York. At least, he was the only person I talked to on a regular basis.

Mike enjoyed our time together, too. I know he did, because he must have fixed the wall at the top of the stairs ten or twelve times over the next few months, and he laughed every time. "They like it," he said. "Let them play."

And like it they did. I mean, these were two enthusiastic dogs, and they loved to go after each other. They sprinted, even though the staircase was only a few feet wide, and when they hit each other, they hit hard. Wellington was small, but he was a muscular brute.

"He runs like Emmitt Smith," Mike said proudly. And it was true. Emmitt Smith, the great Dallas Cowboys running back, had a low center of gravity and a powerful running style that relied on quick cuts. Welly ran the same way, turning Tuesday around as he plowed relentlessly from side to side, except he was bowlegged, twitchy, and incessantly shook his behind like he was blending margaritas with his stubby tail. When they wrestled, they worked hard at getting the upper hand, and when they fell down the steps they rolled hard, head over tail, still snapping and clawing, with no thought of stopping until they hit the floor.

I soon realized that if Tuesday and I were going out, I needed to leave an extra half hour in case Wellington mugged us. Twenty minutes were for the dogs to play. It usually took that long for Wellington to collapse, panting in exhaustion and sprawled out on the cool floor at the base of the stairs. Tuesday often joined him; he was usually smoked by then, too.

The other ten minutes, unfortunately, were to clean the Welly-slobber out of Tuesday's ears. Tuesday has big floppy golden re-triever ears, and after Wellington bit and tugged at them for twenty minutes, they were dripping like dish towels. Tuesday was my buddy. I couldn't let him out of the house like that. It had to be cold. And uncomfortable. And, um . . . gross.

CHAPTER 16

HOPE AND CHANGE

You gain strength, courage and confidence by every
experience in which you really stop to look fear in the face. . . .
You must do the thing which you think you cannot.

—ELEANOR ROOSEVELT

WITH TUESDAY BREAKING THE SOCIAL ICE WITH WELLINGTON, and with my optimism about the future growing by the day, I decided to attend Barack Obama's presidential inauguration on January 20, 2009. From a PTSD perspective, the event was potentially as disastrous as the party at my professor's apartment in November: hot, loud, and crowded. And instead of twenty people, there would be twenty thousand. At least I wouldn't be making a public presentation.

But the situation was different, too. I was more comfortable with Tuesday, and we both knew much better how to handle public gatherings. I was no longer naïve about the challenges of a service dog, especially in a crowd, and I was mentally prepared to confront them. And perhaps most importantly, instead of being in a negative place about the event, I was ecstatic. The George W. Bush era was over (I won't say Republican era, because the two have little in common), and I was enthusiastic about the new direction Obama was promising. Hope and change. Change and hope. In the three months since the election—the three months I had spent with Tuesday—I had lived the reality of those words.

In the years since, like many people, I have been disappointed. I never thought things would change overnight. My life has taught me that only through continuous hard work, by progressing one step at a time over a protracted period of time, can worthwhile accomplishments be achieved, whether that's training an army for combat or learning to thrive with war wounds and a service dog. I think the concept of hard work, in the end, was a major stumbling block for Bush. He never really worked for his rewards, especially as a young man, so he didn't understand how much hard work was involved in, for instance, invading a country and establishing a democracy in a deeply divided society where none had ever existed before. He assumed it would be easy, and he planned accordingly.

President Obama, who came from a middle-class background, understood hard work. I think he appreciated our soldiers' extraordinary daily effort and meant to do right by them. He increased the budget for the Department of Veterans Affairs, for instance, which has alleviated the problem of inadequate care for veterans, though, unfortunately, has not come close to solving it. But he missed the most important thing for me and a lot of other voters who were primarily interested in military affairs: he never demanded accountability. The commanders who wrecked the war effort through terrible planning and egotism, from Secretary Rumsfeld on down, were given a free pass. The real officers who created the environment of abuse at Abu Ghraib were never named, much less punished. Gen. Stanley McChrystal, a man deeply involved in the unconscionable lies about the death of Pat Tillman—a former professional football player turned Army Ranger (who was killed by friendly fire, as it turned out)—was the president's handpicked leader for the war in Afghanistan. It's like the country was staring over the cliff at the shattered remains of a bus, but Obama, like Bush before him, refused to acknowledge someone was driving it. Accountability indeed.

Of course, that was in the future. On January 20, 2009, I was celebrating possibility—both of a new direction for the U.S. military mission and a new life of my own. On the train to Washington, D.C., that weekend, with Tuesday at my side, I felt free. I was going to the kind of event that, less than three months before, would have produced crippling anxiety, and I wasn't even thinking about the crowd. Instead, I was watching Tuesday and laughing. The dog loved trains. He loved the noise, the motion, the people passing by in the aisle, and the land sweeping by out the window. We were moving, Tuesday and I, in the right direction.

At the party in November at my professor's house, everything went wrong: bad dogs, bad memories. and a service dog snout in a tube skirt. In Washington, it was exactly the opposite. Everything went right. Tuesday and I were guests of the Iraq and Afghanistan Veterans of America (IAVA), so we were with a group of like-minded people. Most of the event was outdoors, so it was less claustrophobic. Tuesday was the only dog, other than the bomb-sniffing German shepherds lurking at every entrance, so there were no yipping purse-puppies to distract him.

And Tuesday was focused. I've always felt, as his companion, that it was my responsibility to give Tuesday a life he enjoyed. I didn't know how he'd feel about his first full-scale party—the music, the lights, the balloons and streamers—but I was prepared to slip him enough refreshments under the table to keep him happily at my side. I didn't need to worry, though. Tuesday never left me. Never. Not once. Not even when the waiter came by with a full tray of donkey-shaped dog biscuits (okay, that didn't happen). But we did ride in a crowded elevator together. That's one of those things you never think about, riding in a busy elevator with an eighty-pound dog. At every floor, people sauntered on, then stopped abruptly when they saw Tuesday staring at them. "Service dog," I told them. I don't know if they knew what that meant. They might have thought he was a Secret Service dog for all I know, or a military service dog back from a tour in Iraq, but they never questioned it. By halfway down, poor Tuesday was smushed in and staring at derrieres, but that didn't seem to bother him at all. (And no, he didn't sniff . . . I don't think.)

At the party, everybody wanted to meet Tuesday. When they heard I was a wounded veteran and Tuesday was my service dog, they wanted to give both of us hugs. I didn't let them, of course; we weren't ready for that. When I ran into two attractive women at the bar (literally ran into them, it was very crowded), Tuesday was a perfect gentleman, bobbing his eyebrows while they commented on his beauty and deportment. *What the heck*, I thought, *it's a party. Let them pet him.* You'd have thought I let Tuesday catch the chuck wagon from those old dog food commercials, he was so ecstatic. Lynette and Jeri were from Miami, and since I'm a Cuban American with several relatives in Miami, we transitioned easily into other subjects. Life stuff. Normal people stuff. We talked for twenty minutes, and I'm not ashamed to say it was the best and longest conversation I'd had with anyone, outside of my family and landlord, in more than two years. I even got a phone number, but after the high of the party wore off I chickened out and never called.

Soon after, Paul Rieckhoff, the executive director of IAVA, pulled me aside. He wanted me to meet someone. When Paul walked into the VIP-only section, Tuesday and I followed. I don't know why we weren't stopped by the bouncers, but it was a magical night, everything was going right, and they let us pass without question, even though we were far from VIPs. I guess a man with a cane and a service dog doesn't seem like much of a threat.

"There he is," Paul said, walking toward a man on the other side of the enclosure. He tapped the man on the shoulder—"Hey, Al!" he said—and there I was, face-to-face with that old *Saturday Night Live*–starring, *Trading Places*–mugging, senator-to-be (the election was still being disputed in court at the time) Alan Stuart Franken. I mean, the guy was almost a senator, *and* he knew Eddie Murphy—back when Eddie was the funniest person on the planet.

"This is Captain Luis Montalván, a wounded Iraq veteran," Paul said, "and his service dog, Tuesday."

As it turned out, Al Franken wasn't just a great *actor* (ahem), but a friendly, intelligent, down-to-earth gentleman. He was genuinely interested in my perspective on the war, and we talked briefly about my two tours of duty and my injuries, both mental and physical. He was most interested, though, in Tuesday. Al Franken was a serious dog lover, and in between stories about his own dogs, I told him about Tuesday and what a difference he made in my life. While the senator-to-be was down on one knee petting Tuesday (how could I refuse?), I told him it would mean a lot to many people if he considered championing the cause of service dogs for veterans. We talked for a long time, but I didn't think much about it, even when he asked me detailed questions about Tuesday's training and the program that had matched Tuesday and me.

Eventually Franken moved on, and Tuesday and I spent the next few hours wandering the VIP section—no way we were leaving, now that we were inside—in a low-key state of joy. So many well-known, recognizable people approached us to talk to Tuesday that, by the end of the night, I really did feel like a VIP—or at least the wingman of a dog that was a pretty big deal. When the fireworks finally blasted into the sky to close the night, Tuesday and I took a cab to my parents' house and, exhausted but happy, fell into bed like best friends on a spring break trip to Cancún.

"You're a true VIP, Tuesday," I said, stifling a yawn. "Or maybe a VID: a very important dog."

Tuesday licked my face, a gesture both goofy and sweet, and laid his head on my shoulder. On the edge of sleep, I felt him rise out of the bed and, peeking out of one half-closed eye, saw him wander to the window, where he stood looking out at the moonlit yard.

A few weeks later, I received a call from Al Franken. He had been moved by our story, and he wanted to ask me more questions. We spoke several more times in the coming weeks, and it soon became clear that he was serious about service dogs. In fact, he planned to introduce a bill to help provide them to wounded veterans—if and when the court cases ended and he officially became a member of the U.S. Senate. Tuesday, I realized, really was a star.

CHAPTER 17

THE BACK OF
THE BUS

─────────

Am I mad, to see what others do not see, or are they
mad who are responsible for all that I am seeing?

—LEO TOLSTOY

PRESIDENT OBAMA'S INAUGURATION WAS AN EXCEPTION. I WAS
not, in my ordinary life, much more comfortable with crowds than
I had been before. I avoided them as much as possible, in fact, just
as I did social interactions, subway rides, and sit-down restaurants.
What I did feel better about was walking around New York City
during the day. Although Tuesday and I had both missed the de-
ranged alley cat, I felt more and more comfortable as the winter
progressed with Tuesday's ability to recognize danger.

He had a few quirks. He didn't trust homeless people, for instance, and always alerted me to their presence. I understood his
concern. Homeless people were often situated in unusual places,

─────────

Leo Tolstoy, the Russian author of the masterpieces *War and Peace* and *Anna
Karenina*, served in an artillery regiment during the Crimean War. At the war's
onset, 2nd Lt. Tolstoy was transferred to the front where his "experiences in
battle helped stir his subsequent pacifism and gave him material for realistic de-
piction of war's horrors" in his later literary work.

like dark vestibules, behind bushes, or at the bottom of the subway stairs. They didn't act like other people, either, sitting where most people walked, gesturing toward you as you passed, or fishing around in garbage cans. I know it was wrong to single them out, especially since so many were wounded veterans with problems similar to mine, and I tried to reach out to them as best I could. On good days, I talked with them briefly and offered spare change and assistance. On bad days, when I was too anxious to interact, I walked by them without making a scene. Tuesday often watched them a little too intently for my comfort, even after we passed, but I can't fault him for that. He was trained to notice people behaving strangely and to alert me to their presence. His profiling of homeless people, in an unfortunate way, proved he was doing his job.

It was ironic, then, that a similar sort of profiling was the biggest source of trauma in my new dog-based life. It started the first night, when I went into the convenience store for my usual after-midnight food purchases.

"No dogs, sir."

"Excuse me?"

"No dogs."

I explained that Tuesday was my service dog, not my pet, and by law he was allowed to stay with me at all times. I had been to this store probably a hundred times. I knew the clerk questioning me. But this was the most I'd ever spoken to him.

"Okay, okay. Go." Not friendly, but resigned. As in, *Shop and get out of here as quickly as possible.*

The incident bothered me. I didn't like drawing attention to myself, and I didn't like having to explain that I was wounded. I was never comfortable walking into stores anyway because there were too many blind corners and not enough exits, and during my time without Tuesday in Sunset Park I had narrowed my errands to a small number of places, maybe ten, where I knew the staff. It was difficult for me to trust, so I liked to see the same faces. Establishing familiarity is fundamental to dealing with PTSD, which is another reason it's unconscionable that the Brooklyn VA hospital made PTSD-suffering veterans see a different resident every appointment, especially when that resident's first question was always, "So what's wrong with you?" It's like nobody in the system understood the most basic aspect of the most disabling disorder among veterans today.

It was a betrayal at the VA, and it was a betrayal in Sunset Park. That's how I felt when a familiar clerk questioned me about Tuesday. The first few times, I didn't think much about it. I was able to push it out of my mind in the exuberance of those early weeks with him. But as the incidents piled up, often three or four a week, they started to wear me down. People I trusted were turning on me. A few questions were fine, but I was blocked at the door of my favorite bodega. I was harassed at the counter of the one deli I felt comfortable in, first by the employee taking orders and then by a customer. One restaurant refused to seat me. Another took my money and gave me food, then had the manager throw me out of the dining room. There was a sign on the door that said NO PETS ALLOWED EXCEPT ASSISTANCE ANIMALS. I tried to point that out to the manager, but he threw me out again.

"No, no," the owners of the mom-and-pop shops said. "You can't come in. One dog hair and they shut me down."

"But this is my service dog. He has to come in."

"No. Dogs against the law."

"He's my *service* dog" I said, pointing out the red vest and medical cross that marked him as a working dog. "It's against the law *not* to let him in."

I understood the problem. Many of the shopkeepers were immigrants with limited English. Others were low-paid clerks trying to get through the day. They didn't understand the intricacies of

American law, and they lived in fear of the New York Department of Health and Mental Hygiene, one of the most dog-phobic sanitary patrols in the country. But these store owners were discriminating against me. They were violating my civil rights. They were playing with my mind. PTSD is a dwelling disease, where the mind fixates on an issue or image and relives it over and over again. Death. Dismemberment. Betrayal. Every time I entered a store, I felt all the past instances of discrimination. I felt every betrayal, from not having enough soldiers at Al-Waleed to being tossed out of a deli the night before. "No dogs" felt like a push out of the ordinary world, a rejection because I was broken and different and less of a man.

Imagine if a store owner said every day to a customer, "Sorry, no wheelchairs. We don't want people like you in here." Horrible, right? Well, that's what physical barriers like steps say to wheelchair-bound people every day. And that's how it felt every day with Tuesday, who was as vital to me as a wheelchair to a paraplegic. The store owners, the government, society—they didn't want me here.

It wasn't just a matter of hurt feelings; these encounters damaged my health. In addition to the PTSD, since Al-Waleed I had been dealing with traumatic brain injury, the result of my initial concussion and subsequent blows to the head. For years, I had lived with tinnitus, a constant ringing in the ears. I had such humiliating memory problems that, before I left my apartment, I always wrote down in a little notepad where I was going, why I was going there, and when I was expected. Bleak moments of confusion forced me to consult that notepad on almost every excursion, even when I was only going to the corner store. I remember glancing at a man selling newspapers by a subway entrance one day, feeling the world suddenly spin away from me, and tumbling down the stairs, severely bruising my tailbone. Before Tuesday, I would occasionally "gray out," as I termed these episodes to my therapist, and find myself thirty blocks from home, unable to remember how I got there. That's a long way to wander, especially since at the time I limped badly, used a cane, and walked at the pace of an eighty-five-year-old man.

The worst aspect of the TBI, though, was the migraines. To call them headaches is to compare a firecracker to the atom bomb. A headache is a little man inside your skull, pushing to get out. A migraine is two enormous hands slowly squeezing your head into the size of a golf ball, ratcheting up the pain centimeter by centimeter until, finally, in a fiery cataclysm, your skull explodes and splatters your brain all over the room.

They came in a variety of ways, these atomic explosions. I was sensitive to both light and sound, and sometimes too much of either would set the crushing machine in motion. Sometimes, the head pain seemed to bleed out of physical discomfort in my back or knee. At other times, it seemed to arise for no reason at all. The most reliable trigger, though, was extreme tension and anxiety, and the most common reason for this level of agitation was discrimination by shopkeepers.

It wasn't just verbal confrontations. It was also more subtle issues, like being singled out and watched. The *supermercado* near my house, for instance, had an employee follow Tuesday and me around the store. I don't know why they thought this was necessary, but you probably realize by now that being followed is not a good thing for a PTSD-suffering veteran. It triggered all my symptoms: anxiety, hypervigilance, alienation, outrage, and perhaps most importantly, the overwhelming feeling of imminent danger and threat. I was as tight as a cord, and within a few minutes, I could feel the pressure in my head. At that point, I knew it was inevitable, the migraine was coming, so I struggled home, pulled the blinds, turned off the lights, and lay down in the darkness just as my skull came apart. In that state, I couldn't move. I couldn't think. Even opening my eyes was like jamming two sabers into the pain center of my brain.

If I was lucky, the migraine lasted only an hour or two. That was the best kind. The other kind, the bad one, lasted two days. Usually, I lay in the dark the whole time, in exquisite pain, trying not to move, while Tuesday, who was aware that even the jostling of a paw on the bed would send shock waves through my brain, waited patiently on the other side of the room. Once, I remember, the pain became so intense that I couldn't take it any longer. I stumbled to the bathroom and turned the shower on scalding hot. I could hear myself yelling, as if from a great distance, but I stood under the burning water for twenty minutes until I felt my knees buckling and knew I was going to pass out. I stumbled back to the bed and slept for hours, and when I awoke the pain was gone. It felt like I was coming out of the worst stages of the flu, but for that time, at least, I was cured. The experience was so intense, though, such a shock to my system, that I have never tried it again.

Instead, I stopped going to the *supermercado*. I stopped visiting all the stores, in fact, that questioned Tuesday's presence. I tried to limit those experiences, to wall them off from the rest of my existence, because despite spending probably 20 percent of my time in mental or physical pain, that was a vast improvement over where I'd been a year before. There was no way I could allow bad days and worse incidents—no matter how distressing—to undermine the positive aspects of my life with Tuesday. For the first time in years, I felt comfortable most days and confident about the future. I wasn't just surviving; I was beginning to build a life and a productive career. My freelance editorials were gaining attention, especially several articles on how the actions of New York's mayor, Michael Bloomberg, were not backing up his public pronouncements of support for veterans, and I soon found myself being invited to speak on veterans' issues.

In the past, my public speaking engagements had been like a mound of greasy french fries: something I couldn't turn down, but which always left me feeling nauseated and remorseful. In March 2008, for instance, eight months before meeting Tuesday, I traveled to Washington, D.C., to participate in the Winter Soldier rally mobilized by Iraq Veterans Against the War (IVAW). As a captain, I was the highest-ranking veteran present, so I felt compelled to accept their invitation to speak in front of several thousand people. I have only a vague idea of what I said. I had doubled my medication to combat the anxiety, and I was loaded to the gills on rum. That's how I did things back then, when I did anything at all. The effort left me sick in bed for almost a week.

With Tuesday, public speaking was different. He gave me confidence, but even better he gave me something to talk about. How could anyone, after all, not love hearing stories about a beautiful and specially trained golden retriever? It was mostly speaking panels and community events, but I took it seriously because there might be one person in the audience, one caregiver, parent, or sufferer of TBI or PTSD, whose life I could change. Sure, I was opinionated. But I had done my research. I was passionate. And, thanks to Tuesday, I was usually stone-cold sober, too. I still don't remember what I said most of the time, or even what most of the panel discussions were about, but I remember the woman in charge of one of them. She was beautiful, smart, opinionated, and socially conscious, exactly the kind of woman I like.

So I asked her out. I hadn't been on a one-on-one situation with a woman since my last girlfriend left me with an apology and a picture she had drawn of me with half my face stripped off and replaced with barbed wire, guns, and grenades. I hadn't gone out with anyone, anywhere, even for a coffee, in more than a year. That's the size of the difference Tuesday made in my life. He changed everything in me, right down to my heart.

She agreed to meet me at my apartment in Sunset Park, a necessity since I would never make it through an evening in a new neighborhood. I planned a night at a Lebanese restaurant I knew in Bay Ridge, a short bus ride away. The trip was complicated, at least in my condition, but the evening was special. It felt like a turning point, an entry back into normal life, and as always I went all the way.

The date started out perfectly: The woman was fantastic. She loved Tuesday. And after a day spent steeling myself for conversation, I was my old sociable self. She made it easy, and so did Tuesday. I didn't even have to be entertaining because Tuesday handled that part for me. He gave us something to talk about and filled the awkward silences, and that helped me relax and enjoy myself. By the time the bus pulled up on Fifth Avenue, we were laughing and having a good time.

I let my date step up first, like the traditional gentleman my mother had raised, then stepped into the small entryway with Tuesday.

"No dogs," the bus driver barked.

"Oh, this is my service dog," I said with a smile, expecting her to let me pass.

"I said no dogs, sir."

"But this is my service dog."

She looked Tuesday over, her lips pursed. "That's not a service dog."

"What?"

"I said that's not a service dog, sir."

"Yes, Tuesday is my service dog. See his vest. See my cane."

"Service dog don't wear a vest like that. Service dog has a big handle you hold onto."

"That's a guide dog for the blind," I said, trying to hold myself together. "This is a service dog for the disabled."

"Sir, I know a service dog when I see a service dog, and that ain't no service dog."

I pulled out my cell phone. "Then call the cops," I said angrily, "because I am not getting off this bus."

I was sweating. Big Time. It was winter in New York, probably 30 degrees outside, but I could feel the sweat dripping down the back of my neck. I was trying to impress a beautiful, intelligent woman, the first woman I had talked to in a year, and I couldn't even get on a city bus. I mean, it was bad enough having to bring Tuesday with me. I love him, but it doesn't exactly say "boyfriend material" when a man has to bring a golden retriever on the first date just to keep it together.

I looked the bus driver straight in the eye. I held out my phone. There was nothing else to do. I couldn't look at my date. I couldn't even look in that direction, because I knew every passenger on the bus was staring at me, and that thought made my PTSD-addled brain reel.

"Please," I said quietly. "I'm on a date. Please let me on."

"No, sir," she said loudly, trying to embarrass me.

"Then I'm calling the police," I said angrily, "because you are violating my rights. I hope you are ready to explain to your boss why you wouldn't let a disabled person on your bus."

She gave me a nasty look, waiting for thirty seconds to see if I would back down, then let me pass with a grunt. I felt like throwing up and I was probably shaking, but I had won. I had made it onto a city bus.

Hold it together, Luis, I told myself, as I took a seat beside my date and Tuesday settled between my knees. *Hold it together.*

"Are you all right?"

I took a deep breath and petted the back of Tuesday's head. "I'm okay," I said. "That happens sometimes. Right, Tuesday? Right, good boy?" I talk to Tuesday when I'm nervous, even in the middle of conversations.

"I'm sorry."

"Don't be," I said. I looked at her. Smart, beautiful, understanding. She smiled, patted me on the arm, and . . .

"That ain't no service dog."

I looked up. It was the bus driver. She was talking to a woman in the first seat, presumably a friend, but she was intentionally talking loud enough for the whole bus to hear.

Keep it together, Luis. "I think you'll like this restaurant . . ."

"I've been driving this bus a long time," the bus driver continued, clearly trying to embarrass me. "I know service dogs."

My mind was crumbling. "I think you'll, um, I think you'll like . . ."

"Service dog's got a handle."

She was like the voice of PTSD always playing inside my head, bringing up the betrayals.

"Ain't no service dog. I know a service dog."

She was harassing me, and she wouldn't stop.

"He thinks I don't know a service dog. I know a service dog."

"I'm not deaf," I said in a raised voice. "That is not my disability."

Some of the other bus passengers laughed. Tuesday turned and nuzzled me with his snout. I grabbed him around the neck, and he leaned into my chest. I could tell by Tuesday's reaction more than anything that I had been shouting. This bus driver was pushing me, harassing me, trying to make me snap.

"Sorry about the dog," she said sarcastically to the people at the next stop. "Man *says* it's a service dog."

I went inside myself. I held Tuesday and tried to beat down the anger. I could feel a migraine coming, but I pushed it away. *Just a few hours*, I thought. *A few hours and it will be over.*

We made it to the restaurant, but the host who knew Tuesday wasn't working that night, so I had to explain that he was my service dog, that he was not only allowed in the restaurant but it was illegal to keep him out. I got angry, more so than I should have, but nothing happens in isolation. I was deeply embarrassed by the time I walked into that restaurant. My head was pounding, and I was nauseated from the stress. This was a big night and it was all going sideways. There was no way, at that point, I could separate the restaurant's polite refusal to seat me from the mean-spirited harassment on the bus—or being thrown out of a dining room halfway through my hamburger, or having shopkeepers I trusted tell me they didn't want my business anymore, or being violently attacked with knives by my supposed allies in Al-Waleed.

I wanted a normal life. That's all. A normal life. Tuesday made me believe I could achieve it. And I could have. Easily. But the presence of Tuesday, the very thing that made it possible, was also taking it away.

I never saw that woman again. I said good-bye after the meal and, unlike the gentleman my mother had raised, took a car service home. She was polite and understanding, but a few days later she emailed to say she would rather not go out again. It was hard enough to open myself to human companionship for the first time. After crashing and burning on a bus ride? After barely making it through a meal? After rejection? No way.

The atom bomb exploded in my head, fueled by frustration and disappointment, and the migraine was so severe it kept me in bed for days. Even Tuesday couldn't comfort me. But he stuck with me every minute, until I was finally able to make it out of bed in the middle of the night and walk him down to Rainbow Park, where I flung tennis balls against the concrete wall as hard as I could, for as long as I could, until both Tuesday and I were completely smoked.

It was more than a year before I asked another woman on a date.

CHAPTER 18

TUESDAY'S HANDLE

*And I remember . . . I . . . I . . . I cried, I wept like some
grandmother. I wanted to tear my teeth out; I didn't know what
I wanted to do! And I want to remember it. I never want to
forget it . . . I never want to forget.*

—Colonel Kurtz, *Apocalypse Now*

I GUESS I SHOULD EXPLAIN TUESDAY'S HANDLE, SINCE THAT'S
what caused the fracas with the bus driver. After all, she didn't look
at me and assume I wasn't handicapped, as some people do. Or that
I'm not "handicapped enough" to warrant "special treatment."
That's part of the challenge of PTSD; the wounds don't leave visible
scars, so some people assume they don't exist. I suppose I'm "lucky"
that my back and knee injuries force me to walk with a limp and a
cane, two outward symbols of the damage done in Iraq.

Tuesday's outward symbol is his red vest, known as a cape,
which he always wears when he's in public. That's what marks him
as a working dog. I've added three patches since I purchased the
vest after completing the training at ECAD: one from Disabled
American Veterans (DAV), one from the Military Order of the
Purple Heart (MOPH), and one from American Veterans (AM-
VETS). I'm proud of my service, and those patches are a show of
support for my fellow veterans.

Some assistance dogs also wear harnesses that have a large solid
handle, intended for use instead of a leash. The handle is shaped

like the top of a crutch, with two bars on the side, a large bar across the top, and a gripping brace across the middle for extra stability and control. This is what the bus driver was looking for. This type of handle is excellent for those with vision impairment and physical disabilities because, since it is only a few feet long, it keeps the dog at your side. From there, the dog is able to accompany its owner through tight obstacles and brace her against possible falls.

I never used the handle, even though I had serious balance and coordination issues. After the assault at Al-Waleed, I had gone from a coordinated Terminator to an injury-prone man, much to my enduring frustration. Most of it was physical. I was compensating for my disabled back, which threw my entire body out of alignment. That caused my training injuries in the summer of 2004 and contributed to my devastating knee injury in 2006. My traumatic brain injury was also a major contributor. Just as serious, though, was my loss of confidence. The world no longer felt benign, and I no longer felt natural in it. I felt like I needed to watch every step, but with my mind usually reeling from hypervigilance I was unable to focus on my feet. My legs stopped trusting my brain, and my body rebelled. I had taken a dozen serious falls since Al-Waleed.

Tuesday helped with all these issues. He realized pretty quickly I didn't like broken sidewalks, so he pulled on the leash to alert me to changes in the concrete. He slowed down on rough ground, letting me set the pace. As soon as I felt dizzy, he sensed my distress and moved against me, allowing me to grasp him around the neck and support myself until the episode passed. With Tuesday so attuned to my needs, I regained confidence. I knew he was going to be there if I stumbled and that knowledge, along with Tuesday's vigilance for cracks and other hazards, caused me to fall less. He was my stabilizer; he helped me gain control of my mind and body, even without a hard handle to hold.

Stairs were still a problem, but there was a cloth handle on Tuesday's vest for that. Since stairs never surprised me, I simply stopped, ordered Tuesday to my side, and used the cloth handle to balance myself. After a few weeks, I didn't even have to order Tuesday to my side. When he saw stairs, he moved against me and waited for me to grasp his vest, then carefully supported me up or down.

The rest of the time, a hard handle would have been a nuisance, or even worse, a hindrance. While balance and falls were a problem, my most pressing issue was psychological. Public spaces often brought on intense periods of anxiety, and any sort of unexpected social interaction—even someone bumping into me by accident—made me jumpy and paranoid. The sidewalks of New York were usually filled with people, so I needed Tuesday as my buffer. A leash allowed him to walk a few steps in front of me, so he was the one to meet oncoming pedestrians, driving them to the side and away from what my mind perceived as possible confrontation. Ironically, the trait Lu Picard worried about most—that Tuesday often walked slightly forward of his trainer—turned out to be a valuable asset.

It was even more important with crowds, which were unavoidable in New York City, especially since I rode the subway to the VA hospital and Columbia. A New York rush hour subway crowd—oh man, that was bad. The space on the platform was tight; it was underground; there was a vague sense of agitation among the commuters; and there was no real way to avoid it. Those crowds gave me a flashback to a particular moment in Iraq: the first time I faced a riot at Al-Waleed.

I don't want you to misunderstand when I say flashback. I didn't think the multiethnic, semipatient crowd of New Yorkers was a mass of rioting Iraqis. The tunnel didn't turn into the desert, as it would in a movie, and the drop-off to the tracks didn't turn into the dirt berm that marked the border of Iraq. As I pushed through the crowd, I sometimes saw flashes of faces from the crowd at Al-Waleed, but I didn't turn businessmen into smugglers or mothers into enemies. It wasn't a visual flashback; it was a psychological one. What I experienced was the *feeling* of standing in front of that crowd in Iraq, thinking my life was over.

This was in January 2004, shortly after the attack on me at Al-Waleed. Saddam Hussein had been captured a few weeks before, but the American occupation was fraying. When the order came to close the border, we locked it down within minutes. There was no explanation, but the reason could have been anything—a blocking maneuver while raids were conducted in Baghdad, a large cache of unexploded ordnance (UXO) missing from a former Iraqi Army ammunition supply point (ASP), the sighting of a high-value target (HVT) from the deck of cards. I mean, most of us believed there were weapons of mass destruction. We thought it was only a matter of time before they were discovered or, even worse, used, and that the fifty of us at Al-Waleed might be the last and only line of defense against their free movement into or out of Iraq.

Nothing dramatic like that happened. Instead, within a few hours of blocking the gates, there were hundreds of cars and trucks in line at the border. For an entire day, these people waited patiently, accustomed to bureaucratic delays. Around dusk, some started to leave their vehicles to ask for an explanation. Would they get through before nightfall? What about the next day? There was no cell phone service this far out in the desert; Iraq was a dangerous society rife with sudden violent death; their relatives would be worried. They were polite, but unfortunately there was nothing we could tell them. We didn't know why the border was closed. We had no idea when it would open again. We were merely following orders.

I'm not sure how long the border was closed. I'd estimate a couple of days, although some closings during our time at Al-Waleed lasted longer. There would have been a riot in the United States after ten hours; believe me, I've seen it in airports. The Iraqis were relatively calm. They endured a hard life under Saddam, and it had made them resilient. They always carried enough food and water for a few days because they were so used to having their lives interrupted.

On the third day, though, the mood turned ugly. We suspended our patrols and stuck close to our base, aware that the primary source of trouble was at the border checkpoint. By then, there were thousands of people piled into the two-kilometer-wide no-man's-land between Al-Waleed and the Syrian border station. Most had been living in their cars for days, in cold desert temperatures. Food and water were running low, and those with compromised health—small children, the elderly, the sick—were suffering. People's financial futures were spoiling on trucks. Dead bodies were rotting. The Muslim faith calls for the dead to be buried within three days, and dozens of people came to the gate every day, weeping, telling us they were trying to take their relatives home for burial. I knew it was true, because I could smell it; the bodies were decaying in plywood coffins.

"*Ana aasif,*" I told them, "I'm sorry. I'll see what I can do."

I radioed squadron headquarters at FOB Byers, asking for permission to open the border, but the orders came from the top, without explanation or time line, and they were not subject to change.

"*Ana aasif,*" I told the increasingly frantic Iraqi border guards, who were tasked with holding back the crowds. "Don't let them through."

By then, the Iraqis were leaving their vehicles en masse. Hundreds of them, it seemed, were pressed against the barrier that marked the border. They shouted at us, shook their fists, but I had no idea what they were saying, and I had no choice but to turn my back and walk away.

It must have been the third night, or maybe the fourth, when I received a frantic call from the Iraqi border police asking for reinforcements. I grabbed four of my men and raced down to the crossing. The scene was chaos. Enormous, close-packed chaos. It looked like one of those big outdoor concerts with a sea of people surging en masse, but instead of being raised above the chaos like a rock star we seemed to be running below it, with the whole crowd shouting from on top of us. It was so clear the crowd had reached its breaking point that two of my men ran straight to the barrier and started swinging their rifle butts to drive people back. It was the faces on those men in front, the ones screaming and clawing a few feet away, that I glimpsed sometimes in the crowds in New York.

"What should we do, sir?" one of my biggest guys, Staff Sgt. Danhouse, yelled over his shoulder, still swinging his rifle.

I looked at the Iraqi border policemen. They were standing back from the barrier, frozen in fear. When trouble started, they would run. I knew it, and so did the crowd.

Then I looked at the four men from my team. There was no doubt. They would stand and fight.

Having been through riot control training as an infantryman, I knew exactly what to do: snatch the two or three biggest trouble-makers and drag them off to detention. That took the boil off a crowd. But we didn't even have enough men for a snatch team, let alone riot control. I looked into the face of the rioter nearest to me. He was a typical middle-aged Arab, except that he was dirty, hungry, and enraged. I saw his desperation, and I knew the rioters were going to breach the gate, and when they did, they were going to trample us to death. For a moment, it was that clear. I saw the chain snapping and the crowd descending on us, and I knew I would go down firing.

I unholstered my pistol. Glaring, I raised it toward the crowd. The men in the front looked at me, and they knew I was in charge.

A number of them turned and pushed backward, trying to avoid the inevitable confrontation.

I aimed my Berretta at the most angry and vocal Iraqi in the crowd. I put my finger in the trigger well and thought about the effects of shooting him. Would it quell the rioters? Or would it enrage them and escalate the situation? These weren't combatants. These were frustrated civilians, including women and children, and I was prepared to shoot them down. In fact, I was convinced I was only seconds away from opening fire.

"Just stand your ground," I told my men, lowering my pistol and taking a defensive stance.

That is the moment that comes back to me in a New York City crowd: the feeling that I will be overrun and crushed, and the awareness that I will go down fighting. In Iraq, I stood my ground. I didn't have any other choice. It was my job, and I believed in it. To lose control of the border, at that moment, could have meant a key Saddamist escaping or weapons of mass destruction unleashed on Jerusalem, Jordan, or a major Army hub of operations where thousands of troops were gathered.

I see it differently now. There weren't any weapons of mass destruction, of course, and now I'm not even sure there was a reason to close the border. I suspect it was just the whim of L. Paul Bremer or some other stiff at the top, an action that seemed harmless—and possibly, just maybe, helpful. I wouldn't be surprised if, after a few days, they forgot they'd closed the border, or that they intended to rescind the order but waited for the next meeting to bring it up.

Meanwhile, every time we closed the border, damage was done. Every day at Al-Waleed, Iraqis drove through the checkpoint, got out of their cars, and kissed the ground. They raised their arms to the sky and praised Allah, then turned and thanked us, the Americans, for their deliverance. Many had been exiled for twenty years, waiting for the fall of the dictator. Many never thought they'd live to see this day, and they were practically tearing off their disdashas in joy. It was a passion I understood. I will do the exact same thing on the day the Castro brothers fall. I will get to Cuba any way I can, and I will kiss the ground, because my homeland is free. I will remain an American, because I was born here and this is my home, but I will work myself to death to make sure the new Cuba succeeds.

Sure, there were terrorists and smugglers crossing the border at Al-Waleed, truck drivers and entrepreneurs, con men and jihadis, but when I'm in a crowd in New York or Washington, D.C., or some small American town hall, I always remember that a vast majority of the people at that riot were ordinary citizens coming home enthusiastic, optimistic, and ready to work with us to create a new Iraq. Instead of freedom, they found chaos. Instead of an ally, they found an American occupation overstretched, confused, and incompetently run. They found armed foreign soldiers allowing corrupt Iraqi "allies" to destroy ordinary lives. We tolerated our own corrupt contracting process, figuring nobody would miss $10 billion in a war zone. We coddled overpaid and arrogant security contractors, then shielded them from their own crimes. We paid and protected unscrupulous Iraqis whose existence poisoned the country against us, because there was too little planning and too few soldiers to seek out and empower the honest citizens.

We lost them. Whatever the reason, that's far too clear. I have no doubt that many of the Iraqi exiles kissing the ground and hugging me at Al-Waleed were shooting at us two years later in south Baghdad.

That too was part of the cocktail shaken up in my brain when I encountered a crowd: not just the memory of almost being trampled, not just the knowledge that I was capable of killing innocent people, but the guilt over our failure to protect and empower those honest citizens, the betrayal of our efforts on their behalf by corrupt and incompetent leaders, the pointless spiral of violence that got so many of my friends and fellow soldiers killed.

In New York, unlike Iraq, I often fled. I didn't run, but there were dozens of times when I simply turned around and left the station.

Tuesday, though, changed the calculation. With Tuesday, I could say, "Go forward, Tuesday." I used a six-foot leash, and the "Go forward" command told Tuesday to walk to the end of it and keep going. Tuesday didn't have any qualms about nosing through a crowd; he would part people like the Red Sea and guide me along in his wake, safe in the comfort zone he created.

"Left," I'd tell him. Or right, or wherever the crowd was more manageable, usually at the very end of the platform.

"Stop," I'd tell him, pulling on the long leash. "Side, Tuesday. Side." He'd come back and sit down beside me, supporting me just as he would have with the wooden handle, while I waited for my heart rate to slow and Tuesday's ears to perk up, the first sign of an approaching train. It wasn't salvation, because the train was often worse than the platform, but I always knew that, in a pinch, I had the extra six feet of leash, and the safe zone only Tuesday could provide.

That's why I used a leash instead of a guide dog handle. That's why I don't look exactly like a typical disabled person with a service dog. I'm sorry I didn't have time to explain that to the bus driver.

CHAPTER 19

TUESDAY TALKS

---

*Don't walk in front of me, I may not follow. Don't walk behind
me, I may not lead. Just walk beside me and be my friend.*

—ALBERT CAMUS

NOTHING IS ENTIRELY BAD. GOOD CAN COME OUT OF ABJECT
failure, which is one reason I press so hard for accountability in
Iraq. We can do better, and we will, if we're honest and learn from
our mistakes. The incident on the bus was an abject failure on many
levels, and it had a serious impact on my confidence. After the humiliation of that date, I was hesitant to talk to anyone new for most
of the spring, and it took six solid months, at least, to work myself
out of my shell.

But the incident was also an awakening, the moment that finally forced me to acknowledge, publicly and privately, that I was
part of something larger than my personal circumstances. I'm a
joiner by nature, a pack animal that loves to be part of a group. In
my life, I had thought of myself first as a son and a brother, then as
a Cuban American, then as a soldier, then as a wounded veteran,
always with a responsibility to speak for others like myself. In the
spring of 2009, I realized I was something else as well: disabled.

That may not sound like much, but it's an important self-
realization. Most wounded soldiers never use the *d* word, preferring

to say things like "wounded" or "recovering" or "struggling to adjust." It's hard for the newly disabled, whether the cause is a car accident, a disease or an IED in Iraq, to admit just how much their lives have been altered. The word "disabled" acknowledges the seriousness of that change.

This is especially true for PTSD. Most soldiers spend years denying they have it, or being told by loved ones it's all in their heads. It *is* in their heads, but it's a real wound nonetheless. Even if they accept the diagnosis, most veterans assume PTSD is temporary. *I'm going to beat this*, they say. *In a year, I'll be fine.* Everyone knows you don't grow back a leg that's been blow off by an IED, but everyone assumes you can heal a brain that's been scarred. You can't. You can restore trust. You can reconnect with the world. You can live a full life. But the experience is with you forever.

It doesn't have to be a burden. You don't have to give in to the opinion of people like my father, who wrote to me that vets who admit to being wounded are "deepening their own disability and strengthening their desire to live on the dole." I am not a charity case, and I am not weak for addressing my wounds. The truth is the opposite. I lived for three years in denial of my problems, burying them under an avalanche of effort and work. It only made me sicker. When I finally acknowledged that I was disabled, I discovered a fractured back, a traumatic brain injury, and PTSD weren't just limitations on my life. They also offered new challenges and opportunities. My life was not the same after the attack in Al-Waleed and the subsequent betrayals and traumas, but it didn't have to be worse. Being disabled offers each person something different. For me, it was a new way to serve.

My activism started as therapy. When I began writing about the failings of the war effort in 2006, I was trying to find a way to explain my feelings of guilt, betrayal, and anger and make my sacrifices and those of the American soldiers and Iraqis I respected—no, that I loved and admired—worth the effort and loss. If we turned our strategic problems around, I felt confident we could succeed.

In 2007, when I moved into veterans' issues, I was working through feelings of betrayal and neglect from the Army I had served and battling the creeping fear and isolation that were tearing apart my life. By grouping myself with hundreds of thousands of other wounded warriors (350,000 veterans of Iraq and Afghanistan are currently being treated by the VA for PTSD), I felt less vulnerable to the system—and less alone.

Tuesday, I now realize, was my first move beyond veterans' rights. By adopting him, I was acknowledging that my condition would continue for years, and that I needed help beyond the counseling and medicine the Department of Veterans Affairs provided. I didn't think about that consciously. At the time, I was desperate for a way to survive on a daily basis. But underneath, in my subconscious mind, I was moving into a different category. Service dogs weren't for veterans; they were for the disabled. Period.

So when Tuesday and I faced discrimination, I fell back on my usual therapy: writing. The Army expects its leaders to make on-the-spot corrections and write memoranda to identify problems and recommend solutions. Why would I stop this practice just because I no longer served in uniform? If the offender was a local business, such as a laundromat or a small convenience store, I simply tried to educate them. If the offender was a corporation, I wrote to its regional office or headquarters, letting people there know what happened, its physical and psychological consequences, and how they could improve their treatment of the disabled with service dogs. Like my life in the Army, the emails were purposeful work intended to better the lives of others. They also helped me relax and, by getting my feelings down on paper, stop dwelling on individual incidents and move forward with my life.

The bus was different, though. After that humiliation, I was too stressed and sickened to write. I lay in my bed for days, even after my migraine subsided, lost in my own mind. Tuesday, as always, was stalwart at my side. On the worst days, when I couldn't even communicate my desires, he crawled onto the bed and, with a soft sigh, curled up beside me. It reminded me of my childhood dog, Max, and how his happy presence took me away from my weekly bully-beatings. But with Max it had been accidental. With Tuesday, it was intentional. His dedication and loyalty were more than I could ever ask from my parents or my siblings or any human being. It was something only a dog could give. When he lay beside me with his dog-breath sighs, it was as if he was saying, *Give me your sadness. I will take it, as much as you need. If it kills us both, so be it. I am here.*

As part of my public advocacy, I was scheduled to speak around that time at Hunter College in Manhattan. The conference was for mental health providers, mostly therapists and staffers at community outreach centers. The focus was "hidden clients": those who need help but were reluctant to come forward, a category increasingly dominated by veterans as the sixth anniversary of continuous war approached. It was an important subject, and after the setback on the bus I wasn't sure I was up to discussing it. In the end, encouraged by Tuesday's patience and strength, I decided to attend.

I can't remember if my remarks were planned. I remember being in front of the audience and feeling the crushing return of my PTSD symptoms: nausea, anxiety, a pounding in my head that made the room swim. As always when I was in trouble, I looked down at Tuesday. I could see his concern, but also his confidence in me. There was something about his eyes, when he looked at me, that always said, *I believe in you, Luis.* I looked back at the audience, a shadowy faceless crowd. Then, instead of talking about veterans' issues, I talked about Tuesday. I had been an alcoholic, I told them, trapped in my apartment and nearly suicidal before Tuesday arrived. But this dog stood by me. He helped me with my anxiety and phobias. He kept me from falling. He monitored my breathing. He knew 140 commands . . .

I paused. "Does anyone want a demonstration?" I asked, surprising myself.

"Yes," someone yelled through the clapping and encouragement.

I had spoken before gauging Tuesday's feelings about performing, but one look at his eyes, upturned as always toward mine, and I wasn't worried. He was ready for anything. So we started with the basics: sit, jump on, shake, retrieve, tug. We must have gone through sixty or seventy commands, and although the audience clapped for each one, it soon felt like Tuesday and I were alone together enjoying our regular practice session. When I finally gave Tuesday a piece of paper, and he delivered it to a volunteer with her hand in the air at the back of the room, the audience gave him a standing ovation. When he trotted back to the stage, I greeted him with my most enthusiastic hug. He put his head on my shoulder, and I think the audience saw the true affection we had for each other because the clapping went to a higher place. I know they saw the affection, because after the session several people came up to us with tears in their eyes.

The Hunter College conference led to other "Tuesday Talks," where I used public appearances to demonstrate what a service dog could do. I remember several high schools and a lot of discussion panels. Most of my appearances, though, were at community outreach organizations and independent living centers for the disabled (ILCs). These organizations ranged from large church-sponsored gyms to hole-in-the-wall storefronts, but they shared one thing: they were the first point of contact, the place a psychologically troubled or disabled person was mostly likely to seek help, and the staffers knew all too well the extent of the suffering in the veteran community. But they had never really watched an animal like Tuesday before. They had never considered how much good a dog could do.

My appearances were uneven experiences because PTSD is an uneven condition. Some days I felt great, and my talks were energetic and optimistic. Other days I was sick and anxious, and I dwelt on the negative aspects of my life. It wasn't just the bus; dozens of incidents of discrimination had shaped my interaction with the ordinary world, and some days I couldn't shake them. Tuesday and I would demonstrate his abilities for half an hour, until the audience was completely in love with him, and then I'd ask, "Now how could anyone discriminate against this dog?"

They would murmur shake their heads, *No, not possible.*

"It happens," I told them. "It happens all the time. In fact, it happened ten minutes ago when I was getting a coffee around the corner." This was depressingly true; I usually stopped for a coffee or tea (alcohol replacement) to calm my nerves before an appearance, and there was often an objection to Tuesday.

Slowly, though, as I talked more about Tuesday, my perspective changed. Veterans groups had always been responsive to my message—they were incredibly supportive, in fact—but the civilian disabled community was different. The disabled people who used the independent living centers often came to my talks, and many of them had guide dogs or service dogs. Among veterans, I was unique; there were at that time, I suspect, fewer than fifty wounded veterans with service dogs in the United States. But at the ILCs, there were people who understood and had experienced similar challenges. Clearly, the disabled community had a vast network of outreach and support, because within days of my first "Tuesday Talk" I started to receive emails from people with service dogs from all over the country who had faced similar discrimination.

Soon, I recognized a pattern in the responses: while I was angry about discrimination, most of the writers were desperate or resigned. Not everyone with a service dog has a difficult time in social situations, of course. Some owners, especially those who are blind (because society is accustomed to guide dogs) or who have been disabled for a long time, are able to shrug off discrimination as simply part of their lives. But others are not so lucky. People with service dogs are by definition in a fragile mental or physical state; that's why they need the dog. Fighting discrimination is tiring, especially for a group for whom ordinary chores or social interactions are often physically and emotionally draining. I received too many letters, far too many, from people with service dogs who had all but given up. Their history of confrontations, and the thought of another one, kept them essentially housebound. They were writing, for the most part, to thank me for taking a stand.

I felt energized by their letters. Suddenly, I wasn't alone with Tuesday in Sunset Park, trying to convince storekeepers to let me buy a microwave pizza; I was part of a large group of people struggling for acceptance. When I wrote emails, the best outcome wasn't an apology and a coupon for free food but a promised change in training methods and business practice. I'm an organizer and a pack rat by nature. By this time, I had about forty letters to companies, chronologically filed, detailing our interactions. Quite by accident, I realized, I had created a record of underlying discrimination, the kind easy to dismiss as minor—"Oh, they didn't mean it, they just didn't understand"—when talking about one store, but in its totality was clearly the kind of harassment that wears people down.

I knew this record was important. It showed, in a concise visual way, why I so often lost my patience with store clerks and restaurant hosts. In that sense, it made me feel better about my inability to control my feelings of helplessness and annoyance, especially on my worst days. But it also made me feel I was contributing to a cause. I believed—and I still do—that one day there will be a serious discussion in our country about service dogs. When that time comes, I am going to put a stack of letters a foot high on the table and say, "Here, ladies and gentleman, is what life with a service dog looks like."

It was a gratifying time. Intensely gratifying. It was also simply intense. With PTSD and TBI, my mind forced me to relive, in vivid detail, the worst moments of my life. Now my advocacy was forcing me not just to remember but to talk about those traumas. In essence, I was taking one of the worst aspects of my disorder and incorporating it into my daily life. I was giving my memories a purpose, and that was empowering, but I still had to relive them, and my public appearances often left me stewing long after in my own private hell. I walked away many times in a mental and physical fog, with only Tuesday to guide me home. I didn't have as many flashbacks or migraines, though, because Tuesday recognized the symptoms. No matter where we were—on the street, in my apartment, in the middle of a talk—he nudged me as soon as my eyes glazed and my breathing grew shallow, not stopping his banging and pawing until I looked down into his concerned eyes, then leaned forward, tussled his neck, and told him, "I'm here, Tuesday. Don't worry. I'm here."

They happened so frequently, these little reminders from Tuesday, that after a while I took them for granted. I was so up and down, so prone to dwelling on traumatic events from both New York and Iraq, that Tuesday's interruptions became the rhythm of my life. He was keeping me so grounded, in fact, that I didn't realize I was pushing myself too hard, thinking too much, and letting my sleep schedule run amok. I didn't think much of it, since my life had been haphazard for so long, until the hours before dawn on the fourth night of absolutely no sleep, when Tuesday started to cry. If you have ever heard an animal whimpering in the dark, you know what a heartbreaking sound it is. Those sobs, so raw and genuine, cut through my chest like a serrated blade and then, like a key in a lock, pierced right into my closed-off heart. I rose from my bed, walked over to Tuesday, and gave him a hug that lasted until dawn. Then I put on his cape and, together, we went to the emergency room.

A few days later, Tuesday quietly crossed our apartment as I read a book and, after a nudge against my arm, put his head on my lap. As always, I immediately checked my mental state, trying to assess what was wrong. I knew a change in my biorhythms had brought Tuesday over, because he was always monitoring me, but I couldn't figure out what it was. Breathing? Okay. Pulse? Normal. Was I glazed or distracted? Was I lost in Iraq? Was a dark period descending? I didn't think so, but I knew something must be wrong, and I was starting to worry . . . until I looked into Tuesday's eyes. They were staring at me softly from under those big eyebrows, and there was nothing in them but love.

When I put my hand on his head, he stepped onto the couch and raised his face to my own. We stared at each other for a few seconds and then, slowly, Tuesday licked me. Yes, on the lips . . . and the chin . . . and the nose . . . slobbering all over my face with that big slow-moving tongue. That's the moment when Tuesday, after all his caution, stopped being just my service dog, and my emotional support, and my conversation piece. That's when he became my friend.

CHAPTER 20

SUMMER DAYS

Once you choose hope, anything's possible

—CHRISTOPHER REEVE

BY THE SUMMER OF 2009, IT FELT LIKE EVERYTHING WAS COM-ing together. Ali, my former translator from Al-Waleed, had ar-rived in the United States from Jordan and settled in New Jersey. He was having difficulty finding work, his two-room apartment was too small for his family, and he was in debt to the U.S. govern-ment for the cost of his flight, but at least he was safe. Or, as safe as you can be in the more urban sections of northern New Jersey.

My medical situation, meanwhile, was improving. I had a great therapist and a great primary-care physician, and my newest course of medicine, more than twenty pills for everything from anxiety to irritable bowel syndrome (my digestive system never recovered after Al-Waleed), was working as expected.

In fact, medical treatment of all veterans was improving notice-ably by the summer of 2009. The Obama administration had in-creased the VA budget significantly, leading to more consistent—if still too often inadequate—care. Traumatic brain injuries, like the one I sustained in Al-Waleed, began making the news after evi-dence surfaced that concussions in football players caused long-term anxiety, stress, and depression—many of the symptoms I shared. At the same time, the nation, and especially the Army, began taking PTSD seriously. There were still deniers and military leaders at all levels who mistreated afflicted service members, but a majority of people understood that war, violence, and proximity to sudden death inflicted psychological wounds and that those wounds need to be addressed. Treatment for PTSD was more available and a little less stigmatized, even among military officers and active-duty personnel. If I had been wounded in 2008, instead of 2003, the course of my treatment, and even my life, would almost assuredly have been much different and vastly superior.

But, as a nation, we still had far to go, and I wasn't about to let anyone forget it.

Between May and July, ten of my articles were published in numerous venues, urging the United States not to become complacent about Iraq and the health of its combat veterans.

What about the atrocities American soldiers were still being asked to commit in Iraq, I wrote in the *Hartford Courant*, from firing into occupied buildings to induce and thereby pinpoint return fire to frequent searches of homes without probable cause?

What about soldiers like Spc. Alyssa Peterson, an Army interrogator who killed herself in September 2003 after being reprimanded for showing "empathy" toward prisoners and refusing to torture them? Her words, as written in the official report of her death, are haunting: "She said she did not know how to be two people . . . [She] could not be one person in the cage and another outside the wire."

What about the thousands of wounded veterans who were being discriminated against in hiring, during a terrible recession, either because their bosses felt therapy sessions for PTSD took too much time or because of the stereotype that combat-wounded veterans were ticking time bombs waiting to explode?

What about the fact that, according to the RAND Corporation, of the 300,000 veterans suffering from PTSD (out of 800,000 servicemen and women who had served at least two tours of duty in Iraq and Afghanistan), less than half sought treatment?

What about the suicide rate among veterans, which was already staggeringly high but wouldn't become a national issue until 2010, when the number of suicides per month surpassed combat deaths?

Even beyond my articles, my advocacy efforts were increasing. That spring and summer, as he promoted his bill establishing a pilot program to match service dogs with wounded Iraq and Afghanistan veterans, Senator Franken often mentioned his meeting with Tuesday at Obama's inauguration. He even spoke about us on the Senate floor, thus entering our names in the *Congressional Record*. This exposure led to national news articles and invitations to charitable events, which in turn led to relationships with several organizations that offered resources to the disabled, most notably the Brooklyn Center for Independence of the Disabled (BCID) and the Harlem Independent Living Center (HILC). I was so impressed, I started working with them on broader issues of acceptance and accessibility. They were kind and accepting people and, in hindsight, I can recognize them as the larger family I had been looking for since leaving the military. They might not have understood my experiences in Iraq, but they understood my struggles, because they had gone through similar circumstances.

The culmination of those efforts, at least psychologically, occurred on July 23, 2009, when Senator Franken's legislation, the Service Dogs for Veterans Act (SDVA), was introduced to Congress. Its passage soon after was a meaningful victory, and one that inspired me with hope and pride, not just because Tuesday had inspired it but because I knew how a service dog transformed a life. That March, Tuesday and I had been the guests of honor at Soho's Animazing Gallery charity event, where we raised service dog awareness and donations to help wounded warriors. The title of a piece I wrote about the event for the *Huffington Post* summed up my feelings when Senator Franken's legislation passed: "For Veterans, Happiness Is a Warm Puppy."

That is not to say life was easy in Sunset Park. Tuesday and I went back recently for the first time in two years to see my old landlord, Mike Chung, and his French bulldog, Wellington, and I became so anxious on the hour-long subway ride I almost threw up. If it hadn't been for this book, and my need to reconnect with those memories in order to write it, I would have turned around and gone home. On every block, a business evoked a negative memory, and there was one where the experience was so egregious the thought of it sent me careening so completely into the past that I grayed out and don't remember the last five minutes of the walk. While I was lost in memories, Tuesday led me dutifully back to our block. My old row house, thank goodness, was a safe zone. Mike was as cheerful and welcoming as ever, and Tuesday and Welly picked up exactly where they left off, barreling into each other and then racing wildly up and down the stairs. Twenty minutes later, they were panting on the floor of the entryway, Welly lying upside down on Tuesday like a passed-out preschooler while Mike and I laughed like old times.

But as soon as we left, I felt the apprehension, something I can only describe as claustrophobia even though Tuesday and I had gone from a four-foot entryway to the open air. I limped four blocks out of my way to the one deli where I felt comfortable, but they didn't remember me, and the man at the counter said, "No dogs." I explained, and with a long hesitation, and then visible reluctance, he took my order. But when he went to make my sandwich, a lady came in and started complaining about Tuesday, so another employee turned to me and said, "Hey, sir, no dogs in here."

"He's a service dog."

"Oh. Sorry."

They served my sandwich, but I spent the next twenty minutes hunched over my table, muttering to myself while the deli employees watched me anxiously, hoping I would leave. Tuesday knew to stay at my feet—it was easier that way, when he didn't call attention to himself—but he stared at me the whole time with sympathy in his eyes. No, life wasn't easy for me in Sunset Park. Not at all.

But there were good memories, too—great memories, in fact—and an upward trajectory to my life, especially with Tuesday. We had moved into a new phase of our relationship, where we could be both a disabled veteran and his assistant, and a man and his dog.

I remember like it was this morning, in fact, the first time I took Tuesday to the dog run at Sunset Park, the large green space fifteen blocks from our apartment for which the neighborhood was named. Dogs were only allowed off the leash for a few hours in the morning, so we'd risen early and made a special trip. I saw Tuesday's ears perk up when he heard the barking, but I played a trick on him and walked past the first entrance. After a brief hesitation, and an audible sigh, Tuesday ignored the sound and focused on the sidewalk ahead. When I turned into the second entrance, he dropped his good-dog act and practically pulled me—"Easy, Tuesday!"—up the short staircase. Sunset Park was a hillside sloping down to the street, with a high wall at the base, and when we reached the top of the stairs we could see for the first time the dogs on the hill, running and carousing, their owners standing in little groups along the top. The concrete path wasn't steep, but it was a slow climb for someone with a cane, and Tuesday walked at the front of the leash the whole way, pushing the pace.

At the top, I paused to catch my breath. Sunset Park isn't one of New York's more picturesque parks—it's mostly grass and benches, crisscrossed with concrete paths, young trees, and garbage cans—but the view from the top is one of the best in the city. Beyond a white tower and three insectlike loading cranes on the Brooklyn waterfront, the Statue of Liberty stands two inches tall in the middle of New York Harbor, looking out toward the sea. Beneath her, the Staten Island Ferry is almost always visible, a dark shadow in the shimmering water, a white wake pushing it toward the glowing rectangles and gray shadows of lower Manhattan. The view extends past the support towers of the Brooklyn Bridge, with their mesh of cables, all the way to midtown, the whole southern half of the island appearing no more than five feet long and half a foot tall where the Empire State Building punctures the horizon. It was a perfect metaphor for my existence at that time. I was part of New York, but there was a distance between us. It was only a matter of time, I realized, before I stepped back into life. Maybe that's why, on that morning, Manhattan had never looked more beautiful.

Tuesday, of course, didn't notice. I don't know if dogs can see that far—Manhattan was at least two miles away—but even if he could, he wasn't interested in the view. That morning, he just stood and stared at me, waiting for the next move. When I bent down and unlatched his vest, his tail started to wag and his feet began to shift.

Until then, I had only taken the cape off in my apartment or after midnight, when Tuesday and I limped past the dark row houses to Rainbow Park. This was a first: broad daylight, people nearby, other dogs. I touched his side as I unhooked his second buckle. I felt the quiver, and I knew Tuesday was ready. I don't know if I've mentioned it, but I move rather slowly. I have always been a methodical person. "Slow is smooth and smooth is fast," as they say in the Army, and I like to get things right the first time. After all, you never know when it will end up being your only shot. Since my physical injuries, I've become even more precise. Or maybe it just takes me longer to perform to the high standard I have always set for myself.

By the time I removed his vest, Tuesday was shaking with anticipation. I could tell by the speed and angle of his tail that he was ready to explode into a sprint, but he took one last look at me, his eyebrows bobbing as he analyzed my face. I didn't have to nod. He could tell from my eyes that I wanted him to run.

"Go play!" I yelled, and before the words were out of my mouth, Tuesday turned and bolted down the hill, out past the last of the dogs, running with such abandon I thought for sure he would tumble over in a ball of fur. But halfway to the bottom he slowed, then turned and doubled back, lowering his head to propel himself up the hill, then swerving into the pack, and, finally, bumping and rolling with the other dogs. Have you ever seen a golden retriever running with abandon on a sunny morning? Have you seen the excitement on his face, the pure joy as he gallops faster than it seems his legs can carry him, his tongue hanging down to his knees? Can you imagine what that must have been like for Tuesday, who was three years old and had never really run that way before?

I could feel it. It was a wave of excitement, rising from his soul as he skidded, then stopped, then took off in another direction, a dog at his heels. The other dogs sensed it, that pent-up enthusiasm, and soon the whole group was sprinting and playing with ferocious joy. I suspect the other owners felt it, too, although I was too nervous without Tuesday beside me to glance in their direction.

But I wasn't paranoid. And I wasn't overwhelmed, even though this was the first time Tuesday and I had been apart in the eight months since I'd adopted him. Instead, I was transported. I hadn't expected it, but when I saw Tuesday leaping and wrestling with the other dogs, I felt like it was me out there, running, jumping, doing things my physical body was no longer able to do.

A few months later, in August 2009, my application for graduate housing at Columbia finally came through. I had been stymied

for a year by the fact that the only way I could afford Columbia
housing was to have a roommate, something I felt incapable of
handling. It was my mother who suggested I inquire through the
Office of Disability Services, an idea I like to think indicates she
was starting to accept the new realities of my life. My therapist, my
priest, my physicians, and Lu Picard from ECAD helped me with
recommendations and paperwork.

That's something special about ECAD. All service dog providers are required to recertify their dogs every year for public-access
training. Most providers, like ECAD, also have a follow-up system
to keep in touch with the recipients of their dogs. ECAD went
further by being available and supportive at all times. Even today,
I still call them at least once a week for advice. Is this food acceptable? What's the discipline for this particular problem? What
should I do about discrimination? Almost always, I speak directly
to Lu. She is remarkably busy training dogs and pairing them with
the needy, but she is available nonetheless, whenever I am in need.

When the time came for me to move to Manhattan, Lu even
offered her truck. As I helped her and her husband (and a few volunteers) load my meager possessions, I felt sure that Tuesday and I
were moving on to better things. As we drove onto the Brooklyn-
Queens Expressway, Tuesday with his head out the window and
his big ears flapping, my previous life began to blow away, along
with some of my anger and frustration. After two years of struggle,
I thought, my real postmilitary life was about to begin.

CHAPTER 21

CRASH AND GROOM

I stroll along serenely, with my eyes, my shoes,
my rage, forgetting everything,
I walk by, going through office buildings and
orthopedic shops,
and courtyards with washing hanging from the line:
underwear, towels and shirts from which slow
dirty tears are falling.

—PABLO NERUDA,
"WALKING AROUND"

I SUPPOSE IT WAS INEVITABLE THAT MANHATTAN WOULD NOT immediately live up to my expectations. I had imagined student housing as a social petri dish, where like-minded people would mingle in the halls and almost by necessity forge friendships and relationships. In fact, Columbia's graduate student housing was a typical Manhattan apartment building, full of tiny one-room and efficiency apartments isolated behind locked doors. I occasionally ran into my fellow students at the huge bank of mailboxes in the small entry hall, but otherwise I never saw them. Incidents of harassment and discrimination didn't end either, as Tuesday's presence was questioned everywhere, from the diner on the corner to the Kinko's down the street. It turned out Tuesday and I were even more isolated in Manhattan than in Sunset Park, where at least we'd had Mike and Welly.

I also hadn't anticipated how deeply my mind, still struggling with PTSD, would be unsettled by the change in routine. I may have *ultimately* liked Manhattan better, and *ultimately* felt more comfortable there, but in those first months the place was a warren of new experiences, and the uncertainty threw me into a state of anxiety. New ground meant reconnaissance and surveillance (R&S). What windows were usually open? What people usually passed my building? What did the employees of the local stores look like? What time was the garbage removed, and by whom? I had to know the ordinary, so I would recognize the extraordinary, and in a place like Manhattan, the ordinary was complicated. For the first time since Tuesday and I sealed our bond in the spring, my hypervigilance was in high gear.

By a disastrous coincidence, my move to Manhattan also coincided with the collapse of my support network. Tuesday was the bulwark of that network, of course, but there were people vital to my progress. My therapist, Michelle, had been breaking me apart and putting me back together for a year and a half, since the summer before I adopted Tuesday. She was a former Marine, a whip-smart woman (I found, for some reason, that I couldn't share my emotional experiences with male therapists), and someone I trusted with my deepest personal secrets and fears. Unfortunately, at the end of summer, she moved out of state. Around the same time, a health issue forced my primary-care physician to retire. This was almost as devastating as losing Michelle, because the primary-care physician was the lynchpin of treatment in the VA system. Last but not least, my wonderful psychiatrist moved to California with her family. Without my health-care trinity, I had no one I trusted to discuss problems with and oversee my health. Without their professional approvals, I couldn't see specialists or have prescriptions refilled. Suddenly, after a year of excellent care, I was back in the muddy-boots VA bureaucracy, meeting with medical interns as a stop-gap measure and enduring the fast-moving revolving door of "health-care providers."

It took two months to secure a new primary-care physician, and the longer it went on the more anxious and confrontational I felt. A major course of medicine, like mine, needs constant tinkering, since the drugs interact with each other over time. That fall, my sleep medicine, Ambien, stopped working after more than a year. In fact, I was pretty sure it was keeping me up, because I felt wired after I took it. In my first month in Manhattan, I doubt I slept more than two hours a night. My other medicines began to run low, and without a doctor to refill my prescriptions I took half-pills to conserve. My back pain, diarrhea, and vertigo returned, and bad memories crowded my mind. I started hallucinating from either lack of sleep or withdrawal from my medicine, I'm not sure which. At night, I stared out my window, which looked into a glorified airshaft, or surfed the Internet for news, or just lay in my bed with my eyes open, stressed out and wondering for the first time since Tuesday where my life was headed.

It felt different this time because, in addition to my usual symptoms, I was experiencing something I hadn't felt since the confrontation with my father: deep disappointment. In the Army, we are taught to manage expectations. It's important to understand what you are capable of, both as an individual and as a group, and to plan accordingly. Overextending because of unrealistic objectives can be deadly, for both a commander and his troops.

In moving to Manhattan, I had failed to manage expectations. I assumed I had reached a permanent plateau in Sunset Park, and when I was unable to sustain my comfort level—much less raise it, as I had hoped—I felt dangerously let down. I was disappointed with my alienation, with my continued anxiety, with my failure to integrate with campus activities. But I was even more disappointed in myself. Why couldn't I control these demons? Why couldn't I put the past behind me? I knew the answer: I was seriously ill, and I hated that illness for clinging to me so tenaciously. And yet, despite that knowledge, I couldn't shake the disappointment. I still chastised myself every day for failing to meet my own expectations.

In the past, when I fell into despair, I called Father Tim, the Jesuit priest who was by then a legend in underground Alcoholics Anonymous and PTSD support circles. My early-morning calls to California had always soothed my anxiety, and his wise words had always helped put the memories into perspective. But that fall, after years of being a voice on the phone for servicemen like me, Father Tim had joined the Army. I knew he was helping more soldiers in his capacity as an official military chaplain, and that this was undoubtedly his calling, but when he shipped to Iraq and then Kosovo, in eastern Europe, I lost my ability to contact him at any time. In my darkest periods, I had talked with Father Tim every day. Now, he was only available a few hours a week, and in my wretched condition I felt unworthy of taking up his meager free time.

That left only Tuesday, my companion, my better half, my friend. I knew the situation was bad. I could see it in Tuesday. He was exhausted from worry and lack of sleep, his posture was slack instead of alert. He didn't have the energy, much of the time, to hold up his tail, and more than once I spotted him with his head down in what I can only describe as a standing sleep. He had developed a cough for the first time late that summer—probably caught from the dogs in Sunset Park—and that fall it progressed into bronchitis. I took him to the veterinarian for a course of antibiotics, and although his coughing improved he continued dragging through the day and, when he thought I wasn't watching, examining me closely with anxious eyes.

We needed something: a talisman, a routine, a lift out of the rut. To my surprise, the secret turned out to be grooming. Brushing Tuesday had always been part of our daily ritual. It was my responsibility, after all, to keep him looking good, because I took him into places no other dogs were allowed. How could I ask that if I hadn't put in the work to make the situation as comfortable and pleasant as possible? Could I really demand that a restaurant seat my mangy dog? Or even my average dog? If I came into their establishment with a poorly groomed canine, they would have every right, in my opinion, to kick me out. It was my duty as a service dog owner to make sure Tuesday wasn't just passable, but better groomed and behaved than even the best pet dog.

The grooming we did in those first months in Manhattan, though, went beyond anything we had done before. We would sit for an hour sometimes, Tuesday at my feet or across my lap as I focused on the long slow brushstrokes and the supple beauty they brought out in Tuesday's fur. I always started with his back, running the brush and then my bare hands across his shoulders and down his spine to his tail, feeling his heat. I brushed his tail, including the underside, where the long fur was matted. I brushed the top of his head, starting above his eyebrows and progressing straight back between his ears. I held him lightly around the shoulders and brushed a hundred gentle strokes through the thick fur of his throat while Tuesday leaned on my shoulder and closed his eyes. When he'd had enough, he rolled onto his back so that I could brush his armpits and belly, then down his legs to the thick hair along the back of his calves. It may not seem like much, but it was like communion for us, a solemn ceremony of unity, and we passed whole mornings on the floor, with Tuesday pressed beside

me on his back and my arm going back and forth hypnotically as I
pulled every lump and tangle from his fur.

We had a ritual after outdoor trips, as well. I had my courses at
Columbia, of course, and that semester there were several group
projects that forced me to meet with my fellow students outside of
class, so no matter how bad I felt I was often on the move. (And that
doesn't include our trips to the dog run three blocks away in Morningside Park.) When we returned to my apartment, I always spent a
few minutes caring for Tuesday. I kept a container of baby wipes by
the front door, and after removing and hanging up his service dog
vest, I always wiped down each of Tuesday's paws. I had learned the
value of baby wipes, one of humankind's most underrated inven-
tions, in the Army. At Al-Waleed, we often wiped ourselves down
with a handful, since there were no convenient bathing facilities.
We called it a whore's bath, because it removed the worst of the
stink between missions. (Sorry about the imagery. We were soldiers;
this was tame.) Almost every soldier I knew carried baby wipes,
even on long patrols. The sand in Iraq infiltrated everything, and
baby wipes were the best way to remove it from elbow folds, hair-
lines, lips, nostrils, ears, and every other awful place you can think
of. They were also a great way to wipe down weapons. I spent many
evenings, and many water breaks on patrol, wiping down my M4
carbine and Beretta 9 mm pistol with baby wipes. If it wasn't for
Pampers brand butt cleaners, there would be a lot more jammed
equipment in Iraq, and probably a few more dead soldiers, too.

(Of course, the Army doesn't supply them, so baby wipe purchases are out-of-pocket expenses. If you really want to send
something useful to the troops, send baby wipes.)

In Manhattan, I cleaned Tuesday's paws as carefully as I cleaned
my weapon in Iraq. I rubbed each of his toe pads and nails sepa-
rately, before wiping the center of his paw. This wasn't just to keep
New York out of our apartment; it was for Tuesday's health and

comfort, too. Small rocks, splinters, and grime from the sidewalks tended to stick in his foot crevices, and I didn't want him to develop infections.

Tuesday always stood patiently for his foot bath, carefully lifting one paw, then the other. It wasn't his favorite activity, but he tolerated it. When I was done, he usually ran either to his water bowl, if he was thirsty, or to the end of my bed, where the grooming began.

I brushed Tuesday anywhere and everywhere, but our major grooming sessions were on the floor at the foot of the bed. When Tuesday saw me gathering the accessories, he always got excited. This wasn't rowdy excitement; this was Tuesday excitement, like the calm that comes over you when anticipating a nice long bubble bath. He helped me gather my things with a laconic joy, his tail whapping lazily from side to side. When I eased down cross-legged on the floor, with my grooming tools scattered around me, Tuesday calmly moseyed over and settled into my lap.

I usually started with his toenails, which I clipped once a week. I trimmed the hair between his toes and around his footpads, a prime collector of burrs, seeds, sidewalk gunk, and other annoying hitchhikers. Then I brushed him, running first a brush and then a hand across his body. I felt for tender places in his flesh, for signs of bruising, for hot spots and lumps to make sure they were nothing more than muscle knots or insect bites. When I found a cyst one day on Tuesday's side, I sterilized a razor blade, sliced it, drained it, then covered the wound with a bandage. We performed a lot of injury maintenance at Al-Waleed, since the nearest medical tent was sixty miles away, so this little operation was nothing. Combat soldiers know how important it is to keep in top physical condition, and my men never let small problems linger (except the mental ones, of course).

"You have a little blood, Tuesday, a little scrape on your front leg," I told him, keeping up a steady patter. "I'm going under your chin now, Tuesday, just a little brush under your chin." He had an odd way of pushing toward me while I brushed his armpits and chin. There was a butt wiggle in it, and that always made me smile. "That's a good boy, Toopy, just getting the belly now." The nickname was a combination of Tuesday and Snoopy. I don't know how it started, but that fall it became my go-to term of affection. "That's it, Toopy. That's a good boy, Toopy."

After grooming, I cleaned his ears, and he let me scrounge not just the outside ridges but down into the holes. They were grotesquely dirty from the city air, and each cleaning covered eight to ten Q-tips with foul brown gunk. Tuesday never complained, not once, about having a Q-tip pushed three inches into his head. He never complained about my brushing his teeth with specialized equipment I can best describe as a stick covered with chicken-flavored grit. In fact, he loved it. As soon as the tube came out, Tuesday flipped onto his feet with a big grin so that I could rub it all over his teeth. Afterward, he licked his tongue around his mouth, searching out every morsel while I petted him for a few quiet minutes. That was also part of our routine; I gave Tuesday a nice rub before and after each individual task in our grooming ritual.

In the end, after all the Toopy talk was stowed and the accessories put away, Tuesday looked good. In fact, he practically glistened, and since he was the better part of me I assume I looked better, too. I know I felt better—more relaxed, more content, more in the moment—and that not only carried over into the rest of my day but was reflected in Tuesday's mood: his lazy smile and the way he bumped me two times, then rubbed against my shoulder, then licked my neck to return the grooming before settling in for a nap on my cool bathroom floor.

CHAPTER 22

THE LITTLE THINGS

We can do no great things, only small things with great love.

—MOTHER TERESA

IT'S HARD FOR ME TO QUANTIFY WHAT TUESDAY DOES FOR ME. I mean, what doesn't he do? Every morning, as soon as I stir, he walks to my bed. The first thing I see when I open my eyes is his snout plopped on the covers; the first thing I hear is the happy huff of his breathing and the sound of his tail whapping against my dresser. Once he's confident I'm not going back to sleep, he walks to the foot of the bed—his launching spot—jumps halfway to the headboard in one bound, and curls up next to me. I pet him for ten or fifteen minutes, while any lingering anxiety or bad dreams float out the window. There is nothing more calming in the morning than petting a dog.

When I'm ready for the day, Tuesday brings me my shoes. He used to bring my socks, too. He still opens the drawer, but it takes him too long to decide on a pair, not to mention he's a little heavy on the drool, so I retrieve them myself. I brush him first, even on my good days an important ritual, then give him his food while I brush my own hair and teeth. After he's eaten, Tuesday does his happy dance, ducking his front half and raising his behind and sort of pounding his head and shoulders into the rug with a scrape and a wiggle, first one side and then the other. Have you seen this in your own dog? It is energetic, goofily joyful, and mesmerizing. I suspect Tuesday is either rubbing off loose hair or scenting his spot, claiming this apartment as his own, but it's an endorphin rush for both of us. I leave the apartment laughing every morning, and then I laugh again when I drop the leash as we exit the elevator on the ground floor and Tuesday runs to the lobby rug and does his happy dance again. I mean, is there a better way to start a day than that?

He does the ordinary things, of course—he balances me on the stairs, walks me out into the world, and stays alert to all possible dangers, from homeless people in bushes to cracks in the sidewalk. When I'm overwhelmed, he's there for me to pet. When I want to speak up in class, glancing at Tuesday calms my nerves. When I have a tough therapy session, Tuesday rises from where he waits for me under a side table and stands by my side until the anguish or guilt or sadness subsides. That's one of the gifts of a service dog; he can be there for me wherever I am, even when no other dogs are allowed. When I start down the rabbit hole of anxiety or agora-phobia, even in a restaurant, Tuesday can nudge me back to the present with his dog-eyed optimism and tongue-wagging charm.

He can do all the other tasks he's trained for, too: opening doors and cabinets, turning on lights, retrieving medicine, canes, dropped objects, newspapers, and pretty much anything else under ten or twenty pounds. But my physical wounds have begun to heal and I don't need him for that as much. Often, I just need his courage to push me over the threshold, because with agoraphobia and PTSD the first step is the hardest of all. Twice during those terrible months after my move to Manhattan, I planned desperate trips to my par-ents' house in Washington, D.C. My father, especially, had done a complete about-face since the fall of 2007. He had studied PTSD; he had continued to work on himself and our relationship after admitting his mistake. Instead of being my biggest critic, by the fall of 2009, he was my most ardent supporter. I wanted to be with him in my time of trial, but the fear of the crowds and the trains between us made me stop at my door. Tuesday dragged me across, and once I was on the subway to Penn Station, it was relatively easy. Tuesday took over and guided me four hundred miles to home.

It's not just his understanding of me, although that's part of it. With a word, Tuesday can guide me to dozens of places. He can be my surrogate or a mirror to my heart. He was like a child at my parents' house that fall, discombobulated by joy. Papá, I think, was the only person he ever jumped on. He loved to jam his head under Papá's arm to read the newspaper and to lounge in his comfortable chair. That excitement and comfort were invaluable to me. It reminded me that this was my safe place. That these were the people who loved me and, despite everything, still cared.

It's that sociability, that eagerness to interact with the world, that I find so valuable. Wherever he is, Tuesday emanates happiness and affection. He wants to be noticed; there is something about him—I think it's in his eyes and maybe that goofy grin—that invites people to approach him. After class, or even out on campus, pretty girls I don't recognize say, "Hi, Tuesday" and smile. People wave on the street, or stop to say, "What a beautiful dog." I still hate going to the VA hospital, but even on my worst days, when I don't want to look at anyone, Tuesday's vibrancy and affection pull me through. I see him sitting beside me, looking at me, and I know he wants a hug. So I hug him, and the buzzing lights and grimy walls don't seem so bad.

On better days, when I don't feel compelled to sit quietly and leave as quickly as possible, I'll even nudge him, then motion with my head toward a veteran nearby. Tuesday's eyes, when he looks in your face, are so innocent and playful that they draw you in. He's almost impossible to ignore.

"Do you want to pet him?" I ask.

I'm a pretty good judge of affliction; I know when a veteran wants to be left alone or when he's completely around the bend. (Too common, I'm afraid, far too common.) I can't remember a single time when the man or woman didn't want to pet Tuesday. Usually, that leads to a few questions about him and then, "He reminds me of my dog."

Maybe it's the dog back in their apartment. Maybe it's a stray their unit picked up in Da Nang or Tal Afar. Maybe it's a dog from their childhood. Whatever the link, Tuesday's a conversation starter, a way back to the human side in a dehumanizing institutional waiting room.

Not often, but a few times, I've noticed someone sitting alone on the other side of the room and walked Tuesday over to see them. It's always a younger veteran, one who reminds me of the soldiers I had the honor of serving with. Maybe they remind me of myself too, not so long ago, sitting under those drab lights, trying to hold it together until I received my next round of meds, feeling like a number, a high one, and not one anybody cared too much about.

"Do you want to say hello to Tuesday?"

I'll never forget the way one young soldier hesitated, then reached out and rubbed Tuesday on the back of the head without saying a word. Tuesday started to lean toward him, then thought better of it and sat back. The young man petted Tuesday for what seemed like minutes, without ever looking at me. My back was stiff and sore, my weight pressed onto my cane, by the time he took his hand away.

"Thanks," he said, glancing up. Then he retreated, almost visibly, back into himself. Maybe he was thinking of his combat tour. Maybe he was thinking of a dog he'd known. Maybe he was thinking of a buddy he lost. I don't know. As we crossed the room, Tuesday and I glanced at each other knowingly, then looked away as we plopped back into our seats. Neither of us said a word.

That's confidence. That's trust in your service dog and belief in his value. I think moments like that developed out of Tuesday's kiss that spring, and that first day at the dog park, and the knowledge that after months of hard work I had earned his respect. It's funny, because when I say that I think of young Tuesday, the happy puppy at ECAD. Like him, I never realized something was missing in my heart. Then Tuesday assured me, as only a dog can, that he loved me unconditionally and would never leave my side.

It's the little things, in the end, that create that bond. Removing the rock from his paw the second he limps. Finding him a sheltered place to relieve himself as soon as he drops his haunches. Throwing tennis balls and playing tug-of-war and biting his ears when we wrestle, even though they fill my mouth with hair, because that's what he likes, the rough dog-play of the pack. It's the way Tuesday picks up an object as soon as I drop it, then holds it up to me with a gentle look in his eye that says, *Here you go, buddy. I've got your back.* As soon as I feel bad, Tuesday is at my side. When I notice he's uncomfortable, I drop everything and give him Tuesday time.

I remember when Tuesday was attacked by a pit bull in Sunset Park. It was a typical morning; Welly and Mike were with us, and Tuesday was running with Welly like a halfhearted forward blocker for an overexcited Emmitt Smith. I saw the pit bull arrive with a young Puerto Rican guy, but I didn't think anything of it until the owner released the catch on the leash and his dog sprinted down the hill and dove straight at Tuesday's throat.

I started running immediately, digging my cane into the ground. There is a difference between play-fighting and aggression, and I'd been around dogs and Tuesday enough to know this wasn't a friendly greeting. The pit bull was driving up underneath Tuesday's chest, snarling and maneuvering for a clean bite at his neck, but if the dog thought Tuesday was a soft target, it was badly mistaken. Tuesday may have been well-trained and handsomely groomed, a follower not an alpha, but he was a powerful fighter. He launched into a snarling defensive attack of his own, and the dogs were twisting at each other's throats and snapping wildly when I threw down my cane and dove into the pile, grabbing the pit bull around the throat.

The dog was still lunging and snapping its jaws when another hand reached in and grabbed it by the collar. The pit bull lashed forward, pulling its owner down, and for a second we were all grappling and pushing until the young man found enough leverage to hold on to his dog. I released my grip around the pit bull's neck, and as he began yelling, "*Calma! Calma!*" I turned my attention to Tuesday, who slid over and lay in my lap, his chest heaving.

I ran my fingers through the thick hair under his chin, inspecting him for wounds. My bloody left hand left red streaks in his golden fur, but I couldn't find anything wrong with his neck or throat. I felt his snout and his ears, then his head. Tuesday watched me, his eyebrows drawn down. I could tell he was coming off an adrenaline rush because his body was shaking, but his eyes weren't concerned. They kept staring softly at me, without turning away, as if to judge his own condition best by reading the reactions on my face.

"I'm sorry, man. *Perdóname.* It's my wife's dog."

I looked back briefly. Blood covered the pit bull's snout and dripped down the young man's arm. I turned back to Tuesday, running my hands over his body, flattening his fur and feeling for cuts. Nothing. Either the dog had bitten its owner, or Tuesday had gotten a hard strike on his attacker, because the blood wasn't ours.

"It's all right," I told Tuesday, running my hand over his body, soothing him. "It's over."

He lay his head on my leg. He was trembling, but I could tell he felt safe.

"Are you crazy?" a voice said. I looked over my shoulder again. The young man was gone, but Mike was standing in his place. "You don't jump on a pit bull!"

I wasn't crazy. I was a soldier. A soldier never lets a fellow warrior down, no matter the situation, no matter the odds. Jumping to Tuesday's defense was instinctive. In the Army, the smallest unit is a buddy team, two soldiers who look out for and are responsible for one another. Tuesday and I were a buddy team, and there was no way in hell that pit bull was going to harm my buddy.

But if that was the moment that proved my devotion to Tuesday, as I'd like to think, it was the situation with my old friend from ECAD, Sgt. Mary Dague, that proved how indispensible he was to me. In the spring of 2009, about six months after we received our dogs, Puppies Behind Bars accused Mary of not taking good enough care of Remy. She was overweight, they said, and too social for a service dog, so they threatened to take her back.

The news made me sick. And I don't mean metaphorically. When I heard Mary might lose Remy, I threw up. Her arms had been blown off by an IED less than a year before, and in the six months since ECAD she had been through four painful surgeries and extensive rehabilitation therapy at Brooks Army Medical Center (BAMC) at Fort Sam Houston, Texas. I know that was probably hard on Remy, to see her friend laid up like that, and the dog probably hadn't gotten the exercise she needed, but it had been harder on Mary. Far, far harder. Remy was her lifeline. I know that from seeing them together for two weeks, and from the loving way Mary bit dog treats from the tape on her stumps and fed them to Remy with her teeth. Losing her service dog, at that stage of her recovery, would have been devastating.

I wasn't just sick for her, though. The thought of that happening to me, of losing Tuesday, completely emptied me inside. In the summer of 2009, I had received an unexpected opportunity to travel to Cuba to engage in, let's just say, anti-Castro activities. The trip involved slipping into the country and traveling light, so there was no way to bring Tuesday. I almost didn't go for that reason, but in the end, I decided to do it. I left Tuesday in Lu Picard's loving and capable hands and slipped off to fulfill a dream of my youth. The trip nearly killed me, not because of our actions—there was no violence, either planned or accidental—but because it took me from Tuesday. In fact, I suspect the separation, and its psychological toll, contributed to my breakdown that fall.

And that was only ten days! To lose Tuesday forever? No, it was inconceivable. I may not be able to quantify everything Tuesday does for me, but I can tell you the sum total is this: I can't live without him.

(And don't worry, Mary kept her dog. I am proud to report that she and Remy are still living happily together.)

CHAPTER 23

FOR VETERANS EVERYWHERE

*The best remedy for those who are afraid, lonely or unhappy
is to go outside, somewhere where they can be quiet,
alone with the heavens, nature and God. Because only then
does one feel that all is as it should be and that God wishes
to see people happy, amidst the simple beauty of nature.*

—ANNE FRANK

AS THE END OF THE YEAR APPROACHED, I WAS FEELING BETTER about my move to Manhattan. I had a new primary-care physician, a new psychiatrist, and a new course of medicine. I took a break from my advocacy for veterans and the disabled, and I would soon have a winter break from classes. An episode with a professor, in which we heatedly disagreed over whether reporters should be allowed to do whatever they deemed necessarily in a war zone, turned out to be the turning point of my fall. After that, I hugged Tuesday and, over the course of a few days, felt my tension ease. I became more comfortable in my classes and more familiar with the rhythms of my neighborhood. By Thanksgiving, I was frequenting the three restaurants along Broadway with outdoor tables, where I could keep an eye on traffic and pedestrians while

relaxing with a cup of coffee. Tom's Restaurant, the beloved Sein-
feld restaurant on the corner of 112th Street, had practically become
my second home. The Greek waitresses would always shout, "Hey,
Tuesday" as soon as we walked in the door, then usher us to a tight
Formica booth, where Tuesday would curl at my feet, invisible to
the other customers except for the tip of his nose, which he would
push above the table to ask for sausage. Tuesday loved Tom's
sausage.

He loved it so much, in fact, I sometimes ordered him a link.
Sure, it was greasy, but it was only once or twice a week, so I figured
it couldn't hurt, and Tuesday deserved a treat. It was important to
gain his respect, as I had that spring. It was joyous to discover that
we could spend time together in public parks and dog runs, as we
had that summer. But it was life-changing to test his love with a
major crisis, and for Tuesday to sacrifice his own health and happiness to stand by my side. When I told him to rest, at the depths of
my anxiety, he wouldn't leave me. When I tried to call out in despair, he was there before the words, as if he had read them in my
mind. The real battle wasn't with the pit bull in Sunset Park, when
I came to Tuesday's aid. The real battle was with myself in my
apartment in Manhattan, when Tuesday came to mine.

So maybe the timing of the AP reporter was unfortunate. Or
maybe not. Maybe it was better that his phone call occurred during a good period that winter, because while as an outspoken veteran I received calls from reporters all the time, many of whom
questioned some of my policy positions, I had never received a call
from a professional this hostile or personally insulting. I had never
met or spoken to this reporter, but he acted as if he knew me—and
"knew" that I wasn't injured in Iraq.

So I hung up on him.

A few hours later, he sent me an email acknowledging that I
was attacked, stabbed, and wounded at Al-Waleed, but claiming

that Spc. David Page, who had finished off the wounded attacker, and officers in my chain of command had given differing accounts of the incident. (Not surprising, given the circumstances.) He even questioned whether two attackers were present, although the official report and sworn statements indicate there were. He then used the fact that I "returned to duty within days, with little apparent difficulty," to jump to an accusation of fraud.

"Without a doubt, PTSD is a subjective thing," he wrote. "Two people standing side by side can be affected in vastly different ways by the same event. But I am also told that it is one of the easiest psychological disorders to feign."

In my years of advocacy, I have been called many derogatory names. My articles have been attacked and my website befouled by pornographic rants against my opinions and ideas. These days, that's just part of putting yourself out there for a cause you believe in. There will be critics, which is fine, and many of their criticisms will be vindictive and personal, which isn't. A traitor for being critical of the war effort? A commie? Okay, I know where you're coming from, and I respectfully disagree. But a faker? That I didn't understand. Why would an AP reporter make such wildly unfounded accusations? Had we really, as a culture, sunk so low?

I learned his intentions four months later, when he published an article on May 1, 2010, entitled "In Tide of PTSD Cases, Fear of Fraud Growing," which insinuated that veterans were perpetuating a massive fraud against the VA. The article, which did not allude to me in any way, included no proof of any systematic fraud, but simply stated that "experts" claimed fraud *could possibly* occur. The reporter's only "proof" was a 2005 report that one-quarter of the 2,100 PTSD disability claims studied by the government lacked proper documentation of a stressor. In fact, as Veterans for Common Sense (VCS) pointed out in a rebuttal to the article, the official government press release on that 2005 study stated: "The problems with these files appear to be administrative in nature, such as missing documents, and *not fraud*" (italics mine).

"In the absence of evidence of fraud," the release continued, "we're not going to put our veterans through the anxiety of a widespread review of their disability claims." And yet the AP article used the report to state exactly the opposite, going so far as to say if the findings were extrapolated to the whole VA "questionable compensation" payments that year would have totaled $860 million.

Even the inclusion of Dr. Dan Blazer from Duke University, the "expert" quoted as saying PTSD was among the "easiest [psychiatric] conditions to feign," was dubious. As *Veterans Today* pointed out in another rebuttal on May 7, Dr. Blazer is a geriatric psychiatrist specializing in mental and physical problems among the elderly, and he has no public affiliation with the armed forces. He was a fringe figure at best, and not one of the hundreds of reliable experts on PTSD that could have been consulted.

I don't belabor the point for personal reasons, although the reporter's accusations were deeply hurtful and would have no doubt, in another period of my life, sent me spiraling into outrage, anxiety, paranoia, and despair. The consequences are still with me today. In my anger, I'd posted his email on my Facebook page and somehow it found its way onto Gawker.com. In a post from Mara Gay on AOL.com that identified me as a *Huffington Post* blogger—I am proud to have had published articles on that site, but my articles appear in numerous other publications as well—it was claimed that "[AP reporter Allen] Breed seems to be on the verge of revealing Montalván as an outright fraud." The original title of the article, now labeled as "War, Lies and HuffPo: Vet's Tall Tale Coming Undone," even contained the word "hoax." The word was removed from AOL.com the next day, but not before other websites picked up the original version.

Far worse than the personal attack, though, were the damaging attitudes inherent in Breed's article. *Veterans Today* was correct, I believe, when they called it a "deliberate hit piece on America's veterans" from a reporter with "a fetish for Stolen Valor." The article's underlying premise was that streamlining the disability process made fraud by the rafts of malingering veterans almost inevitable (if not yet provable). I'm not saying there isn't fraud. The Inspector General's report for 2008–2009 found about one hundred cases of fraud per year, out of about one million veterans receiving disability benefits (or only 0.01 percent), and this report covered the end of the Bush administration, which was vigilant in its effort to deny claims.

In fact, the real problem is the opposite of the one speculated about in the article: the difficulty of the VA system means tens of thousands of veterans give up on receiving the help they need, with devastating consequences for their lives. While the article dwelt in loving detail on the cases of three veterans convicted of fraudulently claiming benefits, *none of whom had served in the military or filed claims for disability in the last fifteen years*, it dismissed the suicide of a veteran from New Mexico, who had placed a letter from the VA beside his Purple Heart before killing himself, as mere emotional manipulation. It's a tragedy when a veteran claims to have been in the Tet offensive in 1968 when he didn't reach Vietnam until 1969, the article implies, but to care about a Purple Heart recipient who committed suicide after being turned away by the VA during our country's most recent war? That's for soft-hearted crybabies.

This fixation on fraud—even in the face of hundreds of suicides from veterans who cried out for assistance, not to mention rampant alcoholism, isolation, homelessness, and anonymous death—is an outgrowth of the attitude exemplified by my father when he told me that seeking help for my disabilities meant I was descending to the "lowest common denominator" of humanity and associating myself with people whose real purpose was "helping each other take maximum advantage of disability benefits." It's a belief that those who suffer from PTSD are malingerers by nature, and that if they were just stronger, like real warriors, their affliction would be cured. It was a damaging attitude from my father, because although I never seriously considered suicide, his words sent me into the valley of death, where I contemplated my end often and, on too many nights, welcomed its coming.

It's far more dangerous, though, when that attitude poses as news from a venerable association like the AP, because it legitimizes those views. It emboldens the old school officer who abuses his soldiers for the "cowardice" of their psychological damage. It inspires the loving mother or father, terrified by the change in their child, to show them the "tough love" of dismissal and disbelief rather than helping them with their suffering. It encourages the young veteran to believe that his problems are a matter of weakness, that real men don't suffer pain, and that admitting to nightmares, anxiety, and antisocial behavior would be an embarrassment to himself and his family.

And all of those scenarios, played out every day in this country, have devastating real-world consequences.

But the article heartened me, too. Not the article itself, of course, but the reaction. Veterans and their loved ones from across the country, and from all our modern wars, stood up and said no. We're not going back to the horror of Vietnam, when our battle-scarred veterans were mocked and shunned. We're not going back to the image of the returning soldier as a shiftless burden on society. We're not going to stand at a safe distance and judge trauma by the shots fired or the blood on the uniform; we're not going to engage in intergenerational pissing contests over who had it worse; we're not going to allow society to dwell on a few negative examples when a million men and women have given everything to this country and have come back damaged by what they've done and seen. Maybe PTSD really is triggered by a single incident, a stressor, as it's known in the psychiatric community, and maybe the attack at Al-Waleed was that stressor for me, but as I have learned in the intervening years, I was not damaged by that moment alone. In fact, while there are specific memories that resurface with some frequency, like the suicide bomber in Sinjar or the border riot at Al-Waleed, I find myself most traumatized by the overall experience of being in a combat zone like Iraq, where you are always surrounded by war but rarely aware of when or how violence will arrive. Like so many of my fellow veterans, I understand now that it is the daily adrenaline rush of a war without front lines or uniforms, rather than the infrequent bursts of bloody violence, that ultimately damages the modern warrior's mind.

War isn't like regular life. In war, every soldier routinely experiences trauma and makes judgment calls beyond the pale of civilian existence. In January 2004, for instance, Iraqi border police arrested a young man driving a truckful of fake medicine. A two-man U.S. Army counterintelligence unit—a category three translator and a military intelligence staff sergeant—rotated through Iraq's western border posts on a regular basis, and they happened to be in Al-Waleed when the man was brought in. The two men interrogated the driver for about an hour, but when he wouldn't cooperate, they threw him on the concrete floor, elevated his legs, blindfolded him, stuffed a rag down his throat, and poured water into his mouth. For ten minutes, I watched as U.S. Army interrogators waterboarded a truck driver, his screams of agony and terror muffled by the wet cloth in his throat.

That incident is a scar on my mind. I still hear the splashing of the water, and especially those muffled, desperate screams. I still see the way his head thrashed against two strong hands, and the way the tendons clenched and the blood vessels popped in his neck. It is a black mark on coalition forces. I wish we hadn't done it. But it doesn't haunt me, not like so many other things I did and saw. I don't blame myself for not stopping it. The act didn't violate Army protocol, as I had learned it, and in the absence of orders to the contrary I deferred to the interrogators' judgment. After all, they were professionals. They knew what they were doing. They didn't worry about consequences or calling headquarters to request permission to use strong interrogation techniques. Waterboarding, it seemed, was a regular tool of their job.

This truck driver was no terrorist. After months at Al-Waleed, I knew fanatics. I had stood toe-to-toe with them, and I could recognize the hatred in their eyes. They were different from you and me. This was just a young man paid to drive a truck from Syria to Iraq. A mule. I doubt he even knew what was in it. Does that make waterboarding him wrong?

I don't know. Fake medicine, after all, was lethal. That truckload, especially in Iraq's squalid conditions, might have contributed to dozens of deaths. Innocent children might have died. How many? I don't know. How many other trucks were there in the criminal ring? How far did the black market extend? The driver may not have known, but the guy he was delivering the bogus medicine to probably did. This driver might have been the key to stopping hundreds of innocent deaths.

Is that a hard call, to balance civilized behavior against innocent lives? Well, it wasn't even close to my hardest call in the war zone. I probably made harder calls that same week. In September 2005, at Tal Afar's Joint Communications Center (JCC) during Operation Restoring Rights, we received word from Iraqi police that the women running from a suspected terrorist holdup weren't women at all but armed insurgents in disguise. As the officer in charge of the JCC, I gave an order to cordon off the building, then helped coordinate a U.S. Air Force strike to level it to the ground.

I don't *think* there were civilians in that building, there weren't *supposed* to be civilians in that building, but there *might* have been, and that's why I shy away from Muslim women in head scarves and still see that building sometimes in my dreams.

Again and again, I turned over detainees to our Iraqi allies, even though everyone knew they were torturing, ransoming, and executing prisoners. Waterboarding was nothing—nothing—compared to what the Iraqis had endured over the past twenty years. I spoke with dozens of Iraqis during my two tours, and every single one had either been tortured by Saddam Hussein's men or had a friend or relative who was tortured or disappeared. And I'm not talking about ten minutes of hell, as in Al-Waleed, I'm talking about weeks of being punched in the face or beaten with metal rods, months of living in a small dark hole. That's why waterboarding never worked in Iraq—because the average Iraqi had already endured much more.

And that's why the waterboarding doesn't haunt me, but I am deeply conflicted about walking away from a military jail full of Sunni prisoners in south Baghdad during my second tour. The tortured become the torturers; you can never experience that act from either side without being changed. I knew some of the guards in that Iraqi Army jail had been tortured, and I knew their prisoners were being tortured in return, probably with techniques Saddam Hussein had perfected. I knew some would be executed when I turned my back. I also knew there was no paperwork on any of these prisoners, no official interviews, and no evidence for their guilt. Some were no doubt insurgents; some were innocent men arrested in street sweeps mainly because of their religious sect. To sort them out would take days, and even then it was probably impossible. Any real court would almost assuredly have let them go. But I couldn't do that. And while I worked on this problem, other units of my Iraqi battalion would be arresting other men, holding them in other cells, and executing them without trials. Other Iraqi units would go into combat without adequate training, planning, or backup, leading not just to their own deaths but to the deaths of civilians because of panic and sloppiness. We had six American advisers for two hundred and fifty barely trained Iraqi soldiers, which was fine on a military base but ridiculous in the middle of the Triangle of Death.

So I made a decision to walk away, justifying it by telling myself this was the decision the highest officers in the U.S. Army had already made. I looked those Sunni men in the eye, then left them in the Iraqi Army's hands with a hollow admonition to treat them well. Those men in the cell didn't blink, but I did, and that's why I can still picture them sitting in their neat rows, muttering prayers as the flies buzz around them, waiting patiently for their fate.

That's war. It's messy. It's violent. It's traumatic. It's more real than ordinary life because death makes life tangible, and the closer you are to death's presence the more you experience life's pulse. In Iraq, people died every day because of soldiers' decisions. People died because of decisions my men and I made, and I could feel that power and responsibility pounding through my veins every day. So question my actions if you want. Demand an honest accounting by all means. But please don't tell me the attack at Al-Waleed wasn't traumatic enough or my wounds weren't severe enough or the details weren't solid enough for me to still feel psychological pain. Don't tell any soldier that, especially a friend or your child.

The AP reporter's actions hurt, I admit. The negative insinuations ripped into my psyche and wore me down. It made me angry and confused to have my wounds and service record mocked and to have the pain and effort of the last seven years dismissed as a hoax. At times, the negativity almost tipped me over the edge. But by then, thanks to Tuesday, I was resolute. By then, I had good memories to mix with the bad ones: Tuesday's lick in the spring; our summer at the dog run; the way we laughed, like a real family, when Tuesday shoved his nose under Papá's arm. I took heart in the veteran community's clear commitment to changing attitudes; and I had my father's about-face to prove that change was possible, powerful, and real. When the slander started, after all, it was Papá I turned to for help. And he was there. Always. During the worst of those times, we talked on the telephone every night.

And then, calm in my heart and mind, I could resist dwelling and think back to better times. Times like Christmas Eve, when Tuesday and I visited my sister's house in Manhasset for Noche Buena, the large family meal that celebrates the season. I had been estranged from my sister since my first tour in Iraq, but that night we reconnected somewhere in our hearts, and it felt good. Really good. For hours, we laughed with her in-laws, drank wine, ate traditional Latino favorites like *pernil* (roast pork), tamales, and black beans and rice alongside traditional American dishes like sweet potatoes, carrots, and corn. I had missed the birth of her two children, Lucy and Lucas, while in Iraq, and we hadn't seen each other much in the intervening years, but that night the candles blazed, the decorations shone silver and gold, and we were a family again. I watched the children's exuberance with affection, and I laughed loudly as they played hide-and-seek with Tuesday around the Christmas tree.

By the time Tuesday and I exited the train in Manhattan, long after midnight, it had started to snow. The streets were deserted, and Tuesday walked quietly beside me with his snout in the air so the snow would fall on his face. His fur was sparkling with snowflakes, and the way he shook his head and shoulders into the soft white falling reminded me so much of the Snoopy dance that I could almost hear the Charlie Brown music on the quiet streets as we walked toward home. Inside the apartment, my three-foot plastic Christmas tree was sitting on top of Tuesday's kennel, twinkling with LED bulbs. I didn't say a word or even turn on a lamp. There was no need. I rubbed down Tuesday's feet with baby wipes, slipped off my shoes, and then, by the glow of my Christmas tree's synthetic light, snuggled happily into bed with my great big dog.

CHAPTER 24

A QUIET LIFE

Students achieving Oneness will move on to Twoness.

—Woody Allen

My last semester at Columbia wasn't easy—this was when most of the false accusations flashed around the Internet, after all, and that was a dark, dark time—but it was calm, at least compared to my previous years. Public advocacy became less of my life, and my time was used more for one-on-one interaction with active soldiers and veterans, almost always by email. Many had heard of me through articles, interviews, and events, but others had gotten my name from fellow veterans.

That spring, for the first time, I also started to hear from soldiers I had served with overseas. They had been in denial about the effects of combat, but four years after returning from Iraq they found their lives in disarray. They had lost girlfriends and wives, even children, and some were no longer speaking to their parents. They told me about arguments they didn't understand, jobs they walked out on because they couldn't stand being in the building anymore. They were anxious, wary, and angry about things they never would have been angry about before. They dwelled. They questioned themselves. They were isolated and confused, unable to sleep, disappointed. Several were considering reenlisting, mostly because they were lost in civilian life.

I emailed them all, and I spoke with many on the phone. I suppose that was the U.S. Army captain in me. I felt a responsibility to these men and women, especially brothers I had known in Iraq, and I would never leave them alone in pain. It wasn't easy, but then again being a captain never was. These soldiers were talking about the kinds of experiences that had haunted me since my first tour, and the echoes brought back terrible memories. With guys I knew, it was worse, since the conversations often revolved around events I struggled with, too. Often I could feel their anxiety creeping over the phone like a contagion; sometimes I felt like I was relieving some of their burden by taking it on myself.

In a sense, this was another form of personal therapy. I was lonely, even after six months in Manhattan, and I had fallen back on the solidarity of soldiers. Looking around my apartment now, that's not a surprise. I may have wanted to be part of a university, to be a writer and scholar, but I have always been a U.S. soldier first. I have bookcases full of books, but 80 percent are about the military or war. In my bathroom, I have several framed rum advertisements with pictures of Cuba, but in the main room of my apartment the wall hangings are all mementos of my service, including several certificates and awards. On my dresser, I keep my rack of service medals, including the Bronze Star with an oak leaf cluster, the Purple Heart, the Army Commendation Medal with Valor device and several oak leaf clusters. In the kitchen, out of sight, I keep three knives, including the razor sharp three-inch fixed double-edged blade I carried every day for three years after leaving the Army.

My studio apartment, to an astonishing degree, is a microcosm of my life. To look at it, even once, is to understand me. It is one small room, plus a tiny bathroom and kitchen. The only window looks out on a ten-foot-wide interior airshaft, and because I am on the second floor, it is covered by a heavy-duty security gate. The space is dominated by the queen-sized bed I bought in anticipation of adopting Tuesday, with only a few feet to walk on each side. My desk is in the corner, between my bookshelves and my dresser, but there is no sofa or lounge chair. There is no space, and no need. Sofas are for guests, and I have had few social visitors to my apartment. I don't even have a kitchen table. Most of my life is spent on my bed, with either a laptop or a book and, of course, Tuesday.

I've known some soldiers to leave the Army and become slobs, vowing never to make their bed again with a military fold. I am exactly the opposite. I may have left the Army, but the Army never left me. I still make my bed every morning with a military fold, the corners of the sheets and blankets creased and tucked. I still coil and store my socks in combat rolls. I align my books neatly. I put my laptop back in the center of my desk. I keep my medals in neatly bound rows, right on the corner of my dresser. I sweep the apartment every few days (it's only a hundred square feet) and roll a lint brush over my bedspread to pick up unsightly dog hairs. This is partly because of my mother, who has always been obsessive-compulsive about cleaning. But it is also discipline and pride, two virtues that the Army instilled in me and I have always cherished.

Despite these efforts, Tuesday is everywhere. He is there in the dog bowls on the kitchen floor, and the oversized tennis ball with the thick rope sticking out each side (which he never puts away, the filthy slob). My night table, under which Tuesday sometimes curls on a blanket to nap, is a large dog kennel with the door ripped off. Tuesday's three red service dog vests hang from pegs like an art installation on the wall behind my front door. I have pictures of golden retrievers stuck in the frame of my mirror, but they aren't pictures of Tuesday; they're just cards from friends and family who know how much he means to me. I have hundreds of pictures of Tuesday in my camera and computer, but the only ones in the apartment hang in the bathroom. I don't know why. I guess even in my moment of privacy, I want to know Tuesday is there.

We spend much of our lives in here, Tuesday and I, relaxing on the bed, playing tug-of-war with socks, holding long grooming sessions late into the evening. One morning, while making the bed, I threw the covers over his head, then held them down. I thought it was a joke, but Tuesday thrashed madly, and when I released the blanket a few seconds later he shot out, rolled onto the floor and stood looking at me in a wide stance, panting like he'd just survived a cat attack or an atomic bomb. He stared at me for a minute, as I tried to apologize, then slunk off for a refreshing lap at his water bowl. Ten minutes later, he was back by my side. I don't have a television, but that morning I let him watch all the YouTube videos he wanted: dog popping a room full of balloons, dog riding a skateboard, dog accidentally falling into a lake, dog pulling a little girl's pants down at her birthday party. He loved them all.

I guess I forgot how much he truly hated the blanket trick, though, because a few mornings later I did it again. Tuesday came out of the covers like a scalded cat, huffing and crazy-eyed. He paced the apartment for a few minutes, clearly angry, then lapped down a bowl of water and plopped down in my tiny bathroom, the only private place in our one-room home. It took dog videos *and* horse videos on YouTube to soothe him that time. Since then, he always darts into the bathroom when I make the bed and peeks his head out to watch for me. Ah well, such is life with a dog.

I soothe him with, among other things, mornings in the mulch-covered dog run a few blocks away in Morningside Park. Tuesday loves it not only for its freedom, I think, but for the bizarreness of its characters. Most of the dogs just run circles, but there are definite archetypes. The Odd Couple are the toy poodle and the rottweiler, who can never get enough of each other. A Westie named Louis, owned by an older British woman whose reserved classiness puts us all to shame, is the Humper. That dog would hump a popsicle until it melted, and then he'd hump the stick. Tuesday patiently but firmly nudges Louis away from his back legs, again and again, but sometimes when Louis is too persistent, Tuesday gives me an exasperated look, as if to say, *Hey, alpha dog, can you do something about this?* So I get up and push Louis to the other side of the dog run, then limp back to my bench before he starts humping my cane.

The purple-eyed giant poodle is the Cute One. Two Yorkies who do nothing but chase a ball and argue with each other are the Bachelor Brothers. Sidney, a Chihuahua-dachshund mix, is the Smart One. (He happens to be the Funny-Looking One, too.) I love smart dogs, so Sidney and I are buddies. When he comes tearing toward me on his impossibly small legs, I can't help but laugh, much to Tuesday's displeasure. He's jealous of Sidney, I can tell. As soon as I pick up the little stubby-legged Chihua-shund (or Dach-hua, if you prefer), my big golden retriever comes running.

Tuesday, meanwhile, is the Gentleman. He loves to play, but he never jumps on the other dogs or sniffs aggressively at derrières. Instead, he bends his shoulders toward the ground and wags his tail, asking them to play. He doesn't mind a little roughhousing, and he always holds his own in a play fight, but more often than not he explores alone, happily rooting in the dirt, nosing out sticks, and kissing up to the women because he knows they can't resist his charms. Tuesday's always been a people dog, but he has a special fondness for women. It's funny to see him running from dog to mossy old acorn to young woman and then back again, his tail held high and contentment slathered on his face. He's happy-go-lucky; he sees the good in life and appreciates the little things. Since he's my doppelganger, that attitude brings out the good in me. Perhaps that's why I find it so easy to laugh and joke with the other owners at the dog run—because Tuesday showed me how.

Not that everything went smoothly that spring. The dog run was surrounded by trees, so Tuesday always wanted to play fetch. Usually, that was good. But one afternoon, I faked a toss in one direction, then faked in another, and then to my horror the stick slipped out of my hand, went flying across the dog run, and struck a young woman right in the middle of her forehead. It was awful, sort of like cutting a fart in paradise. The poor woman stumbled backward, shocked and dazed, and, I mean . . . she was bleeding pretty bad. I'm sure it didn't help to see a big Latino with an eighty-pound dog and a Bubba Stik cane hobbling toward her. I apologized and offered a baby wipe and, eventually, we talked a bit about Tuesday, who was standing a few feet away staring at her with soft-eyed concern. She was extremely nice and understanding, especially for someone holding a bloody baby wipe to her face. By the end, we were even laughing about the errant stick. But inside I was frazzled— after all, you don't just recover immediately from blowing the peace of paradise—and Tuesday and I didn't return to the dog run for a week.

Ironically, that was probably one of my longest conversations that spring.

For a while then, Tuesday was confined to the hillside a hundred meters from the dog run. It wasn't a hardship, though, since the hill was actually his favorite place. It was covered with grass, and Tuesday loved the feel of grass on his paws. He was a city dog, confined almost exclusively to a concrete world, and smushing plant life was a special treat. I felt his excitement every time he bounded up the hill, looking for squirrels to chase and then, if no small creatures caught his attention, flopping like a very enthusiastic fish in the grass. He rolled a few times, just for fun, then rubbed one side of his face and neck along the ground, then the other, as he pushed himself along with his back legs before turning over on his back and twisting his whole body from side to side. It was a moment of unbridled ecstasy that was so different from his ordinary manner it always made me cheer him on. Was he scenting the lawn? I doubt it. I think he just liked the feel of cool grass on a warm spring day: the softness, the smell, the way it scratched that unreachable itch. I mean, who doesn't like that?

He is a confident dog. That's what our relationship did for him, in the end: it brought out his natural grace. He loves to please others, even when it is just someone stopping to say, "Oh my, he looks like the Bush's beans dog" (which someone says, by the way, almost every day). He loves it when Rudy, the superintendent for the four or five buildings Columbia owns in the area, yells, "It's Tuesday!" from halfway down the block.

"Go say hi, Tuesday," I tell him, unhooking his leash and giving him a pat on the flank. That is a new command Tuesday and I worked on over the winter, one that was never in the service dog manual. In fact, Lu Picard wasn't too happy when she found out about it.

"He's not a pet, Luis," she said, shaking her head (but secretly smiling at my audacity, I'd like to think). "You can't encourage him to interact when he's working." I get the feeling sometimes that Tuesday and I are like Lu's gifted but exasperating students, always plotting trouble just right when we're about to make her proud.

I'm not worried. Not now. My bond with Tuesday is so deep and ingrained I know it will never come unbound. He knows my scent and my respiration. He can hear my heart beating fast or slow. He knows my inflection—angry or sad—and I know the hunch of his shoulders, the tilt of his head, and the angle of his tail. We trust each other unequivocally; we know each other down to our bones. There are no doubts between us anymore, no hesitations or concerns. We don't even need to practice our commands, although we still do for about thirty minutes a day because Tuesday enjoys it.

Even outside, I only have to tell him what to do half the time, because the rest of the time he already knows. When we cross Broadway, for instance, he always starts right, toward the restaurants with sidewalk tables. I only have to command him when I am going straight or turning left and, honestly, that rarely happens. I am a creature of habit in a hamster-cage world.

"He's a good dog, Luis," Rudy always says with the smile of a wise old neighborhood fixture. "You take care of him."

"Don't worry, Rudy. I will."

On campus, Tuesday is just as popular. There was a buzz that spring when he entered the lecture hall of my largest class, and a hundred eyes followed him when he rose to leave. After class, he had a standing date with his friend Cindy, whom we met at the dog run. I'd unhook his leash as soon as we saw her, and the two of them would sprint down the halls of the journalism school together while I limped behind. Tuesday and I entered the elevator one day with a woman I didn't recognize, and halfway up she turned to me and said, "You know, it's really nice to have a quadruped in the j-school."

A quadruped? "I like that," I told her with a chuckle. "Thank you." And then I petted Tuesday, because I always petted him, that's how we lived, and because I was amazed again that whether it was the National Geographic documentary filmed that spring called "And Man Created Dog" or the halls of academia, he was always a star. At some unrecognizable point, he had crossed over from being "the dog" to "Tuesday the service dog" to "the famous Tuesday."

"Oh," people say when they see him, "is that the famous Tuesday?"

"Say hi, Tuesday," I tell him, and he doesn't hesitate to leave them laughing.

But he has a therapeutic side, too. I remember a waitress at our favorite restaurant walking across the room and asking, "Can I just say hi to Tuesday?"

"Sure," I said.

She bent down and petted him for a while. "Thanks," she said, with a wistful smile. "I was having a really bad day."

There's an assisted-living home on the end of our block, near the Cathedral of Saint John the Divine, and on nice days the residents sit outside with their wheelchairs and walkers. Many are wary of dogs, but they know and love Tuesday. He was trained to assist the infirm, after all, so he understands the equipment. But even if he wasn't trained, he's so gentle and intelligent he would put them at ease. I am always moved to see these wonderful old veterans of life petting Tuesday in the sun. I don't know all of their names, even after all these encounters, but—and I know this sounds weird—Tuesday does. He knows more about these people than I will ever dare to discover.

That's why I always smile when we're sitting out on West 112th Street and someone stops to stare at Tuesday. "I'm sorry," they say finally, noticing me. "I don't mean to intrude, but he's just such a beautiful dog."

"Go say hi, Tuesday," I tell him. "Go say hi."

Tuesday hops up immediately. He knows what I want—the Socializer, the Gentleman—and he wants that, too. I smile as I watch him work his charm on another unsuspecting person, playfully but with perfect manners rubbing against their hand.

"He's so friendly," they laugh, as he turns to let them pat him on the back.

Yes, he's friendly. And helpful. And warm and outgoing. He's dedicated. Loving. Confident yet open, professional and yet personally involved. He's my cane. He's my balance. He's my alarm clock, my medicine schedule, my life coach and emotional monitor. He's my companion. My friend. My ballast. My hope. What else? What more can I offer in his honor?

I shrug.

"He's Tuesday," I say.

EPILOGUE

GRADUATION DAY

In lumine Tuo videbimus lumen

—PSALM 36:9

In Thy light shall we see light.

—COLUMBIA UNIVERSITY MOTTO

WE WALKED FIRST TO THE UNIVERSITY BOOKSTORE, WHERE I bought a light blue graduation cap and gown, then strolled across campus to the registrar's office for my cord. There were eight veterans graduating from Columbia's Graduate School of Journalism in the spring of 2010, a record for the university, and we were each receiving a special red, white, and blue cord to wear around our shoulders and down our lapels. As usual, Tuesday wowed the three women in the office, and we ended up leaving with two special cords, one for each of the veterans of the last two years.

"Kiss-up," I joked as we left. Tuesday glanced at me with laughing eyes and a sly smile. He didn't disagree.

A few days later, I took the gown, the smallest size available at the university store, and cut it in half at the waist. Then I cut off the sleeves above the elbow, rolled the remainder the rest of the way up, and pinned them in a perfect pleat.

"Try it on," I said to Tuesday, who had been watching the prepa-
rations. I slipped it over his head, then around his front legs. There
was some pinning and readjusting, a snip or two at the back, but
Tuesday never complained, never moved more than a foot or two,
and within half an hour he was standing before me in his own light
blue graduation gown, the gold crown of the Columbia insignia visible on each of his shoulders. I wrapped his special veteran's cord
around his neck three times, until the tassels hung down in front
of his shoulders. He snapped at them a few times; they were too
tempting not to bite.

"A true scholar. Mamá and Papá will be impressed."

Tuesday's eyebrows went up and down. *Mamá and Papá?*

"Yes, they're here, Tuesday. This is it. The end of the semester.
Graduation day."

It wasn't the end of anything. Not really. That spring, when I
was sure I would be earning my master's in journalism, I had re-
enrolled at Columbia to complete a second master's degree in strategic communications. After a tough first six months, I felt comfortable
in upper Manhattan, and it was too stressful to think about leaving.
Besides, the Army had started a new specialty branch called Information Operations. This wasn't public relations or communications; those branches already existed. This new field was a merger
of psychological operations, electronics, and cyber warfare. The
Army was training specialized officers to deal with new threats in
the global infosphere, which included training in the art and sci-
ence of propaganda. Since I want to work in policy development
and help induce the honest statements and assessments out of a
military throwing itself openly into media manipulation, I figured
I better understand its strategic communication methodology and
mind-set.

It's funny. I entered the Army partially as a repudiation of my
father's faith in numbers and words, believing instead that the

world can be changed for the better by boots on the ground. I still believe in boots on the ground. I am not an enemy of the U.S. Army. In fact, I love it more than ever, and that's why I want it to change, to own up to its mistakes and actually be the force for justice, honor, and freedom it has always claimed to be. There is no heroism without responsibility; there is no shining example without an honest accounting of actions. There is no valor for the troops at the bottom if there's no honor among the generals at the top.

In the end, I walked away from that world. Like my father, I am betting my life that the pen in my hand (or computer keyboard under my fingers) is mightier than the machine's slow grind.

So for another year, at least, I return. But one day . . .

One day, I am going to leave this place. I am going to have a wife. And children. And a job that makes a difference and some land out west, with a few horses in the back field and a view of the mountains. I wasn't made to live in New York City. I am more of a country boy. In ten years, when Tuesday is retired, I want to see him pushing gingerly through the clean mountain air with the grass beneath his feet, not hobbling through crowded streets with toxic ice-melting salt stuck in the fur between his toes.

It's going to happen. I know it is, just like I knew I would be accepted to Columbia. One day I'm going to hold Tuesday beneath a beautiful blue sky and tell him, "We made it, boy. We did it." I'll give him a hug and kiss him on his head, like I always do, then remind him, "You don't have to give those kids a ride, you know, just because they ask. We have a pony for that."

But that was in the future. For now, we had a lunch date with Papá and Mamá. I could see the pride in Tuesday's eyes, both a reflection of my own and his alone, as I readjusted the gown, rewound the slightly slobbery cord, and placed the cap on his head. He knew something was happening. He felt the excitement. We walked out into a light rain, but nothing could dampen Tuesday's spirit. All along Broadway, people were pointing and smiling, shouting compliments, taking pictures, and Tuesday strolled like a king, casually relishing the stares. By the time we reached Le Monde, one of our favorite sidewalk restaurants on Broadway, Tuesday had shaken off the cap so many times that I finally folded it up and stuffed it in the trash. He was right; he looked better with a bare head, so everyone could see his eyes.

An hour later, after a nice lunch with my parents, Tuesday and I headed off to campus. We had skipped the large graduation ceremony for the entire university, and since the journalism school graduation was less formal I was sporting a jacket, a tie, and some stubble (because, honestly, I had spent so much effort on Tuesday's outfit I ran out of time to shave). That left Tuesday as the star, as he truly was, and we must have posed for a hundred pictures on our way into Lerner Auditorium. Everyone, it seemed, wanted a photograph of the famous Tuesday in his graduation gown. The atmosphere, the crowd, the smiling classmates who suddenly seemed like old friends: it felt great, and I think I laughed the whole way to my seat, both from the excitement of the moment and the goofy, tongue-dangling smile Tuesday flashed for every camera.

They placed Tuesday and me at the left corner of the first row of graduates. I thought that meant we would go first, but when they started calling names, the seating chart didn't correspond to the order. Tuesday and I watched happily, completely in the moment despite the large energetic crowd, as each of our classmates crossed the stage. We waited an hour, through the calling of four hundred names, before the graduates on our row started to stand up and proceed to the stage.

So there was an order, I thought. *The front row is last.*

"And last but not least," the dean announced, after the young man beside us had left the stage, "Luis Carlos Montalván, a veteran of the U.S. Army, and his service dog, Tuesday."

We stepped forward and, with the precision of a drill team, made our way up the steps and onto the stage. I walked quickly, even with my cane marking time on one side, but the journey seemed to take years. Dean Melanie Huff shook my hand and passed me my diploma, then turned to Tuesday and handed him one, too. I was deeply touched; I had no idea of the plan. Columbia had been astonishingly good to me over the last two years, and in that moment, with tears in my eyes, I felt tremendously grateful not just for them, but for all the people who had pulled with me and tolerated me and rooted for me over the years. America, I was reminded, was a wonderful place indeed.

Tuesday was less affected. He took the diploma in his mouth, then with his lips curled in that big doggy grin, lifted his head and held it up to the crowd. The auditorium burst into applause. As we walked toward the edge of the stage, side by side, the applause grew louder and louder, until I raised my hand at the top of the descending stairs and everyone whistled and cheered. The applause wasn't just for Tuesday and me. It was for the whole graduating class, for all my fellow students and everything we had accomplished, but at that moment I felt humbled. I was, as Lou Gehrig once said, "the luckiest man on the face of the earth."

I also felt proud. It had been a hard two years—at times, devastatingly hard. No one knew the depths of my problems when I enrolled, including me; no one knew how hard I'd worked to stand on this stage. Only Tuesday, of everyone in that auditorium, understood.

After the ceremony, Tuesday and I went to celebrate with my parents at Max Caffé. I don't remember what was said exactly, but I know they were proud of me, and their pride was more special to me than the diploma in my hand. Their smiles and congratulations made the struggles worthwhile, and when I hugged my parents four hours (and three bottles of wine) later at the end of the meal, I felt the warmth of their love like a hot blanket around my soul.

And then I went back to my small apartment alone with Tuesday, and curled up with him in our queen-sized bed, and felt not a warm blanketlike love enveloping me but the warm contentment of two hearts melting into one. Because this was my true home, I realized then. Not the apartment or the bed or New York City or even the proud embrace of my parents, but the moment at the end of every day of my life, whether I succeeded or failed, when Tuesday tucked me in.